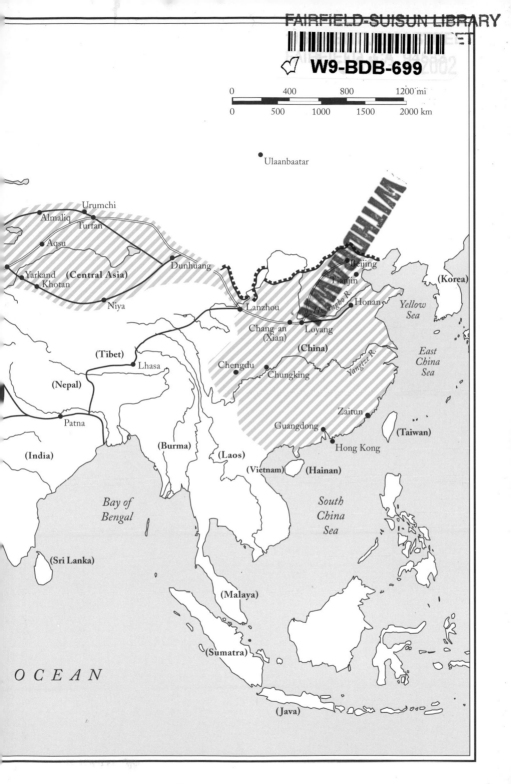

0	400	800	1200 mi
0	500	1000	1500	2000 km

Ulaanbaatar

Urumchi
Almaliq
Turfan
Aqsu
Dunhuang
Beijing
Tianjin
(Korea)
Yarkand (Central Asia)
Khotan
Niya
Lanzhou
Honan
Yellow
Sea
Chang·an Loyang
(Xian)
(China)
East
China
Sea
(Tibet)
Lhasa
Chengdu
Chungking
(Nepal)
Zaitun
Patna
Guangdong
(Taiwan)
(Burma)
Hong Kong
(India)
(Laos)
(Vietnam) (Hainan)

Bay of
Bengal

South
China
Sea

(Sri Lanka)

(Malaya)

(Sumatra)

OCEAN

(Java)

WITHDRAWN

Hoangho R.

Yangtze R.

MORE PRAISE FOR *THE JESUS SUTRAS*

"*The Jesus Sutras* vividly brings to life the partnership teachings of Jesus and their application in a surprising setting. Palmer's account of Chinese communities that honored both women and men and lived equitably and nonviolently is a fascinating story and a stunning contribution to religious history."

—RIANE EISLER
Author of *The Chalice and the Blade*,
Sacred Pleasure, and *Tomorrow's Children*

"Martin Palmer has written a book in the great tradition of English scholars and explorers. He has put together the evidence of the presence of early Christianity, in the first millennium, in China. He has reread and retranslated the Jesus Sutras to present a view of Christianity that was independent of the accepted definitions in the West. He has found in this Christianity, in ancient China, a liberating and healing expression for the whole of the human spirit. Men and women of all the faith traditions will be moved by this book."

—ARTHUR HERTZBERG
Bronfman Visiting Professor of the Humanities
New York University

The Jesus Sutras

REDISCOVERING THE LOST SCROLLS OF TAOIST CHRISTIANITY

Martin Palmer

in association with
Eva Wong, Tjalling Halbertsma, Zhao Xiao Min,
Li Rong Rong, and James Palmer

Ballantine Wellspring
The Ballantine Publishing Group
New York

A Ballantine Wellspring Book
Published by The Ballantine Publishing Group
Copyright © 2001 by Martin Palmer

www.ballantinebooks.com

Library of Congress Cataloging-in-Publication Data
Palmer, Martin.
The Jesus Sutras : rediscovering the lost scrolls of Taoist Christianity /
Martin Palmer, in association with Eva Wong . . . [et. al].
p.   cm.
1. Christianity and other religions—Taoism.
2. Dunhuang manuscripts.   I. Wong, Eva, 1951–   II. Title.

BR128.T34 P35 2001
275.1'03—dc21   2001035320

ISBN 0-345-43424-2

Text design by Holly Johnson
Maps by Mapping Specialists Ltd.

Manufactured in the United States of America

First Edition: August 2001

10   9   8   7   6   5   4   3   2

This book is dedicated to the unsung saints of the Church of the East, and most especially to Jingjing. It is also dedicated to my daughter, Lizzie, in love, admiration, and delight.

Contents

List of Illustrations

Acknowledgments

The sacred texts in this book have been translated in full only twice before, once in 1930 and once in 1937.[1] Both translations are now out of print. The earlier translators were Christian scholars who, though steeped in the Chinese language, had little knowledge of the great sacred books of classical China, such as the Taoist *Tao Te Ching* or the Buddhist *Lotus Sutra*. As a result, much of the meaning and nuance of the texts, contained in terminology, metaphor, and simile drawn from Taoism, Confucianism, and Buddhism, escaped their notice.

The Jesus Sutras takes a fresh approach. Having translated a number of Taoist books in the past, I know how complex they are and so enlisted the help of colleagues who could identify and interpret the insights from Taoism, Buddhism, and Confucianism and from Chinese history. This team worked on the Sutras individually and occasionally together. It has been my privilege to take their work and weave it into what I hope are coherent translations. All the insights I owe to my colleagues; all the mistakes are mine.

I am particularly indebted to Eva Wong, probably the most well-known and respected of contemporary translators of Taoist texts and herself an adept of both Taoism and Confucianism. Her willingness to spend time working with me in England was crucial to the success of the project. Her knowledge and keen understanding led her to discover the extraordinary Tibetan text that was embedded in the Chinese texts.

Zhao Xiao Min drew on Confucian insights and knowledge as well as his profound knowledge of Chang-an, the ancient capital of China at the time of the Jesus Sutras, to help us enter into the classical world from which the Jesus Sutras drew inspiration. He also led us into the rarified world of the Tang Dynasty Court in the capital city. Xiao Min also was responsible for first taking me to visit the temple where, tradition says, ca. 500 B.C., Lao Zi wrote the *Tao Te Ching*, the greatest classic of Taoism.

Li Rong Rong conveyed a deep understanding of Chinese history and culture. Now living in Britain and a recent convert to Christianity, she explored these Sutras as a personal spiritual journey as much as a professional task. Ni Yi Ma showed me the links between the Jesus Sutras and Buddhist Sutras and introduced me to the style and significance of the genre of Buddhist *discourse Sutras*. In China, my organization, the International Consultancy on Religion, Education, and Culture (ICOREC), and our sister organization, the Alliance of Religion and Conservation (ARC), work to preserve the Sacred Mountains of the Taoists. Tjalling Halbertsma, a Dutch anthropologist, brought boundless energy and enthusiasm to the task of directing that work. He also was willing to travel the length and breadth of China with me and sometimes to collect research and prepare information. In particular, it was his detective skills that tracked down the magnificent and previously unrecorded cross of the Yuan Dynasty (ca. 1382) stele that adorns the front cover.

Finally, Master Zhang Ji Yu of the China Taoist Association has taught me, over the years of our friendship and working together, to understand more fully what it means to be a classical Taoist. In doing so he has helped me enter into the worldview of the Taoists with whom the early eighth-century Christians worked, discoursed, and lived. In many ways it has been his friendship that has made the concept of this book possible.

Having said all this, the book remains ultimately my responsibility. Although the translations have been primarily the work of Eva Wong, Li Rong Rong, and myself, in the end the interpretation of their significance is my own. The work of A. C. Moule and P. Y. Saecki and their early translations of the Nestorian Chinese scriptures, however, was invaluable to us. I'm very grateful for the assistance that poet Jay Ramsay gave me in turning the translations back into poetry. In working on this, I was also honored to have the interest and support of the late Ted Hughes, who constantly sought to understand what kind of Christianity could possibly shape the future. I was also greatly supported by colleagues in the BBC, especially Norman Winter. My profound thanks to the many who assisted the key team in working on this book; in particular my colleagues at ICOREC and ARC: Joanne Robinson, Jeannie Dunn, Gena Darwent, and Richard Prime. A special thanks to Lucy Razzell for identifying the stone fragment from Da Qin as an angel's wing; indeed, thanks to all the Razzell family for ideas and enthusiasm. Finally, a very special thanks to Leslie Meredith who forced me to make this a better book. My son, James Palmer, helped me fine-tune the text. Thank you.

Author's Note

The issue of Chinese transliteration into English is a complex one. In general, we follow the modern mainland Chinese system of pinyin: thus, Peking is written Beijing. We also use the pinyin version of Guanyin, though the old style of spelling is Kuan Yin. However, when quoting from texts that use older systems, we retain the older usage. We also retain it for books such as the *I Ching* (which in pinyin becomes *Yi Jing*) and the *Tao Te Ching*, and in our use of Tao and Taoist instead of Dao and Daoist. This follows the methodology of the China Taoist Association.

For reference purposes, we have divided the Jesus Sutras into chapters and verses. It should be noted that these divisions are not present in the original Chinese text.

Introduction

Near the end of the nineteenth century, on the extreme north-west frontier of China, a Taoist priest living a few miles outside the oasis town of Dunhuang broke into a room cut into the rocks of a remote mountain range. Dunhuang was once a great town on the ancient Silk Road, which stretched from the capital of China to Antioch. The town reached the height of its prosperity during the Tang Dynasty (A.D. 618–906), but had long since fallen into obscurity. The room the priest had discovered was a secret library, bricked in with a material that indicated the cave had been sealed around 1005. As he removed the bricks and rubble from the entrance, the priest could see stacks upon stacks of scrolls inside, a vast treasure trove of thousands of books, paintings, and artifacts dating from the fifth to eleventh centuries A.D.[2]

Most of the scrolls were Buddhist, Confucian, and Taoist—the great faiths of ancient China. But carefully stored alongside these works were scrolls from a faith that few knew had even existed in China at that time. These scrolls spoke of "the Visitor," of "the Jade-Faced One," of "the One Sacred Spirit." They told of how the world began and recorded stories told by Jesus the Messiah that were unknown in the West. The scrolls were Christian books, written in Chinese, telling a story of Christianity that is unique and surprising, disturbing and hopeful. It is a story of faith and insight that is relevant to the lives of contemporary spiritual seekers of all backgrounds. The best way to describe these books is collectively, with a term they themselves use: the Jesus Sutras.

To readers used to the conventional language of Western culture and Christianity, the term Jesus Sutras may sound odd, for nothing quite like the documents you are about to discover has ever been found in the long history of Eastern or Western religious beliefs. Their striking version of the Christian faith and expression of the Christ story is as strange, as unusual, and possibly as revolutionary today as Jesus' own life was two thousand years ago.

The word "Sutra" is commonly used in Buddhism for a sacred text. It derives from the Sanskrit word for thread (from which comes the English word "suture") and connotes the idea that a thread of sacred teaching or wisdom is contained within the sacred book. The classic Buddhist Sutras drew a textual picture of the Buddha as a teacher seated in the midst of a throng of souls. In Chinese, the character for Sutra actually means "sacred literature." Thus, the Jesus Sutras are the sacred literature of the Christian Church of China of the Tang and early Sung dynasties—that is, from the early seventh to the early eleventh century A.D. The Jesus Sutras relate the Gospel stories of Jesus and present teachings about the meaning and purpose of Jesus' life.

The Jesus Sutras bring together the beliefs of the Eastern world of Buddhism and Taoism with those of the Western Judeo-Christian world. Although some people today see these two worlds as separate and irreconcilably different, even as implacably opposed to each other, the Jesus Sutras show that these two world cultures can—and did—come together to create an astonishing, accessible, vibrant practice of Taoist Christianity within the context of Confucian China some fourteen hundred years ago.

Today, many spiritual practitioners seek a way to reconcile the teachings and insights of East and West, of Tao and God, of Buddha and Christ. Yet fourteen hundred years ago, the Jesus Sutras had already created a synthesis of Tao, Christ, and Buddha. Their model of spiritual thought and practice shows how ideas, inspiration, and faith can flow across cultural boundaries and still remain faithful to the core teachings of each religion, while providing vital, fresh perspectives on the meaning of life and our place in the universe.

The fragile remains of the Jesus Sutras that have survived are scattered around the world from Paris to Japan. Written on parchment and paper, they are scrolls, although at times I refer to them as books. Some are complete, others decayed or torn so that they break off tantalizingly, leaving us wanting to know more. Yet there are sufficient remains for us to build a clear picture of the ideas, beliefs, and imagery in the writings, preaching, and worship of the Taoist Christians in China. The Jesus Sutras reveal an understanding of Christ and of human nature that is dramatically different from the standard versions of Christianity. Even though they provide a rich spiritual and cultural vision of Jesus' teachings in a Taoist context, they have been a source of embarrassment to Western Christians. For example, Samuel Hugh Moffett's major book *A History of Christianity in Asia* says this of some of the Sutras: "If the four Tun-Huang [Dunhuang] documents discovered in the twentieth century in caves along the Old Silk Road and attributed to the eighth century Chinese church are dated correctly, some weight must be given to the charges of syncretism leveled against Tang dynasty Christianity. At least two of them . . . are more Taoist than Christian."[3]

My own discovery of this Eastern form of Christianity came in 1972, when I spent a year as a church volunteer in a children's home in Hong Kong. I was eighteen years old and my parents and I had agreed that for a year about eight thousand miles between us would be a good thing. Thus it was that, far from home, I fell into a lifelong love affair with China, one of the most fascinating and challenging cultures in the world. I traveled all over Hong Kong, visiting temples and shrines, meeting Buddhists and Taoists and, in those days, Maoists. I celebrated festivals I had never heard of before and ate food I had no idea ever existed. I learned Cantonese, the dialect of Hong Kong, from the children in the home, and classical Chinese by singing hymns with them each night from a Chinese hymn book.

In those days, the Churches in Hong Kong were stuck on trying to be Western. The bulk of Protestant missionaries seemed more concerned about imparting Western values than exploring the issue of faith, although some outstanding Protestant ministers did work there. The Catholics, especially the Jesuits, however, were different. They seemed to have inherited the spirit of what was widely thought to be the first Christian mission to China, which was in the late sixteenth century. Its leader, Matteo Ricci, who arrived in 1581, was the first Jesuit to reside in Beijing. He became so proficient in Chinese and such a scholar of Confucianism and Chinese history that he was praised by the emperor himself. Ricci was a man after my own heart, a Christian who saw and treasured the Chinese world, who loved the fascinating and profound wealth of ideas, history, language, beliefs, and traditions from which Christian faith and practice could learn and within which they could find a distinctive place.

While studying the history of the early Jesuit missions, I made an astonishing discovery. I had taken the Ricci mission to be the first serious engagement between Western and Eastern faiths, but I learned it was not. In the annals of dynastic history in China, I found accounts of an earlier encounter with Christianity, the events of which are as fascinating as any detective story.

In or around 1625, workmen digging a grave in the countryside about fifty miles from Xian in Shaanxi Province found a huge stone stele—a carved stone slab—buried deep in the earth. Weighing two tons, its front was carved with nineteen hundred Chinese characters. More than seventy Syriac names of clergy with Chinese phoneticism were on the stone's side. The inscriptions told of a new religion in China. Dating from the Tang Dynasty (A.D. 618–906) and in fact dated A.D. 781, the text recounted the major events and teachings of an otherwise totally unknown mission of the early Church to China, which had arrived in 635.

A local magistrate in Xian read the text and realized it described the same religion his Western Jesuit friends in Beijing were teaching. He forwarded a rubbing of the Stone to the Jesuits, who translated it. The resulting text left them astonished and delighted. In the most poetic language, it sets out a brief history of the Creation, the path of salvation as offered by Jesus, and how the Religion of the Light of the West was transmitted to China. As a result, the Jesuits revealed to the Church in the West the story of the first known Christian mission to China—almost a thousand years earlier.

When I first learned of the Stone, I became obsessed with obtaining a copy of the text. It took me two years to track down through libraries, but eventually I found and read a somewhat stilted 1930 translation. Even in an uninspired translation, the text fascinated me, for it presented the kind of peaceful, insightful interaction between Eastern and Western cultures for which I had been looking. It united the wisdom and moderation of Taoism and the humanism and compassion of Christianity—the Path of the Buddha and the Way of Jesus.

To my delight—and further obsession—I also found that other texts had survived from this early Church. Here was an ancient Church that had built monasteries and libraries but had written its main teachings in Chinese, using beautiful Taoist and Christian imagery, texts that referred to themselves as Sutras. I felt that if I could locate these mysterious texts, they would yield further insights, perhaps a kind of Taoist-Christian Rosetta stone of the spiritual imagination.

Although very little more was known about the Stone, the

early Church in China, or its Sutras, I searched out, read, and absorbed everything I could. Ultimately, I found translations of more of the Sutras from the cave at Dunhuang. Nonetheless, it was to be nineteen years before, in 1991, I stood before the stele whose writings had so profoundly affected me. I was so overcome with emotion at this first visit I wept. I have visited this extraordinary spiritual legacy many times since, and I always spend at least an hour alone with it.

On my return to England I maintained my links with China, the strongest of which was through my adopted sister, Yan Chi, who arrived from Hong Kong on Christmas Day in my first year at Cambridge, 1973. By 1977 I had moved to Manchester, where I became involved with the rapidly expanding Chinese community and chaired the politically radical Hong Kong Research Project, which worked to protect workers' rights in the British colony. I was mainly engaged in organizing Europe's first multifaith education center, which led me to the task that has dominated my life since: devising practical ways to bring together the worlds of religion and conservation.

In 1993, as part of this undertaking, I began serious work in China, forging links with the Taoist monks on religious environmental projects that aimed to save the Sacred Mountains. Scattered across China, these nine mountains (plus many other, more locally significant sacred mountains) have international cultural, religious, and ecological significance and have been revered for millennia. As a result of this reverence, major areas of environmental importance were protected until recently. Now, however, they are under considerable strain as a result of logging, road building, pollution, tourism, and development. Our role at ICOREC has been to help develop religiously and environmentally sensitive management plans for these wonderful areas, in association with Taoists, Buddhists, and environmental and governmental bodies.

Thus it was that in 1998 I stood again before the great Stone

*The Stone Sutra stele in the Forest of Stone Steles Museum, Xian.
(© Xia Ju Xian/CIRCA)*

in the Forest of Stone Steles Museum, Xian, which I had first visited seven years before. The stele stands twelve feet high, three and a half feet wide, and is about a foot thick, mounted on a huge carved tortoise, as are many Chinese steles. A crude glass covering protects this astonishing stone from the depredations of time and visitors, but frustrates the scholar, who longs to trace with a finger the beautifully carved text in Chinese and Syriac. Even without the tactile satisfaction, however, I could now look at the stele and its text anew, for, aided by Chinese colleagues, I had a deeper understanding of its true significance.

That day in 1998 when we stood before the great Stone was to be a watershed. There in its strange protective hall, a dusty, noisy place of tourists and locals, all of whom cast only a brief glance at this towering stele and then moved on to view the hundreds of others, we began to unravel its full meaning. In the dusty light filtering in through the grimy windows, we began to explore the carved text and images.

The most striking feature of the Stone is the figure at the top of the inscriptions. On a tablet held by two curling dragons, a fairly common device on steles, is a delicate carving of a cross rising from a cloud-wreathed lotus flower. Stylized Western flowers rise on both sides and the top of the cross holds a flaming pearl. The clouds represent yin and the flaming pearl yang. The lotus is of course a Buddhist symbol of spirituality rising above the murky waters of existence. In this wonderful fusion of images, Christianity was skillfully set within the fundamental spiritual images of ancient China.

It all looks so natural. The cross, supported, even embraced, by the forces of yin and yang, firmly rooted in the symbolism of the Tao, is the very embodiment of atonement—"at-one-ment," as Joseph Campbell would say, the reconciling of cultural worlds (China and the West) as well as temporal and spiritual dimensions. A universal symbol of the mystery of life, of the necessity of pro-

Top of Stone Sutra showing the cross rising from a lotus. (© Xia Ju Xian/CIRCA)

found choice at every crossroad of human experience, the cross also represents salvation and hope. As Saint Paul says of the cross, it is the very reason for Christian faith. A symbol of Jesus' life and death, here fixed in a Taoist firmament, the cross shows the way to personal freedom and spiritual liberation, both through the human, physical intervention of Christ and the metaphysical constancy of the Tao. In the cross rising from the lotus, the passion of Christianity finds its place in the Eastern symbol of being rooted in this world but rising above it to full beauty and fulfillment.

Standing there before the tall stone rendering of the cross and its ephemeral clouds, reading again the commemoration of the contribution of the "Luminous Religion" to a grateful people, I felt once again the astonishing power of the spirit and the pull of a long-ago time and people.

This book tells the story of our quest through time and

history. As we unraveled the Stone's mysteries, it would send us across China and deep into the past to uncover the extraordinary story that it had kept hidden for so many centuries. Our visit of 1998 was to be the first of eight sojourns in China in which we explored the Jesus Sutras and the Taoist-Christian world to which they held the key. With each subsequent trip, through archaeology, textual studies, and adventure, we uncovered more of the ancient wisdom through which we can now glimpse the lost world of early Chinese Christianity.

The Lost Monastery

D ust rose in clouds around us as our minibus sped along the country roads of central China in the summer of 1998. Through the windows we could see rural life flashing past: horse-drawn carts, old men on bicycles, young girls walking arm in arm. Earlier that morning we had left far behind us the modern city of Xian, which stands on the site of the greatest of ancient Chinese cities, Chang-an. Some twenty-five miles to the southeast, the great eternal army of the first Emperor of China, Shih Huang Ti, was disinterred. Thousands of slightly larger than life-size terra-cotta warriors and wooden horses there guard the tomb of the Qin Dynasty founder. Enormous tombs surround Xian, however, so even as we traveled the road southwest we passed signs of the ancient city's former glory: temples, gateways, city walls, and huge mounds that cover many acres dedicated to long-gone emperors.

Within an hour we were deep in the countryside. We rumbled our way over a long bridge spanning one of the mighty rivers that flows down from the mountains south of Xian. In the river-bed, truckers loaded boulders flushed down by the winter storms.

Now, in the heat of summer, the river flowed shallowly through the ravine carved by its full force over millennia.

On we went through small towns whose main roads doubled as a marketplace and displayed all the confusion and variety of contemporary China, from Mao jackets to fake Gucci bags. Decrepit buses belching fumes roared straight at us in the continual game of chicken that constitutes driving in China, passing at the last possible moment with but a hairbreadth to spare.

Smog made it difficult to see beyond the small towns and villages through which we sped. The haze of heat and pollution from countless fires and the fumes of trucks and buses create a dense miasma that blankets the countryside up to thirty miles away from Xian. Tall trees planted along the roadside further block the traveler's view.

Thus it was that the Qingling Mountains and the Pass to the West, the traditional route out of China to the mysterious West, came on us suddenly. The towering walls of the mountains, rising like some vast curtain sealing us from the rest of the world, appeared and disappeared, only to appear again through the dust, smog, and clouds. As we drew nearer, the mountains solidified into a range that rose dramatically from the flat plains. It was now clear why the Pass to the West was so fabled and important. Without it, the mountains would have been impenetrable.

Had you asked my friends, as we headed out of Xian toward the Pass to the West, how they thought the day would progress, you would have had an almost unanimous response: it was mad but fun, so they had come along for the ride. We were a motley group: Zhao Xiao Min, head of my group's China office, a historian and classical Chinese scholar; Tjalling Halbertsma, a Dutch anthropologist who works with me in China and Mongolia; Jay Ramsay, poet and thinker with whom I have worked on translations of ancient Chinese books such as the *I Ching* and Taoist classics; Val de Monceau, a feng shui specialist; and Jane Routh, photographer.

We were in China primarily to help preserve the sacred mountains of China. My research for the Jesus Sutras, however, had convinced me that it was just possible that in a mountain range (not one of the sacred mountains!) south of Xian, near the Pass to the West, the remains of a once major Christian monastery might have survived fourteen hundred years of wars, uprisings, dynasties, empires, and earthquakes.

The particular bit of research that had led me to this remote area was an old book on the early Church in China, published in English in 1937 by a Japanese professor, Saeki. In it, Saeki reproduced a small, mysterious map he had somehow acquired. The map marked the site of a pagoda, or tower, identified as the Da Qin monastery, all that remained of a much larger structure that could be as much as fourteen hundred years old. The pagoda was believed by Saeki and other China scholars who had visited the site in 1933 to be associated with the early Christian Church.

I contend that this map was almost certainly drawn by Japanese spies who had visited the area in the late 1920s or early 1930s to determine what Chinese military installations in the region could mount resistance to the planned Japanese invasion of 1936. At that time, it was common for such spies to pretend to be archaeologists, geologists, or botanists, so their notice of an ancient pagoda on the terrain they were mapping would have been in keeping with their disguise.

Professor Saeki noted that Da Qin means, and would have been an old Chinese way of saying, "the West" or "the Roman Empire" or "Christian" monastery. Sadly, Saeki never had the opportunity to visit the site, although he provided directions to it along with the map.

Unfortunately for me, the map was very obscure. It indicated only temples in the region and gave no indication of where they or the Da Qin monastery might be in relationship to towns and cities. In addition, the directions to the location that Saeki gives in the book are strangely misleading and virtually useless for

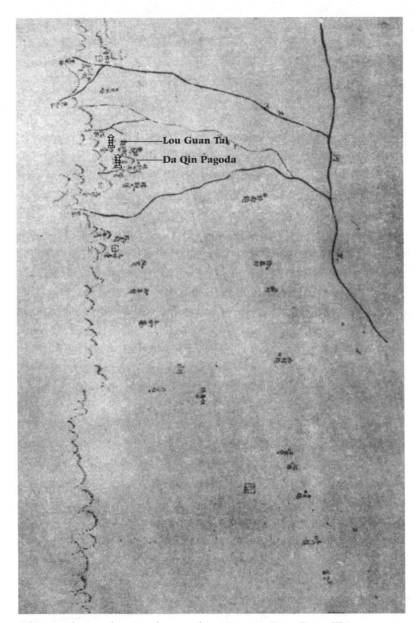

The pencil map showing the pagoda set next to Lou Guan Tai.

someone who wants to find it. Despite much research, I could find no record of any visit after that of the Chinese to help clarify how to get there. Frustratingly, the pagoda at Da Qin, after one thousand years, had slipped back into the obscurity from which it had briefly and peculiarly emerged, leaving not much more than a trace.

It was only by the most extraordinary of circumstances that I discovered the true location of the site. This coincidence still makes me shiver with the strangeness of it. Since I had first come across the professor's book, I would repeatedly and frequently peer at the sketchy map to try to work out where Da Qin might be. Finally, in 1997, seventeen years after I had found the map, I got out a huge magnifying glass, put the map under a strong light, and seriously turned my attention to the different names written in tiny Chinese characters that indicated the other temples. Suddenly the name Lou Guan Tai leapt out at me and I realized I knew exactly where the pagoda was. Not only that, but I had actually been there just a few months earlier while recording a four-part series for Radio 4 (the equivalent of National Public Radio in the United States) on the history of China! I had been within a mile or so and had had no idea it had any relationship to the site of the elusive Da Qin pagoda and the Taoist Christians!

Fourteen hundred years ago, Lou Guan Tai had been the most famous Taoist center in China. Today, very few Chinese even know of its existence and not a single Western travel guide to China of which I know mentions it. From working on a translation of the classic Taoist book, the *Tao Te Ching—The Book of the Way and Its Power*, as it is sometimes translated—and researching the origins of this great teaching, however, I had learned the legend of Lou Guan Tai. There, in the mid–sixth century B.C., the great sage Lao Zi is said to have written the classic *Tao Te Ching*. Traditionally, Lao Zi is thought to have been an adviser at the emperor's Court. Famous throughout the country for his wisdom, he eventually grew tired of the corruption he saw at Court. Believing that all China had become as degraded as the Court, he decided to leave.

The story goes that a watchman, told by the gods to be vigilant for a sage leaving China, built a lookout tower at the Pass to the West. One day he saw a sage riding upon an ox and rushed from his tower to invite him to stay the night. Recognizing that his guest possessed great wisdom that would be lost when he left the country through the Pass, the watchman pressed Lao Zi to write down his philosophy of life. The next morning, legend says, having stayed up all night writing, Lao Zi shook the dust of the kingdom from his feet and departed for the West, never to be seen again. But his book, which became known as the *Tao Te Ching*, survived and is the foundation of Taoism.

For centuries, the site where Lao Zi was supposed to have written his book remained obscure. Then, in the seventh century A.D., a new dynasty, the Tang, arose. The founder of the dynasty was a peasant who found it necessary to claim that he was from an ancient family of nobles. Specifically, he claimed to be a descendant of Lao Zi, and so he elevated Taoism, the only indigenous faith of China, to most favored religion. Huge sums were poured into building shrines, temples, and complexes to honor and practice Taoism. Chief among these chosen places was the little temple at Lou Guan Tai. By the A.D. 630s the site had been declared the Imperial Ancestral Temple and had grown so vast that it covered hills and valleys with dozens if not scores of temples and shrines. Today, though much is in ruins, Lou Guan Tai still dominates the landscape, its grandeur and majesty still very much apparent.

Thus it was that my friends and I were heading resolutely toward Lou Guan Tai that day, toward the nearest recognizable landmark to the purported Christian monastery. Knowing of my deep fascination with any hint of early Christianity in China, they were happy to indulge my latest pursuit of what I am sure they were convinced would be a dead end. As they kindly pointed out to me, since the 1933 visit of Chinese scholars to Da Qin, the

*The Tao. The path leading to Lou Guan Tai.
(© Tjalling Halbertsma/CIRCA)*

Japanese had invaded China, World War II had occurred, and civil war between the communists and nationalists had raged over the area. In 1949, communism had become the only political force in China and the Party had declared war on all that was old, religious, or feudal. The Cultural Revolution from 1966 to 1976 had destroyed probably three-quarters of all religious sites and virtually all religious statues and artifacts in China. There was little chance that even the ruins for which we were searching could have survived. Furthermore, despite initial inquiries on my behalf by my Chinese colleagues in Xian, we had no evidence that Da Qin had any more significance than any of the other hundreds of Tang Dynasty pagodas in the area.

At last we bumped our way up the foothills of a mountain to the hilltop temple of Lou Guan Tai. Covered in dust, we clambered out and made our way up the winding path to the main temple. The 1933 report indicated that the pagoda of the Da Qin monastery site could be seen from this spot at the entrance, but we had no idea in which direction to look. Remembering something I had read in the 1933 report, I looked to the East. Nothing. My heart sank. Then we all turned and looked, as common sense should have told us, to the West. And there it was. Across the valley, about a mile and a half away, a solitary, magnificent pagoda rose like an elegant finger pointing to heaven. Excitement rose in us all. Now we had to find out if this really was the building we were looking for.

Sitting beside the temple entrance was an old woman selling amulets. We turned to her and, after gently declining to buy a cheap plastic amulet of Lao Zi, asked who the pagoda belonged to.

"It's Buddhist," she said, again offering us a cheap plastic Buddha amulet. My heart sank again. Thanking her, I turned away.

"But it hasn't always been Buddhist," the old lady said. Turning back I asked her what she meant.

"Oh no. It used to be Taoist."

Disappointment hit me like a brick. Thanking her again I turned once more to go away.

"But it doesn't really belong to either of them," continued the enigmatic old lady. I turned again and asked her to elaborate.

"Before either of them it was founded by monks, who came from the West and believed in One God."

Her words stuck me like some ancient prophecy. They were words I could never have dreamed of hearing. Monks from the West who believed in One God could only mean Christians. Thanking her, tipping her generously, and still refusing the plastic amulets, we rushed down the hill. Inquiring among the small

The view of the pagoda and its terrace running east-west. (© Xia Ju Xian/CIRCA)

groups of local people, sightseers, and Taoist worshipers, we soon found a guide willing to take us across the valley to the site.

By now I was in a state of high excitement. Not only was the pagoda still standing, but local legend said it was Christian. Now we needed physical proof. As we drove the old dirt roads across paddy fields and through tiny hamlets of surprised peasants—no foreigner had been seen here for decades—the pagoda slipped in and out of our vision like a mirage. I was so afraid that it would prove to be only an ancient Buddhist pagoda. As we drew closer we could see that it had seven stories and that sprouting from its terra-cotta–colored walls and roofs were bushes, shrubs, even a complete tree! Somewhat alarmingly, the entire edifice leaned like a Chinese version of the Tower of Pisa, looking as if a good push would send it crashing down.

At last we arrived at the foot of the hill, halfway up which stood the pagoda. Below us were mud-and-thatch houses and many villagers, oblivious to our sense of excitement but fascinated to see so many foreigners. Looking up at the towering pagoda, we could clearly see its classic Tang design—as well as the toll that the centuries had taken on it. As we began to climb the dirt track up to the pagoda, we stumbled over fragments of decorated terra-cotta tiles and molding, most a dark earthy color but occasionally a piece with traces of green and even blue glazing. Such finds are common at ancient Chinese temple sites and most were standard designs of the sort to be found on sites from the fifth century A.D. onward: flowers, dragons, and scrolls.

But among all these pieces, one stood out as very different. It was a leaf design, classically Greek in style, and it would not have looked out of place in the great churches of Constantinople or on the pillars of the Byzantine churches of Ravenna. Western styles and in particular classical Greek-style designs and motifs entered China around the fifth century A.D. with the coming of Buddhism, yet they were also used in early Christian churches.

After climbing for ten minutes my colleagues and I reached a plateau cut into the steep hillside where the pagoda and other remains stood. A small Buddhist temple, a couple of farmhouses, and a tiny house for the nun who cared for the Buddhist temple occupied perhaps one-tenth of the site. The local people, farmers, and some Chinese visitors were surprised to see us, but all made us as welcome as if we were dear friends. Among them, the elderly Buddhist caretaker nun informed us she was 115 years old. Wizened but vigorous and sharp, she was delighted to have such visitors. She had become a nun in the first few years of the twentieth century and had survived the collapse of the empire, the war lords of the 1920s, the Japanese invasions of the 1930s, the civil war of the 1940s, and then the increasing persecution of people of religious faiths under communism from the 1950s onward. The Cultural Revolution of 1966–1976 had nearly killed her, but when more liberal attitudes toward religion arose in the late 1970s she had reopened the temple here.

As she and her young assistant busied themselves making tea for us, we wandered the site. The plateau was large, about three hundred feet long, and toward the eastern end stood the impressive seven-storey pagoda, rising maybe eighty feet into the sky. It was badly damaged with a great crack up the northern side and it tilted slightly to the west. We had been told by the nun that it had been hit by an earthquake in 1556 and that since then no one had been able to climb up inside. Around that time, she said, its entrance had been sealed. She did not mention its origin and I was too nervous at that point to ask.

Instead, I excused myself and roamed the site, hungry for anything that might declare to me that it was unequivocally Christian. No crosses leapt out at me; no statue of Jesus or inscription declared this to be a Da Qin site. The pagoda was very fine, of a classic late Tang design (ca. eighth century A.D.), but it bore no distinctively Western features.

Fearful of the gentle scorn of my friends, I sought sanctuary by climbing higher up the hillside so I could look down on the site. Settling myself on the grass, I was across from the tower's fifth storey. It started to rain. Peering up through the drizzle, I surveyed the ancient pagoda. Then I looked down at the scurry of activity our arrival had created. Local people were climbing the hill from the village below. The diminutive, kindly nun was busy finding food to accompany our tea. To the west I saw the little fields and tiny house of the farmer who now occupied most of the site. Haystacks perched like little thatched houses beside the farm and its outhouse. Low stone walls separated much of the site into garden plots in which vegetables were growing. The little Buddhist temple was immediately below me, to the east of the pagoda itself. Lazy smoke rose from the nun's house, drifting across the plateau.

View of Da Qin pagoda from up the hill, from which point the author realized the east-to-west orientation of the plaza. Note the grasses growing from the pagoda's roof and ledges. The eighteenth-century Buddhist temple is just visible in the bottom right-hand corner. (© Martin Palmer/ CIRCA)

To the east, I could just see Lou Guan Tai, from where we had come. It was a scene that had not changed much in hundreds of years.

Suddenly I realized that the plateau of our pagoda ran east to west and I leapt to my feet with a triumphant cry. It is an immutable design of every Chinese temple, Buddhist, Taoist, or Confucian, that it runs north to south. Any plateau cut into a steep hillside like this for a Chinese temple would have been cut to run from the north to the south. Yet this one ran east to west, as does every Christian church, facing east to celebrate the rising sun. For example, the third- or fourth-century church at Wroxeter in Shropshire, England, runs thus, as do all the oldest extant churches from Britain to Jordan. Here was the first firm piece of evidence that this was no ordinary Chinese religious site but one whose feng shui, whose spiritual orientation, was classically Christian. If this site also followed standard Christian design, then the pagoda would have been part of the monastic buildings as its library, for that's what pagodas were built for. To the west of the pagoda would have been the church itself, now covered by a mound of rubble and earth, and to the east would have been the monastic burial ground.

I bounded down the hill, shouting out my discovery. The commotion below increased, and the nun asked why I was so excited. I explained that I believed this site had once, long, long ago, been a most important Christian church and monastery.

A stunned silence fell as the villagers looked at the ancient nun. Drawing herself up to her full five feet she looked me in the eyes with astonishment. "Well, we all know that! This was the most famous Christian monastery in all China in the Tang Dynasty." The locals nodded in agreement.

I was speechless, so she continued. Local legend had kept alive the memory of the Christian monks who had built the church, the monastery, and later the pagoda, and who had worshiped here from the seventh to ninth century A.D. Indeed, there was considerable local pride in this fact. Then they began to tell us of the discoveries made here: how in ca. 1625 A.D. the great Stone, now in the Forest of Stele Museum, describing the coming of Christianity to China had been dug up on this very site; how in the 1920s another inscription with a Christian cross had been dug up but was stolen during the Japanese Occupation and had never been seen since.

Looking back, even then it was quite clear to us that we had indeed found the lost monastery of the early Church in China. Lost, that is, to the West, and lost to most of China, but loved, honored, and remembered by the local people. I was elated beyond belief, and I was also humbled. Years of work would be

Fragment of a statue found at Da Qin in 1998 that is part of a wing of a large stone angel and dates from the seventh century. (© Tjalling Halbertsma/CIRCA)

needed to confirm the truth of our discovery to the satisfaction of historians and scientists, but the people of this ancient place had never lost the deep certainty that theirs was a site of spiritual importance, imbued with the spirit of centuries and of many cultures' sacred beliefs.

We talked and talked that afternoon. Various finds were brought for us to see and identify. A small fragment of what we at first believed to be a marble statue's robes classically Western in appearance was shown to us. We later were able to confirm that this fragment is actually a piece of an angel's wing and is similar to that in a mural found at another site in China that dates to the fifth century. A carved mythological creature—half dog, half lion—that must once have guarded some sacred site here. The Chinese character for "horse" carved on an ancient stone slab. And many pieces of terra-cotta molding, mostly traditional Chinese, but a few whose style hinted at an origin in the West. Most were from buildings erected long after the Tang Dynasty, long after the Christians had gone. Meanwhile, Tjalling had been busy photographing everything, Val and Jane sketched maps, and Jay, Xiao Min, and I wandered the site looking for more evidence of its Christian past but mostly speculating as to what might be just beneath our feet.

Angel with wings comparable in style to the fragment we found at Da Qin. This wall painting was found in 1903 at Miran in Xinjiang Province, China. It comes from a Manichaean site of the fifth century A.D. there.

As dusk fell we prepared to leave, packing up the many rolls of photographs we had taken, the drawings and maps we'd sketched, and the people's stories we had written down. As we were about to descend the hill, I paused for a moment and the old nun gently touched my arm. "You want to pray, don't you?" she asked and I nodded, wondering how she knew. "Go ahead then. They will all hear you."

As night drew in and the features of the Christian pagoda of the long-lost Da Qin Christian monastery slid into the darkness, I stood where I guessed the church had been. I stood where fourteen hundred years ago Christians had faced east and prayed, and I too prayed. I felt I had finally come home after twenty-five years of searching for that home, of never really knowing if it did, in fact, exist. Yet here was evidence of a living Tao of Jesus, a once-vital practice of Jesus' teachings in a Taoist context. I wept for joy, for love of my faith, for the gentleness of the Buddhist nun, and because my heart was full to bursting.

Western-style stone capital (top of a column) from Da Qin. (© Martin Palmer/CIRCA)

That was in 1998.

A year passed before I could return to Da Qin again. Meanwhile, my colleagues in China had notified the provincial government and the national government of our discoveries and their significance. Within a month the pagoda had been cocooned in scaffolding and work had begun to heal the great crack, right the whole edifice, and restore it inside. During the course of the restoration, two unusual statues were found inside the pagoda and as a result I was invited back by the government. I was eager to see them and learn from the authorities what the future might hold for Da Qin.

On a warm May day in 1999 I once again watched the pagoda come into close view as my friend Zhao Xiao Min, a scholar of the Tang Dynasty, and I climbed together up the slope. A reception committee of the site manager, local magistrate, and two art experts from the Provincial Museum in Xian awaited us. The Cultural Relics Bureau of Shaanxi Province, the local branch of the main Chinese government agency responsible for antiquities, had sent Mr. Yin and Mr. Zhou, specialists respectively in Buddhist and Taoist antiquities, especially statues. To our great sadness they

Work under way in 1999 to straighten the leaning pagoda of Da Qin. (© Xia Ju Xian/CIRCA)

The tomb of the Buddhist nun who befriended the author and his team. Behind is the pagoda in its restoration scaffolding. The topmost character of the gravestone says "Buddha." The characters on the pagoda proclaim that this is the great Christian monastery of Da Qin, now being faithfully restored. (© Tjalling Halbertsma/CIRCA)

told us that our friend the nun had died a month after our visit. Her beautiful tomb near the pagoda records her 116 years, a dignified reminder of a long life. We laid the flowers we had brought with us to give her on her tomb, said a prayer for her spirit, and then turned our attention to the pagoda.

The site had been changed radically. A new dirt road had been

Restoration of pagoda in progress. (© Tjalling Halbertsma/CIRCA)

cut to the plateau; shrubs and brush had been cleared from around the base of the pagoda; building materials were stacked up where previously there had been mounds of soil or dirt tracks. The whole scene, so peaceful a year ago, was now full of people, engines, backloaders, bulldozers, and noise. The restoration work on the external structure included the creation of a concrete raft to secure the base of the pagoda, repair of the crumbling bricks and stone work, and removal of the trees and other growths on top of the pagoda.

After the formalities of our reception and an inspection of the work under way, we were invited to climb up inside the pagoda to see the two statues. We had been told that the site team and art experts they brought in thought them strange, so we were particularly eager to get to them. The great crack in the pagoda was not yet completely mended, however, so we could not yet use the original ground-level entrance, but had to climb the scaffolding to get in.

Because of a terrible fear of heights and especially of climbing ladders, I stood weak-kneed at the bottom of the structure, knowing that I was going to have to go up. Adding to my anxiety was my responsibility for recording a program for BBC Radio on the discovery of the site and the work in progress. This meant I not only had to climb the awful structure but would have to do so with a microphone in one hand and the equipment slung over my shoulder. Every part of me shook with fear, but there was no way out of this. I had to do it.

With my good friends from the site ahead to encourage me and Xiao Min behind to catch me, I inched my way up the scaffolding. The members of the Chinese team working on the site all waited patiently while this terrified Englishman slowly, so slowly, made his way up. They even gave a cheer when I got to the top!

With knees like jelly and legs like blancmange I stood in the window of the pagoda and prepared to go in, Xiao Min graciously insisting that I go first. Wrapping the cord of the microphone around my arm as I had been taught, I switched on the recorder and stepped into the gloom of the pagoda. Crouching, I began to crunch my way across centuries of debris. Broken tiles, splintered remains of wooden stairs, bird and bat droppings, and dust and dirt were everywhere. In hushed tones I described all this into the recording machine to be broadcast to the gentle listeners of Radio 4. Scuffling the ground for added sound effects, I moved toward the center of the pagoda, keeping a careful eye on the ground, for the floor was missing in various places and the distance down to the next level was a plummet of a good twenty to twenty-five feet.

When I stood up, I saw a huge statue towering above me, looming unexpectedly out of the gloom, dwarfing and awing me. I was so astonished, so frightened, so excited that I fell back on the language of a rather misspent youth, yelling a grievous profanity loud and clear and straight into the microphone. Later, as this sort of thing could never be broadcast on our station, I had to go out and come back in again as if for the first time and exclaim something more acceptable.

Rising ten feet high and five feet wide, made from mud, plaster, and wood, was a huge statue set into a grotto. It was immediately clear to me that this was no ordinary Chinese statue, although the surrounds were classically Chinese. The basic shape was that of a sacred mountain. Indeed, it was the symbolic form of the Five Sacred Mountains of Taoism. Revered for more than two thousand years, these mountains are frequently used in traditional Chinese art. Set into this basic outline was a cave, within which were the broken remains of a human figure. Everything about this late eighth- to early ninth-century sculpture was grandly and beautifully Chinese—except the figure itself. Seated on the ground in a posture unknown in Chinese religious art, the figure's left leg was fully extended. Rising behind it was its right leg, bent at the knee. No Chinese deity has ever been depicted in such a way. (This was later confirmed to me by the two Chinese art experts from the Cultural Relics Bureau.)

Because of my background in Christian religious art, I believed that I knew immediately what I was looking at. For many

The eighth- to ninth-century Nativity scene on the second floor of Da Qin pagoda, with the remains of the Western-style legs of the reclining Mary. The outline that overarches the sculpture is the Five Sacred Mountains of Taoism. (© Xia Ju Xian/CIRCA)

years I have had the privilege of working with Orthodox Christian churches from Russia to Greece. In the monasteries and churches, icons and paintings from over a thousand years of religious tradition are still highly prized, and their style and symbolism are still observed and replicated by leading icon painters today.

Several artists had taught me their meaning and significance, in particular Brother Aidan, a monk of the monastery of Iveron on Mount Athos, Greece, the very heartland of Orthodox religious art.

In the Orthodox tradition, the icon of the Nativity of Christ is completely unlike that of Roman Catholic and other Western art. For reasons that I have never been able to understand, Orthodox icons take their images of the Nativity not from the Gospels of Matthew and Luke, but from a strange and beautiful nonbiblical book, *The Book of James.*

> Mary said to Joseph, "Take me down from the ass, for that which is in me presses to come forth."
>
> But Joseph replied, "Whither shall I take thee? For this place is a desert."
>
> Then said Mary again to Joseph, "Take me down, for that which is within me mightily presses me."
>
> And Joseph took her down. And he found there a cave and led her into it. (12:10–14)[4]

Joseph then heads toward Bethlehem, as he later recounts:

> Then I [Joseph] beheld a woman coming down from the mountains and she said to me "Where art thou going, O man?"
>
> And I said to her, "I go to enquire for a Hebrew midwife."
>
> She replied to me, "Where is the woman that is to be delivered?"
>
> And I answered, "In the cave . . ."
>
> And the midwife went along with him and stood in the cave. Then a bright light overshadowed the cave and the midwife said, "This day my soul is magnified, for mine eyes have seen surprising things, and salvation is brought forth in Israel."

This sixteenth-century Russian icon depicts Mary lying inside the cave in the mountain with her right leg slightly raised and Christ off at an angle to her—as in the pagoda statue. The cave is lit by the star above, while the other figures are from scenes later in the Nativity narrative. (Nativity of Christ, Russian, mid–sixteenth century, tempera on panel, 34 × 23 inches, private collection, USA, Photo Temple Gallery.)

But on a sudden the cloud became a great light in the
cave so their eyes could not bear it. But the light gradually
decreased, until the infant appeared and sucked the breast
of his mother Mary. (14: 1–4, 9–12)

So it is that Orthodox icons, paintings, and statues of the Nativity
usually show a fine high mountain, within which is a cave, within
which lies Mary, right leg raised and bent at the knee, left leg extended along the ground. In her hand or lying beside her is the
Christ Child.

On the statue at Da Qin, the remains of a hand resting on the
bent knee show that the figure had held something, although it is
now gone. Its outline can be seen, however, the outline of a much
smaller figure, the size of a child. That and the style of the robes
made me sure this was a mother holding her child. In other words,
a depiction of the Nativity, made in China ca. A.D. 800 and using
the tradition of the Taoist Sacred Mountains as a backdrop, was
now before me. I was looking at what I believe to be the oldest
known Christian statue in China and a stunning affirmation of the
role of Mary in the early Church of China.

Astonishment, wonder, and a deep sense of being in the Presence of the Other overwhelmed me. I had not expected to find
something as dramatic as this. For nearly an hour I sketched,
photographed, examined, and prayed to this wondrous statue.
Xiao Min called up others from the Chinese team to hear what I
was saying and to record the details. The Chinese were as delighted as I to know what the statue represents.

After about an hour I was ready to see the other statue on the
next floor up. In the center of the pagoda were the remnants of a
wooden staircase that had connected all the floors through a stair-
well that went directly through the core of the pagoda. The earthquake in 1556 and then four and a half centuries of decay had
almost completely destroyed the first eight steps of the staircase on

this level and the remainder hung down at a terrifying angle, with perhaps one step in three still intact.

Once again my stomach and heart quaked as I prepared to go up. While my colleagues held a plank of wood at waist level for me to mount, I reached up to the ends of the broken staircase. Slowly my friends and colleagues lifted me up as I grasped farther and farther up the railings of the crumbling staircase until I was raised some six feet and could step up and onto the staircase. Moving at what must have seemed a ridiculously slow pace that was to me unhealthily fast, I climbed one by one the few remaining steps until I reached the next floor. Here I found most of the floorboards had rotted, leaving just a rim around the edge on which to stand. Slowly, Xiao Min and art expert Mr. Yin also came up, accompanied by all but two of the team, who were left below to catch us if we fell—and to help us down if we didn't.

This time I was so frightened all I could do was clutch the wall and stare across the decayed floor at the opposite wall. There, a much smaller but similarly constructed statue of mud, wood, and plaster stood, about six feet tall and four feet wide. So petrified was I that the brave Mr. Yin had to take photographs for me. Balanced on a thin, cracked floor beam that stretched halfway across the empty space, he took a series of hurried photos.

The statue on this second level depicts a city with Chinese bell and drum towers in the background. In the foreground is a tree, seated beneath which are the remains of another human figure. Once again the posture of the figure is unknown in Chinese art— it is leaning on a stone, one leg stretched out and the other raised and bent behind it—so we have concluded that this is not the Buddha under the bodhi tree, the most common depiction of the Buddha at the scene of his enlightenment. Although at the time I was unsure what this statue represents, several art historians and I have come to believe that the figure is Jonah, resting under his gourd tree outside Nineveh. In the Book of Jonah in the Hebrew Bible or Old Testament, Jonah was told by God to go and prophesy

The eighth- to ninth-century remains of the statue of Jonah on the third floor of Da Qin pagoda. A bell and drum tower can be seen on either side of a central tower in the background depiction of Ninevah as a Chinese city. (© Xia Ju Xian / CIRCA)

doom and gloom to the city of Nineveh. Jonah, however, didn't wish to obey this calling and tried to run away from God, eventually taking a ship to escape. A great storm arose and he was thrown overboard by the crew, who believed he had brought the disfavor of God upon the ship. Swallowed by a whale, Jonah dwelt three days in its belly, only to be thrown up on the shores of the very city from which he had tried to run.

Jonah's three days in the belly of the whale were seen by early Christians as a symbol and prefiguring of Christ's three days in the tomb and his subsequent resurrection. As such, the motif of Jonah was adopted as a hidden symbol of Christianity during the early centuries of persecution, and so could have been exported to the East with the traveling Christians of the time. Even though the Taoist Christians of Da Qin were not originally persecuted, they would have known this symbolism and taken hope and inspiration from it. It is possible, therefore, that we had found the only known statue to depict, albeit symbolically, the death and resurrection of Christ from the early Church in China. We are not as convinced of the identity of this statue as we are of the first floor's Nativity scene, but I can think of no other Christian subject that would fit. Furthermore, Taoist and Buddhist religious art prescribes only a few correct positions for the human figure. This position of the body reclining with one knee raised is not one of them.

As we descended very, very carefully to the first floor, we each knew that we carried with us the most extraordinary news. On the second floor, we stood—five Chinese and one Englishman; Christian, Communist, Taoist, and Buddhist—in awe before the statue we had begun to call Our Lady of China, something greater than us all holding us there in silence. For a moment, we bowed our heads and stood captive to the presence and magnetism of a mystery that spanned centuries and cultures. Then we turned, going back down the ladder and into the world to tell of what we had seen.

To understand why, in a remote part of present-day China, the remains of an early Christian Church still stand, why the Nativity is shown in the context of the Five Sacred Mountains of Taoism, why a Buddhist nun recalled with pride the monks from the West, and why virtually no one else has ever heard of the extraordinary Church of the East in China and its astonishing version of the Christ story, we need to travel thousands of miles to the west and go back to the earliest centuries of the first Christian millennium.

Beginnings of the Church
in China: The First Sutra

In the year A.D. 635, a formal delegation of Christians arrived in Chang-an, now Xian, having traveled from lands west of China, most likely from Persia. They would have journeyed along the Silk Road, traversing deserts, mountains, and plains, all the time on the lookout for bands of marauding thieves. If, as seems likely, they set off from the most eastern part of Persia, or from lands further east, they would have traveled for many months, possibly even as long as half a year.

Upon arriving at the city gate of Chang-an, the capital of Tang Dynasty China, they were formally greeted. The huge gateway would have spoken clearly of the power and might of China. Rising over twenty yards high and being some twelve yards thick, it was made of rammed earth, faced with brick and topped by stone. It formed part of a wall twenty-three miles long, embracing a city of some one million people.

The leader of the delegation, a man named Aluoben, was led in through the mighty gate by a noble of the imperial household and brought with the others of the Christian group before the Emperor Taizong. We know from the Chinese records that the Christians

The Persian delegation led by Aluoben were not the first Persians the Chinese had seen. Discovered a mile from the Da Qin monastery is this Tang Dynasty carving of a Persian decorating the top of a hitching post. It could possibly be a representation of a visitor to the area or the monastery. (© Tjalling Halbertsma/CIRCA)

were dressed in white flowing robes and carried before them icons of Christ, Mary, and the saints as well as copies of their sacred books. The Tang Court was used to exotic foreigners coming to trade with China, for example, musicians and performers seeking their fortune in the rapidly expanding Chinese Empire. One wonders what they made of those Christian priests and their bishop—for so he was—Aluoben.

To the Persians in the entourage of the Church, the emperor's Court must have seemed even more gorgeous and wealthy than the Court of the Sassanian shahs of Persia. For this was a young and vigorous empire to which riches from all over Central Asia, Southeast Asia, and China flowed. We know from descriptions and paintings of the beautiful silk robes, the caparisoned horses, the gold and silver vessels, and the stunning architecture of the Tang Dynasty. Militarily, the empire was also impressive. At that time, China had the largest standing army in the world. The ferocious guards of the Tang Dynasty were so feared that they and their armor were immortalized in the fierce demeanor and armor of temple guardians.

The strength and extent of the Tang military might is captured in this quote from the poem "On the Frontier" by Li Ho (A.D. 791–817)

A Tarter horn tugs at the north wind.
Thistle Gate shines whiter than the stream.
The sky swallows the road to Kokonor.
On the Great Wall a thousand miles of moonlight.[5]

The military had helped restore the deserted lands that civil war and poor government had left fallow. This security and productivity are illustrated in this text from the New Tang History written in the eleventh century by Ou-yang Hsiu and Sung Ch'I: "After he [Emperor Gaozu] had subdued the empire he dismissed them all, so that they could return home. Thirty thousand of them still wished to continue as guards, and to them he distributed the rich land north of the Wei river along the Pai-chu [an irrigation canal near Ching-yang in Shaanxi] which had been abandoned by the common people."[6] Traveling through the empire, which in

Aluoben's time stretched far to the west, the Christians would have seen the revived fertility of lands long wasted by civil war and weak government. Armed security meant a stable life for the peasants and safe trading and travel for the merchants. Nearly twenty years had passed since the Tang Dynasty had been established by the capture of the ancient capital city of Chang-an from the fallen forces of the short-lived Sui Dynasty (A.D. 589–618). The Tang Dynasty had restored order after a vicious civil war and was on its way to creating the most powerful empire in Chinese history and the greatest empire of its time.

The formal delegation had come to China on a mission that had been long planned and expected. They were welcomed by the emperor, who expressed his pleasure at their arrival through the words of an imperial edict, which are recorded on the stele found in 1625: **"The Way does not have a common name and the sacred does not have a common form. Proclaim the teachings everywhere for the salvation of the people. Aluoben, the man of great virtue from the Da Qin Empire, came from a far land and arrived at the capital to present the teachings and images of his religion. His message is mysterious and wonderful beyond our understanding. The teachings tell us about the origin of things and how they were created and nourished. The message is lucid and clear; the teachings will benefit all; and they shall be practiced throughout the land"** (3:8–13). The Christian teachings brought by Aluoben helped establish in China what would become one of the most radical and experimental of all Churches ever to have existed.

With the arrival and establishment of Christianity in the seventh century, the Chinese gave this new faith a new name. All the documents referring to the faith in Chinese use one basic title and one extended title. The basic title is "The Religion of Light" or "The Religion of Illumination," indicated by two Chinese characters usually translated as "Luminous" and "Religion."

luminous/light religion

The character for religion is the same as the one used to describe Taoism and Buddhism. To translate the character for Luminous I have opted for the phrase Religion of Light, which seems to represent the original intention of the title and something of the Church's own self-understanding.

The longer title, "Da Qin Luminous Religion," I have translated as "The Religion of Light from the West." As the old woman who pointed out the Da Qin monastery from Lao Zi's temple said, the monastery was built "by monks who came from the West and believed in one God."

The details of the arrival of Christianity in China are primarily found on the Stone Sutra that had so fascinated me as a youth and inaugurated my own mission to recover the history of the Taoist Christians. The Stone of the Church of the East, carved in 781, commemorates this mission of one hundred and fifty years before, in 635.

✍ MISSIONS FROM THE WEST ✎

Christians most likely visited China from the fifth century onward. Traders, members of converted tribes, soldiers of fortune, and possibly even Tibetan Christians visited the reemerging China of the sixth century. Most of these early Christian visitors were likely from the greater Church of the East, not from the Western Churches of Rome and Constantinople. The Church of the East moved and expanded from the heartland of Persia along the trading networks of the ancient East. As its members traveled, they told of their faith and built modest places for worship.

From the third century onward, books and records treasured by Eastern and Western Christians recount that the Apostle St. Thomas had reached India and gone on to China. By the sixth century, Christian churches, bishoprics, and even archbishoprics were well established within a few weeks' journey of the Chinese heartlands. Church documents from the fifth century onward record that the Church was in touch with the Chinese.

From the formal nature of the commemoration of the mission in 635, however, we can tell that this was the first serious engagement between the Church and China. Aluoben was almost certainly a monk and most probably a bishop. He appears to have been Persian, judging from his name, and as a priest of the Church of the East, he would have spoken and read Syriac. Indeed, the Stone of the Church of the East has Syriac script on it, and just as the Church in India still uses Syriac as a liturgical language, so it would seem the whole Church of the East used Syriac as its sacred language. Aluoben is described on the Stone as coming from Da Qin—the Empire of the West, which usually meant the Roman Empire—or more usually just the West. The Chinese described this Christian monk as from the West, just as Westerners would have described a Chinese or Japanese or Indian as from the East. The important thing was that Aluoben had come to China with a new religion. The Chinese were not that interested in how he got there nor where he had been before coming to China.

The name Aluoben, while clearly a Chinese attempt to phoneticize a Syriac religious name, is a mystery. It could be from Aluobeno meaning, in Syriac, "the Return of God," or Rabban meaning "teacher." Some think it is version of the name Adam. It could also be Jaballaha, which means "the Conversion of God"; the Chinese might have dropped the first syllable and provided a classic Chinese ending.[7] Saeki, author of two of the most important studies on the Church in China, in one of which I found the map of Da Qin, claims it is a version of Abraham.

Based on the terms used in the Chinese descriptions of the mission, as engraved on the Stone and briefly mentioned in the Sutra *Let Us Praise*, it is clear that Aluoben headed a well-planned mission that arrived in 635 and was expected. Someone had been in touch earlier to prepare the emperor for the arrival of this dignitary. The mission was escorted into the capital bearing the first collection of the Jesus Sutras, icons, and other paraphernalia of the faith. It is hard to imagine such an entourage was just Aluoben and a couple of servants. In our translations into Chinese of the earliest Jesus Sutras, we found clear evidence that the Church had searched widely and given considerable thought to finding the right ideas, texts, and people to communicate with the Buddhist, Taoist, and Shamanic cultures of China.

There is no record of this mission, however, in the patriarchal correspondence of the seventh-century Church of the East. It is only later, in the eighth century, that specific references to bishops and churches in China begin to appear. This lack of Western records makes it possible to assume that Aluoben and his team were from Central Asia, perhaps Samarkand in present-day Uzbekistan, Herat in Afghanistan, or Merv, also known as Mary, in present-day Turkmenistan. There the Church was strong, numerous trade routes and worlds converged, and Indians, Tibetans, Indo-Greeks, steppe peoples, and Persians mixed and exchanged ideas. From

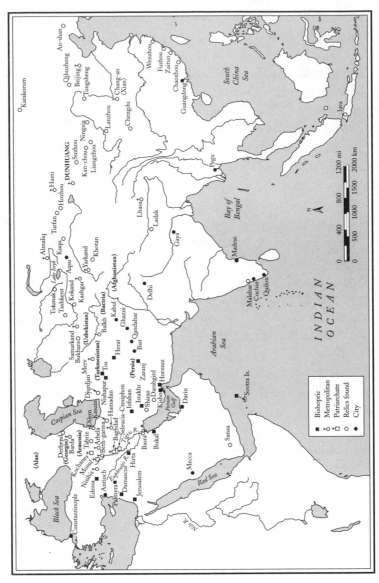

The thousands of miles of the extent of the Church of the East took it from Baghdad to China.

there a team as varied as the 635 mission to China could have been created. From there, too, the many different teachings and books that became the Sutras could have been assembled before the mission embarked. Central Asians would have had real social, political, economic, and religious interest in the emerging Chinese Empire. The Church of the East and the nations in which it resided and the people it influenced would have wanted knowledge of the empire and alliances, which, in those days, often were initially attempted through the contacts of missionaries.

In contrast, patriarchal headquarters in seventh-century Seleucid-Ctesiphon (which later moved to Baghdad, before fleeing that city in 1924) had been troubled for decades by the war between the Byzantine and the Sassanian Empires of the Mideast. By 632, this conflict had exhausted both empires and it is unlikely that either would have had the energy or interest to send a mission to China. Precisely because the Church headquarters had been caught up in what was effectively a war zone, the Church farther to the east, especially around the powerful archbishopric in Afghanistan or the Church center in Turkmenistan, could have gone its own way.

Evidence that such a team came from the eastern edges of the Christian world lies in the Jesus Sutras themselves. These early teaching scripts tell us explicitly that they are early translations of the books brought by Aluoben and they make references throughout to other ancient sacred texts and cultures to help explain these Western beliefs and practices. Besides our physical quest for the origins of the Jesus Sutras, my colleagues and I have also been driven to investigate the Jesus Sutras' literary origins. As a result, we have uncovered a marvelously skillful use of Buddhist, Taoist, Greek, and other scriptures and teachings within the Jesus Sutras that testify to a vital synthesis of cultures and faiths.

Certain key Buddhist Sutras, such as the *Meditation Sutra* (or the *Kasyapaparivarta* or the *Bhavana-Krama*, teachings that form the bedrock of belief and practice), exist only in translation today. This is because the original communities in India where the Sutras were compiled were destroyed in the eighth to eleventh centuries A.D. and their foundational Sanskrit books perished with them. To this day, it is common practice for Buddhist scholars to study Chinese, Korean, and even Japanese translations of ancient Buddhist Sutras in search of lost Sanskrit originals. As my colleagues and I translated the Chinese Christian Sutras, we began to realize that they preserved their own translations of books whose originals in Syriac, Greek, or other languages had long since disappeared. The Christian communities from which they came, with the exception of the Thomarist and the Assyrian Churches, have also been wiped out. The Thomarists, who trace themselves back to St. Thomas the Apostle's mission to India of the first century, survive in India and in fact have become quite strong in some states. The Assyrian Christians are the last remains of the once mighty Church of the East and are so called by the Western Churches to distinguish them from Protestant and Catholic Christians in modern-day Iraq and Iran. Of the other great branches of the Church of the East in places such as Arabia, Tibet, and the steppes, virtually nothing survives. Yet the translated Sutras give voice to their beliefs and their efforts to convey them to others.

After the official reception of Aluoben's mission, according to other historical Chinese sources, the emperor awarded funds and offices in which the delegation could undertake the translation into Chinese of the Sutras they had brought and prepare a report to lay before him.[8] This act of imperial patronage is recorded outside the Christian source materials in Song Min Jiu's eleventh-century *Atlas of Chang-an* in the following entry: "In the north east of the I-ning Ward there was the Persian temple. In the twelfth year of Cheng-kuan (A.D. 638) the Emperor Taizong had it built for Alossu a foreign monk from Da Qin."[9] Alossu refers to Aluoben, and Persian was another term for Western. There, in a foreigners' enclave, the Christians set about translating the Sutras. There, the first Christian monastery in China was built. Twelve years later in 650, according to local records at Lou Guan Tai and elsewhere, the Da Qin monastery that we rediscovered was built in the environs of that great Taoist center. The text of the Stone claims that thereafter monasteries were built in every province of China. This would mean dozens of monasteries arose; later, the text refers to monasteries in every major city.

The first monastery in Chang-an is evidence that the faith had established itself within a decade or so. In the foreign quarter of Chang-an were more than a hundred temples—Buddhist, Taoist, Christian, Zoroastrian, possibly Muslim, and probably Manichaean.[10] Chang-an was a truly cosmopolitan city and it served the needs of the many trading peoples who thronged its thoroughfares.

The founding of the second monastery in the sacred Lou Guan Tai precinct tells a very different story. There is no other evidence that any religion, even Buddhism, was allowed in this most major of all Taoist sites. For a Christian monastery and study center to have been permitted and even encouraged in this area shows that the emperor had come to believe that the Christian faith contributed something different and valuable to his country and his power. Lou Guan Tai itself had risen in the past thirty years to an immense size, wealth, and power because of its official status as the spiritual origin of the Tang Dynasty. The significance of the Christian influence in this Taoist stronghold would be comparable to a new religion being allowed to build a temple within the precincts of Canterbury Cathedral in the Middle Ages, or a new faith being given financial aid and support to build a monastery on the grounds of the White House today. Something important had to have happened to impress the emperor and lead him to grant this new faith its uniquely favored position within the site of his own national and spiritual heritage. Perhaps it was the wisdom of the Jesus Sutras, already being translated, or the lifestyle of the monks that created such a profound influence on the emperor, his Court, and his scholars.

✒ THE EARLY JESUS SUTRAS ✑

The teachings that the first mission to China of 635 had chosen to take with them present a diversity of cultural voices within Tang Dynasty China, but they also represent the core teachings of Jesus and the Western worldview. Most of the books that the Jesus Sutras used as references have completely disappeared from history outside of their preservation in these few fragile Sutras found in China over the past hundred years or so. Yet these teachings reflect the integration of the Jesus story with older traditions and beliefs that produced new versions of the story that had significance to different peoples and cultures.

It is likely that all the scrolls of what we call the Jesus Sutras come from the cave at Dunhuang, where they had been sealed in about 1005. At the cave's rediscovery at the end of the nineteenth century, its contents were scattered through a mixture of adventuring Western explorers who bought scrolls by the sackload and Chinese antiquity robbers and traders who stole or purchased the rest en masse. In 1908 some of the manuscripts were taken to Paris; others, including the Jesus Sutras, began to surface among antiques dealers in China and Japan during the 1920s and 1930s. Few of the scrolls were properly handled or their contents recorded, and many must have disintegrated en route from Dunhuang to the dealers. All the Christian scrolls, the Jesus Sutras, were purchased by either Japanese or European collectors from antiques dealers in and around Beijing in the 1920s. Thus, although we can be fairly sure they came from the hoard at Dunhuang, we cannot be certain. It is just possible that a separate Christian library was found by antiquity thieves and that the scrolls come from there. Sadly, we are unlikely ever to know the exact provenance of the find.

The first set of four were made in or around Chang-an, where Aluoben's translators first worked, but the later ones sometimes tell us exactly where they were written. For example, the Sutra *Taking Refuge in the Trinity* says at the end that it was written in 720 at the Monastery of the West at Shazhou in Gansu Province.

The earliest Sutras present the life of Jesus to people living in cultures where reincarnation and karma were daily issues. They use imagery such as Buddhas and Christ as a raft of salvation and make references to Buddhist ideas of Hell. These images and terms adapt the Old and New Testament worlds to those of the Buddha's life and the *Tao Te Ching*. For example, the four essential ideas in the *Sutra of Returning to Your Original Nature* are based on the core teachings of the *Tao Te Ching*, and the term "Original Nature" comes directly from the Taoist text *Chuang Tzu*. The main savior "deities" of Buddhism, known as Bodhisattvas, are pictured seated in some formal Place of Teaching; this Sutra opens in exactly the same way.

The Jesus Sutras are translated and interpreted in detail throughout the text; here I just want to give an overview of what they are and the teachings they convey. Four of the Sutras date from ca. 640–660 and remain primarily in private collections in Japan. The one that was actually found at Dunhuang in 1908 is now in Paris.

We have called the first *The Sutra of the Teachings of the World-Honored One*. In Chinese the terms used mean "The Lokajvesta [an honorific title for the Buddha as World Teacher] Teaching on Charity, Part 3." It tells us that it was translated into Chinese in 641. Not surprisingly, it is the simplest of the translations, showing that the translators were experimenting with concepts for which the Chinese language did not quite have the right vocabulary. For example, the Sutra confuses left and right when translating the phrase "Don't let your left hand know what your right hand is doing," thus getting it backward. The two characters for left and right are confusingly quite similar. Likewise, the Golden Rule is so badly translated as to be almost unintelligible without knowing the original: "So always treat others as you would like them to treat you" (Matthew 7:12). The translation actually reads "be good, for others like good people, who are good to them, who make goodness back to those who are good to them."

The first is also the most orthodox Sutra in many ways. Indeed, it is almost certainly based on extracts taken from a book, then popular, called *Teachings of the Apostles*, a synopsis of the life of Jesus from the Gospels used throughout the Church of the East for many centuries, but that is now lost except for a few fragments. It is not surprising that this should have been the first book to be translated for the Chinese Court, yet within it are a number of theological surprises showing that the original version of *Teachings of the Apostles* had already undergone some interesting changes and developments. For example, the Syriac *Teachings of the Apostles* draws heavily on the Sermon on the Mount (Matthew 5–7). The original in Matthew is "When you give alms, your left hand must not know what your right is doing: your almsgiving must be secret and your father who sees all that is done in secret will reward you." The Sutra says: **"If someone gives alms, he should do it in the knowledge of the World-Honored One. Let not your left hand know what your right is doing. Pay no attention to outsiders but worship the One Sacred Spirit. The One will become visible to you, and then you should worship only the One"** (1:2).

We've named the second *The Sutra of Cause, Effect, and Salvation*. In Chinese it is called "The First Treatise on the Oneness of Heaven." It is strikingly similar in tone, style, and content to parts of the Indo-Greek Buddhist Sutra called the *Milindapanha*, a teaching about Buddhist cosmology and philosophy thought to have been written between the first century B.C. and the first century A.D. In Sanskrit, its title means "The Questions of King Menander." Also known as Milinda, King Menander ruled from 150 to 135 B.C. and was the most famous of the Greek kings of the region. His name and exploits were even known in Athens during his lifetime.

The *Milindapanha* is a series of discussions between Menander and a Buddhist sage, Nagasena, that deal with classical philosophical issues common to both Theravada Buddhism and Greek philosophy: What is the origin of nature? How do we classify nature? What is it to be human? How does the soul relate to the body? What is true knowledge? How does karma arise? What is reincarnation? Through the philosophical discussion of origins, purpose, and meaning in life and the relationship between physical reality and spiritual reality, the king is shown to have been converted to Buddhism. The Sutra is so Greek and rationalist that many have claimed it is not really a Buddhist Sutra at all, yet today it is still highly revered in the canon of the Theravada Buddhists.

Whether King Menander is the Milinda of the Sutra and whether he ever converted is a moot point, but certainly by around 60 B.C., Greeks with names such as Meridarch Theodorus were dedicating Buddhist temples in the Swat Valley in present-day eastern Afghanistan/northern Pakistan. The book itself says Milinda was king of the Greeks in India. We believe that in the second Jesus Sutra we have found a lost "Indo-Greek Christian" version of the *Milindapanha* that would have been written and used in the Swat Valley by Christian communities that vanished between the eighth and tenth centuries. The Christian communities in this area drew on both classical Greek and classical Buddhist influences in a region that from the second to the sixth centuries A.D. was one of the most important and vital Buddhist centers for art, missionary movements, and philosophy. Though we know from a report of 196 A.D. that there were churches in this area, no other example of a Christian text from this region has been found. We have no way of knowing in what language the original book was written. It could well be Greek, because Greek culture was still strong and much admired. Buddhist texts from this area are written in a special script known as Gandharan and have their base in Sanskrit. It is also possible they were written in Syriac, the international language of the Church of the East, though this was usually reserved for biblical and liturgical books, whereas this is a philosophical, cosmological, and psychological book.

The Sutra, as we have it in the Chinese, opens in a style identical to the *Milindapanha* and uses Greek and Buddhist terms exactly as that text does. It seems to be a deliberate attempt to imitate a book that was highly regarded and used extensively by monks and literate laypeople such as merchants and nobles of the old Indo-Greek kingdoms. Yet the text of this Sutra has adopted certain elements of the Christian Gospel to take into account the existential questions of the peoples of China and Central Asia. In the Buddhist Sutra, a great ruler of one of the most powerful Indo-Greek kingdoms, known for his wisdom, is depicted raising philosophical questions and receiving Buddhist answers from a sage monk. In a similar style, the Christian authors of the second Jesus Sutra write of a ruler who asks comparable questions but who is given Christian answers. For example, the *Milindapanha* opens the discourse on existence thus:

> The king said, "He who is born, Nagasena, does he remain the same or become another?"
> "Neither the same nor another."

The Sutra of Cause, Effect, and Salvation opens:

> **The question is asked: What is the cause of human beings?**
> **The answer is: Humanity is created by that which can be seen and that which can not. (1:1–2)**

The *Milindapanha* uses imagery such as "the architect of a city, when he wants to build one, first clears the site of the town and then proceeds to get rid of the stumps" (II.1.9). This is echoed in the Sutra: **"It is like building a house: the very first thing needed is a place to build" (1.9).**

The *Milindapanha* refers throughout to the four elements—earth, fire, water, and wind—as does the Sutra, and both discuss the Five Skandas, or dimensions of reality, which give the soul the physical space within which to live. First, the *Milindapanha*'s version: "Then the Elder [the monk] repeated the simile of the tree and the seed and said that the skandhas were so many seeds and the king confessed himself satisfied . . . 'where there is an eye and also forms there is sight' " (II.3.4). The Sutra's version: **"The soul has Five Skandas. These are form, perception, consciousness, action, and knowledge. Everyone can see, hear, and speak. Without eyes you cannot see"** (3:1–4).

Even if this Sutra did not come from the Indo-Greek areas and was not influenced by the *Milindapanha* (much more study needs to be undertaken to establish its provenance), it is still an important Sutra that shows Christianity coming to terms with Buddhism as a major belief system with which it needs to coexist.

The third Jesus Sutra may have been translated at the same time as *The Sutra of the Teachings of the World-Honored One*, or a little later than 641. Discovered in a Beijing antiques shop in the 1920s, it is now in Japan. This Sutra is titled in Chinese "Second Part of the Preaching." We have titled it *The Sutra of Origins*, as this is what it addresses. Although the Sutra itself has little in it that helps us identify in which country it originated, it is concerned with the same themes as the second *Sutra of Cause, Effect, and Salvation*. This third sutra, unlike the first two more overtly Christian texts, may have been compiled from various Christian teaching sources expressly to create a new book, an anthology meant for the Chinese mission. It is significant primarily because in it, for the first time, the translators use Taoist terminology that was to become so important in later Sutras. For example, it refers to Yama, god of the underworld, to *qi* as the breath of life, and it uses Tao as a term to discuss the Christian Way.

The last of these early sutras is *The Sutra of Jesus Christ*. In the

Chinese, Jesus is transliterated into what may have been read as Ye-Su and Christ is Mishisuo, the Messiah. A compilation of different Christian books, this Sutra was produced around 645, about a decade after the arrival of the mission. Its use of Chinese is good and its understanding of Chinese religion and philosophy is sophisticated. Its use of portions of the *Teachings of the Apostles* makes the core teachings of Jesus more Buddhist in tone. Most important, it includes text and ideas from the Tibetan Church and materials from a book that shows strong Jain or Hindu influences. It is a fascinating mosaic of ideas current within the Church of the East at that time, a collection of writings from the edges of the Christian world.

✐ THE STORY OF JESUS ✐

The Sutra of the Teachings of the World-Honored One tells us that it was written 641 years after Christ was born. Or, as the Sutra puts it, **"This physical manifestation took place 641 years ago and now all across the world believe."** This date is quite extraordinary, because it is clearly based on the sixth-century A.D.–B.C. calendar system created to make the birth of Christ the pivotal point of world history and time. It is a remarkable testimony to the success of the new calendar that the Church in China was using it less than a century after it had been created. The system was invented by a monk, Dionysius Exiguus, in the mid–sixth century, and one of its earliest uses was by the British Church, which adopted it in 664. To the best of our knowledge, its use in 641 in China is the earliest recorded use of the calendar that has come to define history and time for all world cultures.

    The Sutra of the Teachings of the World-Honored One is a dramatic retelling of the story of Christ and the core of his teachings. It opens and closes with material crafted to make the story more accessible, sensible, and palatable to the Chinese world. As noted earlier, it presents a collection of sayings from the New Testament primarily taken sequentially from Matthew's account of the Sermon on the Mount and appears to be based on the popular second-century compilation of Gospel texts, the *Teachings of the Apostles*, originally written in Syriac. Beginning with the version of Matthew 6:3 quoted earlier, the Sutra then incorporates its version of a section from the Lord's Prayer:

> **Don't hesitate when you pray. Ask first for forgiveness for your sins and at the same time forgive those who have sinned against you. The Heavenly Ruler above will forgive you as you forgive others. (1:5–7)**

Further on is a version of Matthew 6:25–26: "Look at the birds in the sky. They do not sow or reap or gather into barns; yet your heavenly Father feeds them. Are you not worth much more than they are? Can any of you, for all his worrying, add one single cubit to his span of life?":

> **Watch the birds; they don't plant or harvest, and they have no houses to worry about. They do no work yet are fed and watered and never worry about what to wear, because the One cares for them. You are more important than the birds, so why do you worry? (2:15–17)**

A fourth adaptation from Matthew follows (7:3–5). "Why do you observe the splinter in your brother's eye and never notice the plank in your own? How dare you say to your brother, "Let me take the splinter out of your eye," when all the time there is a plank in your own? Hypocrite! Take the plank out of your own eye first, and then you will see clearly enough to take the splinter out of your brother's eye":

**Look for the best in others and correct what is worst in
yourself. Otherwise it is as if you were trying to take a
speck of dust out of someone else's eye while all the time
you had a great beam of wood in your own. We need to get
rid of the beam in your eye. (2:19–21)**

For comparison with the Sutra's first chapter, the full text of
Matthew 6–7 from the Jerusalem Bible is included on pages 69–73.

The Sutra goes on to recount the life, death, and Resurrection
of Jesus. At times, the translator seems to present the view that
Christ was not actually divine, but a human being of transcendent
goodness. For example, at one point the text says, *"The Messiah is
not the Honored One [God]. Instead through his body he showed the people the Honored One"* (4:12–13). Perhaps the writer meant to depict Jesus as a vehicle through whom God worked and was made
visible to humanity. Or it could just be a poor translation into
Chinese of a complex and subtle theological point. It is impossible
to tell.

The Sutra expends a good deal of space recounting and dis-
proving the rumor that the disciples of Jesus had stolen his body,
and attributes this rumor to the Jews of the biblical era. This un-
fortunate prejudice indicates the real tensions that existed between
Jews and Christians in the Persian Empire. At this time, and from
the second century A.D. to the twelfth century, Judaism was still an
active missionary faith that converted tribes in Arabia and rivaled
Christianity in states such as Yemen. Despite the fact that any Jews
who were in China could not possibly have been a threat to Christianity, the Sutra still thunders on this point. As this is a strong
theme in the second-century *Teachings of the Apostles*, it is a further
sign that the Syriac book was the basis of the Chinese translation.

There follows a piece about the Resurrection scene. When
the women come to anoint the body of Jesus on the third day after his death, they discover the empty tomb and see a brilliant
light. The text continues:

The women went to tell all his other students what they had witnessed. As the first woman [Eve] caused the lies of humanity, so it was women who first told the truth about what happened, to show all that the Messiah forgave women and wished them to be treated properly in future, for he appeared and confirmed all they had said. (5:31–32)

A most unusual gloss, but one that explains something of the noted equality of men and women in the Taoist Christian Church in China in the seventh century.

The story moves on beyond the Great Commission (Matthew 28:19–20); when Jesus sends his disciples out to the world to teach and baptize, to explain the significance of his death and Resurrection: "Go, therefore, make disciples of all the nations; baptize them in the name of the Father and of the Son and of the Holy Spirit, and teach them to observe all the commands I give you. And know that I am with you always; yes, to the end of time." It recounts the story of Pentecost and the early Church, with the hardships of the early Church as described in the Acts of the Apostles as well as the persecutions that took place in Persia. It ends with further reflections on the meaning of salvation as provided for the world by Jesus' Incarnation.

This first Sutra is the most clear and conventional Christian account of the Gospel and of Jesus' life in the Jesus Sutras. In trying to tell the story straight, basing it on Western concepts and understandings of the world, however, the early Christians in China ran into a major problem: What was the existential issue or question that Christ had come to solve? The Chinese world believed in karma rather than sin, in repeated rebirth rather than the nothingness of Hell or Hades of the classical Western views of what came after death. To reconcile the two outlooks, the Taoist Christians would eventually make profound theological adaptations.

᥌᥍ THE FIRST SUTRA: ᥊᥍
THE SUTRA OF THE TEACHINGS OF THE
WORLD-HONORED ONE, THIRD PART

CHAPTER ONE

¹The World-Honored One said, If somebody gives alms, they should do it in the knowledge of the World-Honored One.²Let not your left hand know what your right hand is doing.³Pay no attention to outsiders but worship the One Sacred Spirit.⁴The One will become visible to you, and then you should worship only the One.

⁵Don't hesitate when you pray.⁶Ask first for forgiveness for your sins and at the same time forgive those who have sinned against you.⁷The Heavenly Ruler above will forgive you as you forgive others.

⁸If you have a treasure, do not store it on earth where it can decay or be stolen.⁹Instead present it to heaven, where it will not rot or be stolen.

CHAPTER TWO

¹People think there are two important things under Heaven.²The first is God and the second is money.³If you have no money you won't have food or clothing.⁴You'll be as anxious for your family as if they were a child attacked by robbers, anxious about their security.

⁵I say to you: seek just one thing.⁶There is only one sacred spirit who forgives all—if you need clothing you will be clothed.⁷Don't worry about these things.⁸The One knows what you need.⁹If a disciple of the One makes a request to God, it will be granted.¹⁰All ultimately belongs to the One Sacred Spirit.¹¹At birth everyone is given a heavenly soul and the Five Attributes, and at the appropri-

ate time food, drink, or clothing is provided.[12]The Sacred Spirit has no need of these.[13]Watch the birds; they don't plant or harvest, and they have no houses to worry about.[14]They do no work yet are fed and watered and never worry about what to wear, because the One cares for them.[15]You are more important than the birds, so why do you worry?

[16]Be aware of your own qualities and how they relate to others, especially what you see as their failings.[17]Look for the best in others and correct what is worst in yourself.[18]Otherwise it is as if you were trying to take a speck of dust out of someone else's eye while all the time you had a great beam of wood in your own.[19]We need to get rid of the beam in your eye.

[20]Tell the truth in all circumstances, but do not cast truth before swine, because they cannot appreciate it.[21]Doing so won't bring you any benefits and may rouse them to anger; don't you know this?[22]Ask the One and you will receive.[23]Knock on the door and it will be opened.[24]Anybody who sincerely asks something of the One Sacred Spirit will receive it.[25]Knock and the door will open: but if you don't receive what you requested, or the door is not opened, it is because what you asked for isn't right for you.[26]No matter how hard you ask, you won't be given what is bad for you.

[27]If you ask your father for food, you will get food.[28]But if you asked for a stone you would be wasting your time and would never be given it because it is not right.[29]If you ask for a fish, you will receive it.[30]But if you request a serpent, you will be poisoned.[31]So you will not be given one.

[32]If ordinary people make decisions like this because they love you, how much more will your Father, the Compassionate One, do so also![33]He is the One who decides maybe yes, maybe no.[34]There are two issues here.[35]Parents decide what is appropriate for their children; the One decides not on what is wise, or unwise, but only on the basis of who is righteous and who is not.[36]They cannot be reconciled.[37]Those above help those below, but if you don't receive

what you asked for it'll be for good reasons.[38]You cannot be given things that are wrong for you.

[39]Act toward others as you would have them act toward you, and do for others what you would have them do for you.[40]Don't follow the evil way, but go the way of the King's Entrance and find Heaven.[41]Few have achieved this.[42]Others travel the broad path and have a great time, but it leads to the Earth Prisons.

CHAPTER THREE

[1]Some will try to teach you bad ways, but good and evil can be told apart.[2]It is for this reason that the Law has been revealed.[3]The Messiah knew all this and acted accordingly.[4]He shone brightly for three years and six months.[5]He was a student at home until he was killed by being hung on high.[6]There was a Jew who had been a follower but then set his hand against him.[7]The Messiah predicted his death three days beforehand.[8]Any who wish to live after death and go to Heaven can now do so.[9]The Holy acted in a short time to show people what to believe.[10]He taught over three years and six months, after which it is a matter of believing yourself.

[11]The Jews trapped him and he spoke of his understanding of who he really was.[12]He said "I am the Messiah."[13]They said "How dare he say this! He is not the Messiah—not the true Messiah. He is mad and should be arrested. Can you do this?"[14]He went to Bethlehem.[15]This was in the time of Caesar.[16]Even if Caesar had not arrested him he could not have avoided death.[17]He was arrested and tried according to the strict law of the land, and hung up on high.[18]Judged by the law he was condemned to be hung up on high.[19]Caesar said "You people say he must die, according to the law, because of what he said concerning who he was in himself."[20]They said "Who in truth can say 'I am the World-Honored One.' This must stop."

CHAPTER FOUR

[1]Such deceit and problems are not unique.[2]This is how the story has always gone.[3]The first man is the one from whom we all descend.[4]Is it not from his faults that our faults arise?[5]Who can say "I am the World-Honored One?"[6]Wouldn't people see through that straightaway?[7]The first man disobeyed the Honored One's Command and ate freely.[8]The effect of this disobedient act, eating freely, was a change of heart.[9]He began to see himself as able of being equal to the Lord, as enlightened as the World-Honored One.[10]As a result he was no longer in accord.

[11]Anybody who says "I am a god" should die.[12]The Messiah is not the Honored One.[13]Instead, through his body he showed the people the Honored One.[14]He showed the holy transformation beyond all previous reckoning.[15]What he brought was not from being human, but came directly from the Honored One.[16]He showed love to all around him, but the tempter tempts, and this causes problems.[17]This is why the teachings were brought.

[18]As a lamb goes silently to be slaughtered so he was silent, not proclaiming what he had done, for he had to bear in his body the punishment of the Law.[19]Out of love he suffered so that what Adam had caused should be changed by this.[20]While his Five Attributes passed away, he did not die but was released again after his death.[21]Thus is it possible for even those who fail to live after death.[22]Through the holy wonders of the Messiah all can escape becoming ghosts.[23]All of us are saved by his works.[24]You don't need strength to receive him, but he will not leave you weak and vulnerable, without qi [Life Breath].

CHAPTER FIVE

[1]Through the motions of the Law he was hung on high at the appointed time.[2]At that moment the earth shook and the mountains

erupted.[3]The stone rolled away and the beautiful cloth that hung there was ripped in two from top to bottom, as a result of this Holy Event.[4]The virtuous and blessed dead rose from their tombs and the dead walked abroad, seen by many.[5]He was with them for fourteen days in one month.[6]Not a single day passed without them seeing him.[7]Three days had passed since the Holy Event.[8]People cannot see when they dwell in darkness.[9]They can only see and hear when the Holy Event opens their eyes and ears.[10]Because the Messiah was hung up on high he begged to be given firm existence again.[11]It is all as written.

[12]There was a man who was related to the Messiah.[13]He served the World-Honored One and was called Yaoxi [Joseph of Arimathaea].[14]He was a judge of the law of the land and he asked for the corpse.[15]He wrapped him in a new cloth and buried him in a fresh graveyard where a new tomb had been carved into the side of a mountain.[16]A huge stone was rolled in front of the tomb and a seal stamped upon it.[17]The Jewish men also placed a guard.[18]They said "He said he would rise from the dead after three days.[19]Beware— his students will come for his body.[20]They must not be allowed to steal it and then go telling everyone he is alive."

[21]As a result the Jewish men guarded the tomb for three days, watching the sealed place carefully.[22]There were female followers of the Messiah and these women all saw the following.[23]By the tomb stood a flying immortal sent by the World-Honored One and dressed in white, as white as snow.[24]He appeared by the guards, coming down from Heaven to stand beside the great stone.[25]The guards went into the tomb but could not find the body.[26]The flying immortal told them to go and tell the Jews what they had seen.[27]The Jews bribed the guards to keep silent about what they had seen, but the guards spoke of what the One had done, that the Messiah had risen from the dead.

[28]Some women followers, obeying the law, came to where the tomb was.[29]A number of Jews also came at dawn on the third day to the same place.[30]It shone with bright light and the Messiah had

gone.³¹The women went to tell all his other students what they had witnessed.³²As the first woman caused the lies of humanity, so it was women who first told the truth about what had happened, to show all that the Messiah forgave women and wished them to be treated properly in future, for he appeared and confirmed all they had said.³³He came to them all at their place of prayer, so that his students, and then the whole world, should know the truth.³⁴Everyone who saw it went away talking of this.

³⁵His disciples knew what to do.³⁶He told them "Go out and teach everyone, baptise them in water and sign them in the name of the Father, Son, and the Pure Wind to observe everything I have taught.³⁷Know this: I shall be with you until the End of Time."

CHAPTER SIX

¹It is revealed that the Messiah remained here for thirty days after he had risen from the earth.²He taught "You have authority over all living things and will be understood by all."³He promised that the Pure Wind would come from Heaven on those that asked.⁴He was seen in a bright light and then he went into Heaven.⁵A Mighty Compassionate Wind came with true kindness, to perform the great and holy transformation.⁶Everyone saw this.

⁷But evil spirits were roused to evil actions and maliciously attacked all that humanity had been given, throwing everything down to the ground, destroying all that had been gained.⁸The World-Honored One was distressed, and the evil spirits raised their hands against the people, causing terrible suffering and driving them away from the World-Honored One.

⁹Yet all who have faith will be saved.¹⁰Those who have no faith, this is because the evil spirits make it impossible for them to see.¹¹Everyone can see the enlightenment.¹²The True Law brings the religion to those who trust.¹³So have no fear, not even of death; you will live as the Messiah lives.¹⁴Those who believe will be raised after death from the Yellow Springs [Afterlife], every one of

them.¹⁵Ten days after the Messiah ascended to Heaven, he sent the Pure Wind upon his disciples.¹⁶From Heaven he observed the enlightenment the Pure Wind brought to his disciples.¹⁷It came as fire upon them.¹⁸Through the Pure Wind they were inspired to go out and take the true faith to all.¹⁹They took the teachings of the Messiah and helped people see the World-Honored One, who sent the One from the Father to come down from Heaven.²⁰This was the Holy One, the One who suffered for us and brought us freedom.²¹He died, but after three days he escaped from the hold of death, through the action of the World-Honored One's qi.²²Nothing like this has ever been heard of before.

CHAPTER SEVEN

¹Everything in the world has been created for the Messiah.²Before him nobody had ever heard of the dead returning to life.³Through this Law all can be raised back to life from the Yellow Springs, to live forever, after judgment.⁴Every living thing will be judged.

⁵Those who accept the words of the Messiah will live in his realm.⁶Worship the World-Honored One and you will dwell with the Messiah and the Father in the Heavenly Palace.⁷This will be such joy and happiness, nothing will pass and nothing change.⁸The One who was sent was sent by the Father, the World-Honored One.⁹If you do not worship him, you will end up worshiping evil spirits.¹⁰You will be impure and unclean, and you will be dragged into the darkness of the Earth Prisons.¹¹From there you cannot return to the Good Place but must dwell with the Great Evil Ghost [Satan].

¹²To show enlightenment he descended from Heaven and taught the true religion so truth would prevail.¹³His disciples were not just men but were created anew by the World-Honored One.¹⁴In the name of the Messiah these disciples healed and tended to the sick.

¹⁵The Great Evil Ghost called Pa To, who lives on the dead, turned the world against the disciples and stirred up trouble for

them.[16]He pursued the disciples across the face of the earth.[17]They even seized the Jews.[18]He instituted terrible persecutions of both young and old.

[19]Bethelehem is in the land of the Jews, that is, in the West, and here even the king turned against the truth, saying that he was Lord.[20]The Jews were defeated, many killed or scattered across the world, helping to make more disciples for the Messiah.[21]Those who declared for the World-Honored One and served the World-Honored One were hated: yet most people just wanted to continue to believe.

[22]Most of the Messiah's disciples were martyred and their nation was destroyed.[23]Consequently many followed with greater enlightenment and saw the True Way.[24]This Holy Event was for all on earth, and came from the World-Honored One.[25]People need to do right and avoid wrong.[26]The World-Honored One seeks to save all: this is what all the kings and founders of holiness have sought.

[27]But in Bethlehem and in Persia the believers were killed and evil laws passed against them.[28]Those who protested were destroyed.[29]Those who survived in Bethlehem did so only because of the World-Honored One.[30]The Evil Ghost Spirit makes people create false deities, but the World-Honored One sent the Messiah.[31]The World-Honored One caused the Holy Event to touch many throughout the world.[32]Thus did all become clear and falsehood disappear.[33]Seeing this, the Messiah came down from Heaven.[34]This physical manifestation took place 641 years ago and now everyone across the world believes.[35]All can see what has been achieved.[36]You may have been taught that people cannot save themselves.[37]This is why the Heavenly Honored One sends the spirit force to all places to save everyone.[38]It goes to all that live and teaches the truth.[39]This is different from what the various deities and spirits do.

CHAPTER EIGHT

[1]The Messiah chose ordinary people to be his disciples.[2]The true religion comes from Heaven and I teach it.[3]Know this.[4]This is not the way of the Holy Founders and Kings.[5]They chose their disciples from the rich and powerful, and control things through petty people.[6]The Messiah follows the true Law of prayer and liturgy. [7]All will be done, and everyone will know this is what the One Sacred Spirit wills.[8]This holy law is of the house of the One Sacred Spirit.[9]The One Sacred Spirit will save anybody who wants to be saved.[10]The soul returns to Heaven if it obeys the path of the Law—that is, not to trick people, fool or deceive, and not to say false things or do wicked acts.[11]This is the Law.[12]Those who wander from the True Way are sinful and follow not the path of the One Sacred Spirit, but rather a false Way.[13]It is possible to return to the truth, though, for the World-Honored One can bring you back.

[14]There is no other True Way that people can walk.[15]Any other way is judged to be false.[16]Its followers are as bad as those who worship the sun, moon, stars or even the fire gods.[17]They follow the evil spirits, and will go to the fiery Earth Prisons forever.[18]This is because they need greater faith.[19]If they don't follow the One Sacred Spirit, they will dwell with evil spirits and other hell-dwellers and ghosts.[20]This is as written in the Sutras drawn from the true Law teachings of the One Sacred Spirit.

[21]When the time comes for all life to end, evil spirits will seize people and judgment will come from Heaven for all to see.[22]All that is wrong will increase.[23]This is why the One Sacred Spirit took a body and came teaching, saying "I am the Messiah.[24]For three and a half years I came.[25]For three and a half years I struggled with the wicked deeds of the evil ones, and everyone could see this clearly."

[26]Now act virtuously and those who have no faith will be unable to withstand the judgment of the Heavenly Honored One.[27]These

are the evil ghost spirits.²⁸All this the Messiah and the One Sacred Spirit watch closely from Heaven.²⁹When the world ends, the dead will be raised and judged.³⁰Those who believe the teachings, who act virtuously and whose hearts follow the True Way will go to Heaven.³¹There you will be happy forever.

³²Those who know of the True Way of the One Sacred Spirit and have read the Good Book, but do not follow this or the One Sacred Spirit's commands, will dwell with evil spirits and ghosts in the Earth Prisons, and serve the evil ghosts forever.³³In these Earth Prisons they will suffer in a great fire which burns without end.³⁴Listen to this, you who wish to be saved.³⁵Know that what you have heard is true.³⁶If there is anybody not willing to receive this grace, think on your soul and body and their fate.³⁷Anybody displeased, who does not listen, will be cast out and dwell forever with the evil spirits in the Earth Prisons.

MATTHEW 6

Be careful not to parade your good deeds before men to attract their notice; by doing this you will lose all reward from your Father in heaven. So when you give alms, do not have it trumpeted before you; this is what the hypocrites do in the synagogues and in the streets to win men's admiration. I tell you solemnly, they have had their reward. But when you give alms, your left hand must not know what your right hand is doing; your almsgiving must be secret, and your Father who sees all that is done in secret will reward you.

And when you pray, do not imitate the hypocrites: they love to say their prayers standing up in the synagogues and at the street corners for people to see them. I tell you solemnly, they have had their reward. But when you pray, go to your private room and, when you have shut your door, pray to your Father who is in that secret place, and your Father who sees all that is done in secret will reward you.

In your prayers do not babble as the pagans do, for they think that by using many words they will make themselves heard. Do not be like them; your Father knows what you need before you ask him. So you should pray like this:

> Our Father in heaven,
> may your name be held holy,
> your kingdom come,
> your will be done,
> on earth as in heaven.
> Give us today our daily bread.
> And forgive us our debts,
> As we have forgiven those who are in debt to us.
> And do not put us to the test,
> but save us from the evil one.

Yes, if you forgive others their failings, your heavenly Father will forgive you yours; but if you do not forgive others, your Father will not forgive your failings either.

When you fast do not put on a gloomy look as the hypocrites do: they pull long faces to let men know they are fasting. I tell you solemnly, they have had their reward. But when you fast, put oil on your head and wash your face, so that no one will know you are fasting except your Father who sees all that is done in secret; and your Father who sees all that is done in secret will reward you.

Do not store up treasures for yourselves on earth, where moths and woodworms destroy them and thieves can break in and steal. For where your treasure is, there will your heart be also.

The lamp of the body is the eye. It follows that if your eye is sound, your whole body will be filled with light. But if your eye is diseased, your whole body will be all darkness. If then, the light inside you is darkness, what darkness that will be!

No one can be the slave of two masters: he will either hate the first and love the second, or treat the first with respect and the second with scorn. You cannot be the slave both of God and of money.

That is why I am telling you not to worry about your life and what you are to eat, nor about your body and how you are to clothe it. Surely life means more than food, and the body more than clothing! Look at the birds in the sky. They do not sow or reap or gather into barns; yet your heavenly Father feeds them. Are you not worth much more than they are? Can any of you, for all his worrying, add one single cubit to his span of life? And why worry about clothing? Think of the flowers growing in the fields; they never have to work or spin; yet I assure you that not even Solomon in all his regalia was robed like one of these. Now if that is how God clothes the grass in the field which is there to-day and thrown into the furnace tomorrow, will he not much more look after you, you men of little faith? So do not worry; do not say, "What are we to eat? What are we to drink? How are we to be clothed?" It is the pagans who set their hearts on all these things. Your heavenly Father knows you need them all. Set your hearts on his kingdom first, and on his righteousness, and all these other things will be given you as well. So do not worry about tomorrow; tomorrow will take care of itself. Each day has enough trouble of its own.

MATTHEW 7

Do not judge, and you will not be judged; because the judgments you give are the judgments you will get, and the amount you measure out is the amount you will be given. Why do you observe the splinter in your brother's eye and never notice the plank in your own? How dare you say to your brother, "Let me take the splinter out of your eye," when all the time there is a plank in your own? Hypocrite! Take the plank out of your own eye first, and then you will see clearly enough to take the splinter out of your brother's eye.

Do not give dogs what is holy; and do not throw your pearls in front of pigs, or they may trample them and then turn on you and tear you to pieces.

Ask, and it will be given to you; search, and you will find; knock, and the door will be opened to you. For the one who asks always receives; the one who searches always finds; the one who knocks will always have the door opened to him. Is there a man among you who would hand his son a stone when he asked for bread? Or would hand him a snake when he asked for a fish? If you, then, who are evil, know how to give your children what is good, how much more will your Father in heaven give good things to those who ask him!

So always treat others as you would like them to treat you; that is the meaning of the Law and the Prophets.

Enter by the narrow gate, since the road that leads to perdition is wide and spacious, and many take it, but it is a narrow gate and a hard road that leads to life, and only a few find it.

Beware of false prophets who come to you disguised as sheep but underneath are ravenous wolves. You will be able to tell them by their fruits. Can people pick grapes from thorns, or figs from thistles? In the same way, a sound tree produces good fruit but a rotten tree bad fruit. A sound tree cannot bear bad fruit, nor a rotten tree good fruit. Any tree that does not produce good fruit is cut down and thrown on the fire. I repeat, you will be able to tell them by their fruits.

It is not those who say to me, "Lord, Lord," who will enter the kingdom of heaven, but the person who does the will of my Father in heaven. When the day comes many will say to me, "Lord, Lord, did we not prophesy in your name, cast out demons in your name, work many miracles in your name?" Then I shall tell them to their faces: I have never known you; away from me you evil men!

Therefore, everyone who listens to these words of mine and acts on them will be like a sensible man who built his house on rock. Rain came down, floods rose, gales blew and hurled themselves against that house, and it did not fall: it was founded on rock. But everyone who listens to these words of mine and does not act on them will be like a stupid man who built his house on sand. Rain came down, floods rose, gales blew and struck the house, and it fell; and what a fall it had!

This, the most clearly biblical of all the Jesus Sutras, already shows signs of both the problems of translating classical Christian thought into Chinese as well as signs of adoption of certain Chinese ways of thinking. It stands as the most orthodox of the Sutras, yet shows signs of the beginning of a shift from classical Western Christian orthodoxy. It is the doorway into the extraordinary adventure of the Church in China fourteen hundred years ago.

It is time now to go right back to the start of the Christian story itself, to the world of early Christianity—both the physical and the spiritual world.

Panorama of the
Early Christian World

**So God caused the Cool Breeze to come upon a chosen
young woman called Mo Yan, who had no husband, and
she became pregnant. The whole world saw this, and
understood what God had wrought. The power of God is
such that it can create a bodily spirit and lead to the clear,
pure path of compassion. Mo Yan gave birth to a boy and
called him Ye Su, who is Messiah. (5:1–4)**

This passage, so similar to the Gospel in its description of the Nativity, describes the paradox at the heart of Christianity: the birth
of Jesus, Son of God, son of Mary. From *The Sutra of Jesus Christ*,
it was written in China in the seventh century. To begin to understand the meaning of the Jesus Sutras, we need to understand the
physical and spiritual worlds from which they arose.

The Sutras' cultures of origin are in the West, from where the
monks who brought them came. We will trace the physical and
metaphysical journey not just of the monks and the Church of the
East, but also of the ideas, beliefs, and teachings that are to be
found in the Jesus Sutras. For from classical Western Christianity

to the Taoist Christianity of the Jesus Sutras, we travel not just through many countries and cultures, but also through engagements with many faiths. This is a journey in time, belief, and distance that moves from the eastern seaboard of the Mediterranean to bring us ultimately back beneath the pagoda of Da Qin, fifty miles southwest of Xian, China, fast up against the mountains.

✍️ THE POLITICAL GEOGRAPHY ✍️

The world within which the events leading to the foundation of Christianity in China took place was very different from the modern world. Past names of venerable countries of Europe and Asia, such as Mercia, Fresia, Gandhara, and Sugdiana, have now disappeared. Ancient cities such as Antioch and Palmyra have come and gone; others, such as Byzantium, later named Constantinople, then Istanbul, and Alexandria Arachoton in present-day Afghanistan, now named Kandahar, have changed their names two or three times. In the two thousand years since the birth of Jesus cultures have reinvented themselves over and over again. Religions and beliefs have evolved, influenced kingdoms, inspired artists, changed history, and vanished.

The rugged remains of Hadrian's Wall in the North of England, built ca. A.D. 122, give a palpable sense of the scale and power of the Roman Empire. Even after nearly two thousand years, the Wall still strides out across crags and through bogs. The military road that served the wall is still a road today, and the outlines of the forts and houses built by the legions can be clearly seen. This was an empire that left its mark over hundreds of years of existence.

The West—that is, most of Europe, Turkey and the region traditionally known as the Middle East, and most of North Africa—was largely under the control of Rome from the time of the birth of Jesus until the seventh century. The Roman Empire

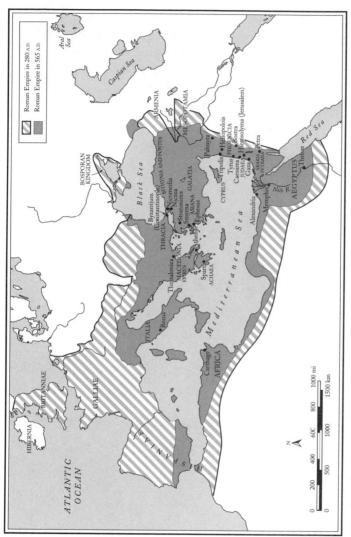

The heartlands of Christianity lay within the Roman Empire, which by the fourth century had become Christian.

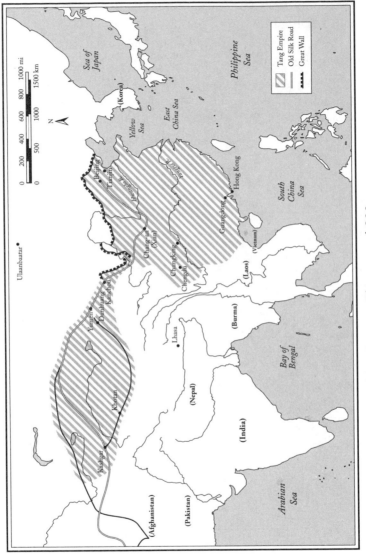

Tang Dynasty China around 800 A.D.

stretched south from Hadrian's Wall, today close to the border of Scotland and England, down through Spain to modern-day Morocco; from Morocco across North Africa, past the ruins of Carthage to Egypt, including present-day Algeria and Libya. From Egypt it moved north through the current countries of Israel and Jordan, even reaching at times deep into present-day Iraq. The whole of what today is Turkey formed the great eastern bastion of the empire, sometimes reaching up to modern-day Armenia. The empire also encompassed most of present-day Europe: Bulgaria, Romania, much of Hungary, Austria, southern Germany, the whole of Greece, the former Yugoslavia, Albania, Italy, Switzerland, France, Belgium, and much of the Netherlands.

At its height, the empire was ruled from its original heartland, Rome, the greatest city in the West until the rise of Constantinople in the fourth century A.D. Yet even at its greatest, Rome was smaller than its eastern counterpart, the capital city of China, Chang-an, near which the modern city of Xian, capital of Shaanxi Province, now stands.

By 635, when the first Christian mission reached China, the capital of the Roman Empire was Constantinople. Symbolically and pragmatically straddling the boundary between Europe and Asia, Constantinople was the largest and most powerful Christian city in antiquity. Yet even by the start of the seventh century, when Constantinople was at the height of its power and influence, the Roman Empire had shrunk considerably. Britain had been abandoned in the early fifth century, Spain and much of North Africa had fallen to the Visigoths and Vandals in the early sixth century, and the Holy Land fell to the Arabs between 635 and 640. The western parts of the empire—England and Wales, France, Belgium, the Netherlands, southern Germany, Spain and Portugal, Switzerland, and the north of Italy—were all under non-Roman, barbarian control, though many of the barbarian tribes had converted to Christianity. The empire had retreated toward its new capital and was barely holding on to the northern coast of Africa. Its strength

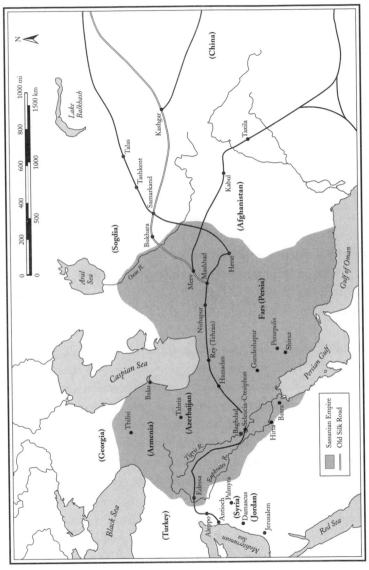

The Sassanian Empire around 600 A.D., heartland of the Church of the East.

came from the area of present-day Turkey, Greece, the former Yugoslavia, the Middle East, and Egypt.

In the areas of present-day Iraq, Iran, and Afghanistan, the Sassanian Empire ruled from A.D. 226 to 642. The Sassanian Empire, sometimes incorrectly called the Persian Empire, took its name from King Sassan, who ruled northern India and Afghanistan in the first century A.D. and whose descendants invaded Persia. The Sassanian heartland was the old area of the ancient Roman Empire's greatest foe, the Parthian or Persian Empire, which ruled the region of present-day Iraq and Iran from 247 B.C. to A.D. 226.

To the east of this heartland of old Persia lay a hodgepodge of kingdoms and states that, in the first few centuries of the Christian era, encompassed a staggering mixture of peoples and traditions. These included much of present-day eastern Afghanistan, Pakistan, the northern edges of India, Tajikistan, Turkmenistan, Uzbekistan, Kyrgyzstan, and southern Kazakhstan. Some of these kingdoms were ruled by tribes from the Mongolian and Central Asian steppes and some were the fragile remains of the Greek states established by Alexander the Great in the third century B.C. These ancient countries, now defunct, such as Gandhara, Bactria, and Sogdiana, had produced a strange mixture of Greek artistic style and lifestyle combined with Indian, steppes, and tribal Afghanistani life. Suspended between East and West, they played a significant part in the story of the creation of the Jesus Sutras.

Today the Gandharan culture is best remembered for having created the two towering sixth-century Buddhas that the Afghan Taliban destroyed with missiles in 2001. The Bamiyan Buddhas, as they were known, were cut into a mountainside about 100 miles west of Kabul, where they rose to 175 and 200 feet. They overlooked a valley where, some fifteen hundred years ago, the trade route between China and India flowed, bringing together languages and religions, including Buddhism, Hinduism, and, later, Islam. These monumental Buddhas, rare for their size and age, rose out of a combination of different artistic styles from India, Persia,

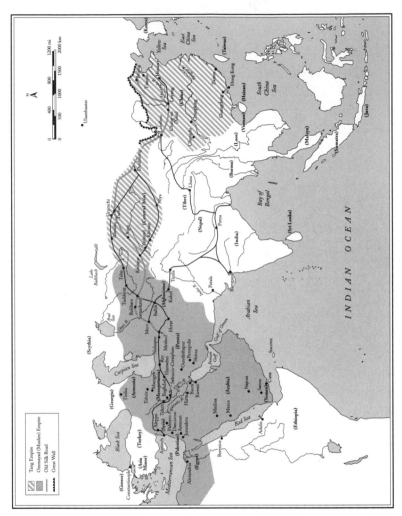

The Tang Dynasty of the seventh century reached farther west toward the Persian Empire than any other Chinese empire before or since. The Silk Road was the main reason for this expansion west.

and Greece that coexisted in the kingdom of Gandhara. The Buddhas' tragic destruction leaves the sculptures in the Da Qin monastery in the position of being the oldest examples in situ of the fusion of East-West influences in religious art.

By the seventh century A.D., many of these ancient kingdoms and states had become part of the Sassanian Empire. To the south of the heartland of the empire lay the vast unknown of Arabia, where tribes moved in a world all their own, occasionally coming into contact with the edges of the great empires of Rome or Sassania. Some tribes had become Christian, some had converted to Judaism. Others were traditionalists, or pagans, who worshiped an array of deities in the strange shrine of the Kaba in Makkah (Mecca), which was built at some time in prehistory to house a meteorite. It was the focus of the many tribal deities of Arabia from time immemorial until Muhammad captured the city in A.D. 630, upon which he had all the tribal deities removed.

Until the very year of the first Christian mission to China, 635, Arabia had been so divided that it posed no threat to the great empires that bordered it. But in 635, Arab armies united under their military leader, Khalid ibn al-Walid, known as the "Sword of Allah," burst out of Arabia and began one of the most astonishing conquests of history. Within a hundred years they had conquered the heartlands of the Sassanian Empire and much of the Roman Empire, including the Middle East, all of North Africa, and Spain.

To the Far East, to present-day Tibet and China, even a thousand years before Marco Polo's visit in the twelfth century, travelers by the thousands had made their way. From around the birth of Jesus until the third century, this region was dominated by Han Dynasty China, one of the longest-lasting empires the world has ever seen (206 B.C.–A.D. 220). Its last two hundred years were marked by gradual decline, ending in brutal civil war. Han China occupied much of the area of modern China but had no lands west of the edge of the Tibetan plateau, the western half of the present province of Sichuan. Nor did it occupy the huge region of modern northwestern China, the present province of Xinjiang and northern region of Inner Mongolia. Between Han China and Rome stood the Sassanian Empire, the Greek-founded states of Gandhara, Bactria, and Sogdiana, and the bulk of the emerging Tibetan Empire. Periodically, the region of present-day Inner Mongolia and Xinjiang was invaded by tribes of nomads sweeping down from the Central Asia steppes and Mongolia. These were, among others, Huns, Kushans, White Huns, Uighurs, Turks, and Khitans. Some of these eventually settled, intermarried, and disappeared from history. Others were dislodged by the next wave of steppes peoples or by Chinese, Persian, or Arab forces and moved on, some to appear in Europe a hundred years later.

When the first Christian mission arrived in China in 635, the Tang Dynasty had recently arisen out of more than four hundred years of petty states, civil war, and short-lived dynasties. China was at its greatest extent ever, stretching from its present-day territories as far west as Sogdiana and Ferghana, present-day Kyrgyzstan, Tajikistan, and much of Uzbekistan. The Silk Road ran through this corridor from China proper via the mountain passes to the west of Mongolia to the legendary cities of Bukhara, Samarkand, and Tashkent. Along the Silk Road traveled convoys carrying silk to the West and returning eastward with gold, silver, and other treasures. Starting in Chang-an, the capital of Tang China, the Silk Road went northwest from the most western outposts of the Chinese Empire, passing on through the Sassanian Empire to the Roman Empire and Constantinople, or to the great trading center and clearing house of Antioch in the Roman province of Syria.

Below the long western arm of Tang Dynasty China lay Tibet and India. The Tibetan Empire at the time of the first Christian mission to China was huge, stretching from present-day northern India and Pakistan to the edges of the old Greek states of Gandhara, Bactria, and Sogdiana. A mighty empire, it reached more than two hundred miles east into what is present-day China proper (above present-day Tibet) and north to penetrate deep into the modern Chinese province of Xinjiang.

India from the first to the fifth century A.D. was an ever changing mass of petty kingdoms, some of which condensed into one mighty empire, that of the Guptas, who, from the start of the fifth century, ruled or controlled much of present-day Afghanistan, all of Pakistan, the whole of northern India, and much of eastern India.

Above the western arm of Tang Dynasty China lay the "badlands." There, in present-day Mongolia and Kazakhstan, tribes rose and fell, forever pushing outward toward the great empires of China, Tibet, and Persia, or onward to the Roman Empire. These tribes, such as the Uighurs, Turks, Kazars, and White Huns, were never united into any great force until the rise of Genghis Khan in the early thirteenth century. However, distinct tribes were often powerful enough to seize control of much of northern China or to seize ancient kingdoms such as Sogdiana or Bactria, sweeping in and out of the history and geography of Central Asia, China, and Persia.

✑ THE GEOGRAPHY OF THE MIND ✑

The physical geography of the regions through which the monks and their Sutras passed is important, but we must also explore the geography of the mind, the conceptual worlds of the peoples who inhabit this history. The thought worlds of these old countries at first may seem familiar, but they prove to be even more remote than the physical and political landscape they once occupied. Early Christian beliefs and practices existed in a chaotic world, in which the first Christians struggled to define themselves and their traditions. Their diverse and often competing worldviews can still be discerned today in the major divisions of the Catholic, Orthodox, Coptic, and Syrian traditions.

The heart of Christianity is the life and teachings of Jesus.

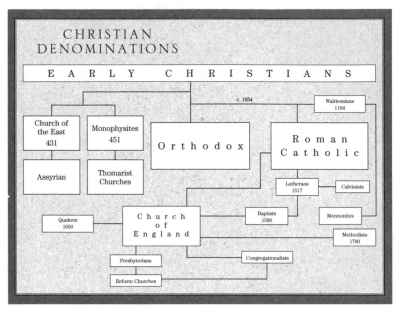

The variety of Churches of Christianity is vividly seen in this family tree of the faith.

The early Church came to believe that Jesus was both divine and human. To them he was one of three divine persons who made up the Trinity, the others being God the Father and the Holy Spirit. "God became human," said St. Athanasius, one of the great teachers of the early Church in the fourth century, "in order that humanity could become God."

The life and teachings of Jesus promise Christians a new life of the spirit, a kingdom of God on earth. According to St. Luke, this new life means a society of justice, compassion, and liberation from poverty and oppression in this life. He tells us that at the start of Jesus' three-year ministry, when he was about thirty, he expressed this vision in his home synagogue at Nazareth. Given the scroll to read the portion of scripture for the day from Isaiah, Jesus quoted.

"The Spirit of the Lord is on me,
For he has anointed me
To bring the good news to the afflicted.
He has sent me to proclaim liberty to captives,
Sight to the blind,
To let the oppressed go free
To proclaim a year of favor from the Lord."

He then rolled up the scroll, gave it back to the assistant and sat down. And all eyes in the synagogue were
fixed on him. Then he began to speak to them. "This text
is being fulfilled today even while you are listening."
(Luke 4: 16–21)

Having taught that the kingdom of God is within every man and
woman, and having profoundly disturbed the culture in which
he lived with his teachings, Jesus was persecuted and killed. As the
Gospels of the New Testament report, after being crucified he rose
again from the dead to bring salvation and hope to the world. Six
hundred years later, when the story of Jesus was told in China, the
Jesus Sutra known as *The Sutra of the Teachings of the World-Honored
One* (see Chapter 2) described the sacrifice that created Christianity:

**As a lamb goes silently to be slaughtered so he was silent,
not proclaiming what he had done, for he had to bear in
his body the punishment of the Law. Out of love he suffered so that what Adam had caused should be changed by
this. While his Five Attributes passed away, he did not die
but was released again after his death. . . . Through the
motions of the Law he was hung on high at the appointed
time. At that moment the earth shook and the mountains
erupted. . . . Because the Messiah was hung up on high he
begged to be given firm existence again. It is all as written.
(4:18–20; 5:1–2, 10–11)**

The first people to be inspired by Jesus' message were almost all Jews. But within a decade after the Crucifixion, non-Jews were being converted and the burgeoning faith was spreading out to the great cosmopolitan centers of the Roman Empire. In particular it was spreading into areas where Syriac and Greek were the dominant languages. Jesus' native tongue was Aramaic, a version of the Syriac language, although he would have read Hebrew and probably a few words of Greek. But the Gospels and all the books of the New Testament were written in Greek, the international language of the time.

In Antioch, a city in the Roman Empire that was nonetheless orientated toward the East and the great trade routes of the Silk Road, Christians were first called Christians. From here the Church went north and west into the heartland of the Roman Empire and simultaneously east and south into the Persian Empire. Until the fourth century, Christianity was a small but growing faith that achieved considerable successes in the Roman Empire in spite of several severe persecutions. Outside the Roman Empire, the faith grew more slowly in places such as Persia and India. By 300, there were Christian communities from England to India and from Egypt to north of the Black Sea.

The early Church is often spoken of as if it were one monolithic institution. In reality, however, the Church grew in different ways and as the result of diverse forces. The early Church experimented with incorporating local beliefs, mythologies, and practices according to the area in which it took root. Gradually, versions of the Christ story that had common elements coalesced and were defined into standard Christian teaching, and those that were too radical or heretical were banished or resisted. The ideal of One Church is a historical invention of the fourth and fifth centuries, after the Western Church had become the faith of the Roman Empire and the empire became known as Holy.

Right from the start, personality clashes and differences of opinion occurred over the meaning and significance of the Jesus story. The apostles Paul and Peter, in particular, clashed vigorously. Peter was by nature more Eastern and cautious, more caught up with tradition and history. Paul had been fashioned by the Greek West and the interaction between Judaism and Greek philosophy. He wanted to create a new faith: more radical, more unusual, and not bound by tradition.

Besides disputes among its founders, the early Church was also bedeviled by theological and practical disagreements: How Jewish should the Church be? Was Jesus more divine than human? Did the Old Testament have any place in Christianity? Was the material world evil or good or indifferent? Early Christianity, from the first to early fourth century, had no formal creed and quite consciously drew on models of belief that it found around it. For example, it adapted the Roman veneration of the sun to its own schedule of worship. The day of the Roman week dedicated to the sun, the day on which Jesus rose from the dead, was turned into Sunday, the day of church services; east, where the sun rose, became the direction of church buildings, whose altars were placed at the east end; and December 25, the sun's birthday, became the birthday of Jesus.

Beginning in the fourth century, Church historians and teachers presented a view of the early Church as a single ship plowing its way steadily through the tempestuous seas of the pagan world, buffeted by the winds and storms of heresy but nevertheless always finding the true path. Perhaps a better analogy would be to see the early Church as a series of small boats, setting off from different places, using different designs, but all under the sail of the personality and teachings of Jesus. Gradually, those boats that were outmanned or outmaneuvered faltered and disappeared. Yet a small armada of boats survived and decided to sail together rather than separately.

Christianity grew slowly, taking many different forms. Some believers held views of Jesus that were later seen as diminishing his divine nature; others, such as the Apollinarians, underemphasized his human nature. Some, such as the Gnostics, wanted mystery rather than truth. Still others in Egypt and Rome simply interpreted the Jesus story in ways that made sense in their own culture. Not until the conversion of Emperor Constantine the Great in 312 did some Christians begin to feel that this diversity was dangerous and unanimity essential. When the empire became Christian it was as if a series of churches that had existed alongside each other were brought together to mirror the single State of the Roman Empire in a single Church. This aim to establish unity was the impulse behind the calling of the councils—formal meetings of the bishops from across the Christian world—which began in Nicaea in 325. These councils came to be seen as the defining moments of true Christianity as understood by the state and its state Church. Those churches that did not adhere to these views were cast out of the fellowship of the Church. Yet the Church that these councils defined was largely confined to the major lands of the Roman Empire, and many local expressions of Christianity had little or nothing to do with them.

For example, the British Church, although in touch with the Church of the empire, went its own quiet way, giving rise over time to the distinctive version of Christianity known as Celtic Christianity. Even a saint such as Patrick, who was in full communion with Rome in the mid–fifth century, felt free to write his own creed as well as to use the formal creeds established by the councils. In his own creed, Patrick takes account of the different culture of the Celts and builds on this in language and imagery that is quite alien to the Greek philosophical terminology of the formal creeds. For example:

> There is no other God except God the Father, nor has there ever been in time past, nor will there ever be in the future. God is the origin of all things, and has no beginning. God possesses all things, but is possessed by none. . . . He has poured down his Spirit upon us, and we

overflow with the Spirit. It is his Spirit which brings us the promise of eternal life. Through the Spirit we learn to trust and obey the Father and with and through Christ, become sons and daughters of God.[12]

By comparison, here is an excerpt from the standard creed in the Book of Common Prayer, based on the Athanasian Creed written around 400:

I believe in one God the Father Almighty, Maker of heaven and earth, And of all things visible and invisible: And in one Lord Jesus Christ, the only-begotten Son of God, Begotten of his Father before all worlds, God of God, Light of Light, Very God of Very God, Begotten, not made, Being of one substance with the Father, By whom all things were made. . . . And I believe in the Holy Ghost, The Lord and giver of life, Who proceedeth from the Father and the Son, Who with the Father and the Son together is worshipped and glorified, Who spake by the prophets. And I believe in one Catholick and Apostolick Church.[13]

Patrick's creed is concerned with generosity and, in a sense, the "family" of God, hence "poured down his Spirit," "we overflow with the Spirit," and "through Christ, become sons and daughters of God." The creed of Athanasius, on the other hand, is concerned with exact Greek philosophical definitions of what God and Christ are, hence the confusing line "Jesus Christ, the only-begotten Son of God, begotten of his Father before all worlds . . . Very God of the Very God, Begotten, not made, Being of one substance with the Father." In a sense, the formal creed seeks to define, Patrick's to express.

For the churches that had arisen in the Persian Empire and farther afield to the east, the councils were of interest but had no binding power, for these churches lay outside the political and military authority of Rome.

Before 325 and the Council of Nicaea, the churches of the Ancient World stretched from Wales to India. These churches kept in touch with their own Mother Church, that particular church from which their key missionary had come. Bishops met each other when they could or when traveling, but there was no single, ruling church from which all took direction. After 325, a process began that sought to draw all the churches into The Church. Yet this was ultimately impossible, because the concept of The Church was essentially an outcome of the conversion of The State—the Roman State. Churches beyond the control and lands of the Roman Empire saw little or no need to form a spiritual version of the state.

As a result, by the end of the fourth century, Christianity had begun to coalesce into distinct blocs. The West, the Roman Empire, in effect, was dominated by the State Church, sponsored for better or worse by the emperors and funded by the state. For this history and for the sake of simplicity I call it the Church of the West. To the east, in the lands ruled by the Sassanian Empire and even beyond them to India and the borders of Tibet, were the lands of the Church of the East. This Church was not and never became a State Church. Apart from these two spheres of influence there were other churches that were in alliance with one or other of the major Churches, but that kept their independence, such as the British or Celtic Church in the British Isles (parts of which were outside any area ever ruled by Rome), the Armenians (who had become the first State Church in 312, unrelated to what was happening in the Roman Empire), and churches in Southern Egypt and Ethiopia.

Heresies of various forms came and went, often leaving a deeper impact on the definition of what it meant to be Christian than the defenders of orthodoxy appreciated. One such heresy was Manichaeism, popular in the Roman Empire, which taught that the physical world was evil, creating a duality of good and evil between the spiritual and physical worlds. This dualism influenced the young St. Augustine of Hippo, and through him left its mark on Christianity, which since that time has had problems with the physical body and denigrated it as sinful and inferior to the spirit. Heresies such as Manichaeism led to a series of acrimonious theological and political disputes that cracked the unanimity of the Church so longed for by the emperors of Rome. The divisions left by these disputes split Christianity to this day and lead us to the origins of the Jesus Sutras.

It is from the Church of the East that the Jesus Sutras emerged. To understand why and how, it is necessary to go into a little of the controversy that made the fifth century such a dramatic time for Christianity.

✐ UNITY AND DIVISION ❧

The core dilemma for Christianity has always been how to describe Jesus as both human and divine. How could he be the historical man of the first century A.D. and also the Second Person of the Trinity, existing before existence, eternal and divine? This paradox is one with which Christianity wrestles to this day. Perhaps the story of the Church would have been a more peaceful, practical, and humane one had the paradox been allowed to remain a source of thought and reflection rather than dogma. But to the early Church, so influenced by Greek philosophy's desire to define, this question of identity demanded resolution.

The first serious attempt to create a definition was made by the Council of Nicaea in 325. It confirmed the generally held view that Christ is coeternal with God. Crudely put, Nicaea resolved the God bit of the paradox by declaring that Jesus is truly God. Later, the Council of Constantinople, held in 381, allowed the other side by saying that Jesus is also truly human.

In the early years of the fifth century, Christianity was dominated by two schools or traditions based on two of the great church centers or patriarchates, those at Antioch and Alexandria. Alexandria veered toward emphasizing the divinity of Christ over his humanity, whereas Antioch saw Jesus as the model of what all humans could become. The Church at Antioch was renowned for its followers' care for the poor, establishment of hospitals, and involvement in what today would be called a Social Gospel. This arose from their belief that humanity was capable of great good because God was capable of becoming one of us and of working through us.

Yet both sides confirmed that Christ was both God and man. The two fourth-century Councils of Nicaea and Constantinople seemed to have achieved a balance with which most Christians could live. But it was all to come apart in the fifth century, with a debate over the identity of Mary, mother of Jesus. This was to be the theological centrifugal force that spun away the Churches of the East and of Armenia, Syria, and Egypt from the Greek-speaking Church of the West. The issue at stake was how to understand the significance and personality of Mary in light of Nicaea's claim that Jesus is God and Constantinople's claim that Jesus is also truly human.

In 428 a young monk named Nestorius was appointed archbishop of Constantinople, the most powerful position in the Christian Church. By the early fifth century the Roman Empire, based at Constantinople, was officially Christian, and huge wealth and influence were entering the Church. Nestorius had been shaped by the Antioch Church tradition and shared its view of the paradox of Christ's dual nature. He preached a sermon about Mary, taking exception to a phrase that described Mary as "Mother of God." To Nestorius and the Antioch party, this description overemphasized the divinity in Christ and attempted to make Mary a deity in her own right.[14]

The cult of Mary as Mother of God had already taken hold, having originated in Egypt, as did the development of iconography that shows her as the idealized Mother, the Divine Mother, holding her Divine Offspring, Jesus. These images are, in fact, a Christian version of the most deeply loved and powerful Egyptian deities, Isis the Divine Mother and Horus the Divine Offspring. Thus, when Antioch, and especially Nestorius, attacked the use of the phrase Mother of God they were touching profound, deep-rooted religious impulses, beliefs, and images that were thousands of years older than Christianity.

The Roman Empire in which Nestorius lived was fascinated by theological debate to an extent that we would find unimaginable today. Nestorius's sermon led to a war of pamphlets, anathemas, and protests between Antioch and Alexandria. To resolve the dispute, a council of the whole Church was held at Ephesus, the sacred port city on the west coast of present-day Turkey, in 431.

The Council of Ephesus was one of the all-time lows of the Christian Church. A rich religious politician named Cyril, then the patriarch of Alexandria, wanted also to obtain the post at Constantinople, with the wealth and power it would bring. He forced through a vote in the council against Nestorius and in favor of the definition of Mary as Mother of God. Mobs fought in the streets, because the issue had become highly politicized and each group had brought its own supporters to the council. The emperor had to send troops to keep the peace; the upshot was that both Cyril and Nestorius were exiled by the emperor.[15]

In the course of time, the Alexandrians withdrew from the Western Church based at Constantinople and Rome. Alexandria became the headquarters of a new Church, the Coptic Church. The Coptic Church became a force of its own, and over the next few hundred years drew in other Churches that had fallen out with the Western Church—namely, the Church of Ethiopia, the majority of the Syrian Church, and the Armenians. Also known as the Monophysite Churches, these organizations believe that there is only one, divine nature in Christ, not two natures, divine and human, as in orthodox teaching.

Nestorius, who remained supported by Antioch, was nevertheless forced to end his days in exile in the remote south of the Egyptian desert, where he died around 451. The Churches east and south of Antioch were alienated from the Church of the West because of this and other theological differences, and by political divisions between the Roman and Sassanian Empires. They became a refuge for the intellectuals who fled the increasingly hard-line doctrines of the Church of the West.

The Church of the East—the Churches in the Sassanian Empire and points further east and south—was more a confederation of Churches than one monolithic entity. From 489 the Church of the East had no serious links with or need for the Church of the West. It was about to launch upon its own extraordinary period of expansion and consolidation. From then on it was what the name implies: an Eastern version of the Christ story and of Christianity.

The Church of the East

On a hill some eight miles from the center of the southern Indian city of Channai (Madras) is a church dedicated to the Apostle Thomas. Crowds come here every day to climb the hill and offer their prayers, sometimes scooping up some dust to take home or to smear on their foreheads. Children, married couples, and old folk moving slowly but with great determination make their way to the top. Well-dressed Thomarist Christians walk side by side with middle-class Hindu families, and both rub shoulders with poor Indian Christians as well as poor Hindus who have also come to pay their devotions to one of the strangest of India's holy places. Here, three thousand miles east of Jerusalem in the middle of the first century, it is claimed, one of Jesus' original disciples was martyred.

The Church established by St. Thomas in India is one of many across Asia that once formed the Church of the East. To understand the story of the Church of the East it is necessary to go back to the rise of the Sassanian Empire in the early third century A.D.

✑ CAUGHT BETWEEN TWO EMPIRES ✑

When the Sassanians came to power in A.D. 226, they established Zoroastrianism as the state religion of their huge empire, an empire that stretched from present-day Iraq to Pakistan. Zoroastrianism is rooted in the teaching of Zoroastra, who lived around 1500–1200 B.C. and taught that there is just one supreme deity, Ahura-Mazda. Opposed by Ahriman, the principle of evil, Ahura-Mazda's forces are locked in a cosmic battle that good will eventually win. Zoroastrians kept sacred fires in the temples and prohibited the pollution of fire and water through contact with the dead or others who, because of their work or some illness, were considered to be polluted.

At first, Zoroastrians and Sassanians paid little attention to the Christians, who were a minority in the land. But the Church grew swiftly, and Zoroastrians began to impede it by making it officially illegal to convert from Zoroastrianism to any other faith and by persecuting converts.

In earlier times, during the persecutions under the Roman Empire, the Sassanians gave refuge to Christian exiles. Yet after Constantine the Great turned Christian in 312, the growing communities of Christians with their links to Antioch and the Empire of the Enemy were perceived by the government as a potential threat. This view was given credence when Constantine began preparations for a huge Roman invasion of Persia, urged on and supported by some within the Church. He was going to war ostensibly to defend Christians from attack in Persia.[16] Although his death in 337 put an end to the invasion, the Sassanians were under few illusions.

For Zoroastrians, the idea of conversion to another faith was literally inconceivable. To be a Persian was to be Zoroastrian.[17] Thus, in 340 began 110 years of ferocious persecutions. The worst moment came in 448 when, in Kirkuk in northern Mesopotamia,

153,000 Christians were murdered and their bodies heaped outside the city.

Soon afterward, around 450, peace was at last established by the Persian Emperor Hormizd III. But by now the leaders of the Church in the Sassanian Empire had learned that any link with Rome, Constantinople, or even the Mother Patriarchate of Antioch exposed them to Zoroastrian suspicions of treason.

Despite the persecutions, Christians eventually grew to outnumber Zoroastrians in the Sassanian Empire, and theirs would have become the faith of the empire had not the Arabs conquered the Sassanians by the middle of the seventh century and introduced Islam.

THE CHURCH OF THE EAST GOES ITS OWN WAY

Today, Antioch, once the heart of the Church of the East, is a shadow of its former glory. All that remains is a modest Turkish town settled within the ruins of the ancient city. Yet the head of the contemporary Maronite Church in Lebanon, which had split away from the Orthodox in 680, is still formally known as Patriarch of Antioch and the Whole of the East.

Relationships between the Mother Church at Antioch and the Church in the West were soured by political and theological problems. As the Church of the West sought to impose its model of theological agreement on the various Christian Churches of the Middle East, some went off to join the Coptic Church and others found welcome in the Sassanian Empire. The Church of the East never sought to enforce agreement in the way the Church of the West did, mostly because, as a confederation of Churches, it could not have done so.

Such inherent openness and diversity on its borders only helped fuel the determination of the Church of the West to expel all who disagreed with the party line. Anyone suspected of having divergent views, especially anyone associated with Nestorius, was persecuted. In particular, the Church of the West took a dislike to the most important theological establishment serving the Church of the East: the great theological college known as the School of the Persians in the Roman border city of Edessa. Here, for two hundred years, leaders of the Persian Church were trained, until the Emperor Zeno finally closed the school in 489. Most of its teachers took sanctuary in Persia, in the city of Nisibis in the Sassanian Empire.

Effectively from this date onward, the Church of the East was cut off from the Church of the West. The Church of the West dismissively labeled the Church of the East Nestorian, therefore heretical and not really a Church. This dismissal continues to this day. All those Churches that have come from the Church of the West—the Roman Catholic, Orthodox, Lutheran, Anglican, and Protestant Churches—have traditionally taken the view that the Church of the East is heretical.[18] Even today, the current edition of the *Pelican History of the Church*, in its volume on Christian missions, devotes only 6 of 577 pages to the Church of the East.[19]

A DIFFERENT SPIRIT

The Church of the West, having won the battle to convert the Roman Empire, began to turn inward, redefining itself as a state religion through intellectual giants such as St. Augustine of Hippo, who explored what constitutes a Christian state. In contrast, the Church of the East developed its own distinct spirit, one that allowed a greater freedom of belief and that was dedicated to preaching the message of Jesus. Unlike the Church of the West, it never dominated its cultural world to the exclusion or suppression of other faiths. Instead, it worked out a modus vivendi by which it could function as a minority among other faiths. This made it a first-class missionary Church.

This missionary spirit was exemplified by Narsai (ca. 410–ca. 503), who bears the delightful name "Harp of the Spirit" for his skill as a writer of hymns, some of which are known today. He began his studies under the great teacher Barsumas at the famous School of the Persians in Edessa, but in 457 his teacher was expelled by the Roman authorities for heresy. So Barsumas and Narsai fled to Nisibis, on the Persian side of the border, where they founded a new school. This was one of the dramatic moments of self-definition for the Church of the East. From here, Narsai passed on his vision of mission to his many students. He saw Jesus as the model for self-giving, compassionate love and paraphrased Jesus thus: "Your [task] is this: to complete the mystery of preaching! And you shall be witnesses of the new way which I have opened up in my person. . . . You I send as messengers to the four quarters [of the earth], to convert the Gentiles to kinship with the House of Abraham. . . . By you as the light I will banish the darkness of error, and by your flames I will enlighten the blind world. . . . Go forth! Give gratis the freedom of life to immortality."[20] Thus, a very different psychology of what it meant to be a Christian shaped the development of the Church of the East, even more so after the collapse of the Sassanian Empire, when Christians and Zoroastrians found themselves under the rule of Islam.

Between the fourth and eighth centuries, the Church of the East was more widespread and more active in a greater range of cultures than any other Church. Its missions were also situated within more highly developed cultures than any other Church. The different Churches in the East did not set out to be part of a thing called the Church of the East; rather, they arose as the Christian message spread out along the caravan trails and sea trade routes that had existed since antiquity. From the Persian homelands to Arabia, northeast Africa, Afghanistan, Central Asia, India, and Sri Lanka, Christian merchants traded and settled, and also brought the Gospel. As local churches slowly grew, so monasticism and bishoprics were created to help them practice their faith. Ultimately, necessity drew these disparate churches together into the loose alliance I am calling the Church of the East.

Against this background, in 635, a mission team from the Church of the East arrived in the western suburbs of China's capital city. From the materials translated for this book, including the early *Sutra of the Teachings of the World-Honored One* and *Sutra on Cause, Effect, and Salvation*, it is clear that this mission was made up of people who had engaged with many different faiths and that it drew on books developed in many different cultures. To appreciate the traditions that came together in that mission team, we need briefly to explore the astonishing cultural range of the Church of the East by the early seventh century.

✍◌ THE CHURCH IN PERSIA ◌✎

The Church in Persia itself dates from the earliest Christian times. Church tradition tells that the first king to be in contact with Christian missionaries was a Persian satrap or client king, Abgar V of Osrhoene. It is reported that he wrote to Jesus and that Jesus sent him a missionary, who converted him.[21] It is likely that the first groups of Christians in the land between the Roman and Persian Empires existed within a few decades of Jesus' death. Certainly, the Church was well established by the second century and was even producing religious literature concerning Churches much farther East, such as India.

The Church in Persia is still in existence. Some of its members have held the highest positions in the current Iraqi government, though they have also suffered as have so many communities from the power struggles and the brutality of the regime. In Iran the communities are protected by the Islamic regime as honorable brothers and sisters of faith. But the Church is greatly reduced in size and influence and has been so since the destruction of Persian life by the Mongol invasions of the thirteenth century and the almost total destruction of the cities by Tamerlane in the early fifteenth century.

At its height, from the seventh to eleventh centuries, the Church was in touch with bishops, archbishops, monks, churches, and Christian communities spread out over thousands of miles. It responded to requests for help from Sri Lanka to China and from Qatar to the borderlands of Russia. It ruled through consensus and allowed the different member Churches to get on with life as best they could. Because of the huge distances and frequent wars, breakdown of civil order, and invasions, communications were infrequent. The rise of Islam also strained the effective operation of the Church. The struggle between Islam and China, which began in the late seventh century and ended in 751, made communication and support for the Church in China especially problematic.

TATIAN'S GOSPEL

From about the end of the second century to the start of the sixth, the Church in Persia used a remarkable document, a book that became more popular than the Gospels. This was the synopsis of the Gospels called *Teachings of the Apostles*, written or compiled by Tatian (ca. 110–180), discussed in Chapter 2. Tatian was born in the old Persian Empire but went to Rome to study. Persecution drove him back to Persia in about 172, where he became a teacher and philosopher and created his masterpiece.[22] Because the canon of the New Testament was not defined until the Council of Rome in 382, many competing Gospels were circulating. Tatian created, in effect, a Gospel that might have become the definitive book alongside or even instead of the Four Gospels, had Church history worked out differently. Indeed, so popular was Tatian's book that, until the eighth century, *Teachings of the Apostles* was used instead of the Four Gospels by Persian Christians. It was most certainly one of several books that were taken to China and influenced the writing of the Jesus Sutras.

⤫ THE INDO-GREEK CULTURES ⤭

When Alexander the Great and his army burst out of northern Greece in 334 B.C., they stormed through the ancient Middle East, capturing what is present-day Turkey, Lebanon, Syria, Israel, and Egypt. Alexander then turned his attention on Persia and defeated its king, Darius. Not satisfied with that, he went beyond the old boundaries of the Persian Empire into present-day Afghanistan. By 326 B.C. he had reached the Indus River and India, where his soldiers refused to go any farther. Before Alexander the Great turned for home, however, he established cities and Greek colonies right to the banks of the Indus. Evidence of these cities is still discernible. For example, the second city of Afghanistan is still called Kandahar, a corruption of Alexander, pronounced Iskandah in Islamic areas.

The Greek soldiers and civilians who were left behind in the cities and colonies in what is now Afghanistan, Pakistan, and India created multicultural, multifaith kingdoms that covered considerable areas. Ruled by Greeks, these were centers of trade, art, and literature to which came peoples from across Central Asia, India, the eastern Mediterranean, and Greece. A fusion of Greek and primarily Indian cultures emerged, known to history as Indo-Greek. The Greek kingdoms survived for more than three hundred years as distinct Greek entities. Coins were struck there for the various kings with quintessentially Greek names such as Diodotus, Euthydemus, and Menander/Milinda. The last known Greek king was Strato II, whose kingdom fell to invaders in A.D. 10. But the Greek influence continued long after this, and the lasting effect of these Indo-Greek cultures is perhaps their best memorial.

◯ BUDDHA AND APOLLO ◯

The Greek influence in India continued and spread long after the last Greek king had been overthrown, in the style of art and sculpture adopted by the Indians. Contact between Greeks in Persia and the former Indo-Greek kingdoms was revived when the region was overrun by the Parthian (Persian) Empire in A.D. 56. Subsequently, in the first century, a marked change occurred in the art of the region. Greek style fused with Buddhist motifs to create the first statues of the Buddha. This distinctive style is known as Gandharan.[23]

Early Buddhist art until the first century B.C. consisted of symbolic representation of the Buddha. Because the Buddha did not wish to be seen as a deity or as divine in any way, but as a simple teacher bringing the truth for others to follow, Buddhists discouraged anything that seemed to elevate him into an object of devotion. In fact, quite soon after his death, relics were being worshiped, but the development of iconographic art did not begin then. It was customary to represent the Buddha as a pair of footprints indicating the way to walk to enlightenment, or as a wheel, the symbol of his first teaching on *Setting in Motion the Wheel of Truth*. It was in this sermon that the Buddha first taught the Four Noble Truths:

1. Suffering exists.
2. There is a reason for suffering: desire and craving.
3. There is a way to end desire and craving and thus suffering.
4. The Eightfold Path of right behavior and thought is the Path to the ending of suffering.

For the Greeks of the Indo-Greek kingdoms who converted from the first century B.C. onward, this was all far too abstract. They wanted images, so they began to create the first representations of

The sun god Apollo was chosen by Greek converts to Buddhism as the model for the first statues of the Buddha, the Enlightened One.

the Buddha. But because there were no extant or current images to copy, they turned for inspiration to their own mythology and iconography, brought from Greece hundreds of years before and sustained by constant contact between Greece and the Indo-Greek kingdoms.

To show the universal sense of enlightenment that was the hallmark of the Buddha's teaching, they looked to Apollo, god of the sun. Usually depicted as a clean-shaven young man with a fine head of curly hair, Apollo looked Greek, not Indian. Yet the Indo-Greek Buddha became a young man with curly hair. Greek iconography also used the image of an extra bump on the top of the head to show intelligence, so the Indo-Greek Buddha also has a bump on his head. Because Apollo was usually depicted with a sun disk behind his head, Buddha, too, was given a halo. In the original Gandharan carvings of the first century B.C., the halo has flames of light bursting out from it like a sun. And, just as Greek Apollo wears a toga, so does the Buddha.

Today, through all the vicissitudes of two thousand years, the essential Greekness of the original depiction of the Buddha can be seen almost anywhere in the world. The toga-wearing, sun-haloed, curly haired, clean-shaven, bump-headed Buddha owes his origins to the artists of the Indo-Greek cultures.

✍️ CHRISTIANITY MEETS BUDDHISM ✍️

In the second century, when the first Christian missionaries arrived, Greek influence in the former Indo-Greek kingdoms was still very strong. Greek-style statues of the Buddha were made in Gandhara until the late fifth century A.D. Indeed, traditions of Greek ideas and beliefs exist to this day in the former Indo-Greek kingdoms.[24] For example, Greek herbal remedies can be bought in the old marketplace in the Afghan city of Kandahar, from where their use is disseminated across Pakistan and northern India.

Christians were active in this area from shortly after the time of Jesus. In 196, for example, a church scribe[25] reports that Christians were living among the Kushan, a Turkic tribe who had swept down from Central Asia in the mid-first century and settled in far-off Bactria. Links with Antioch and Alexandria would have meant a steady stream of traders, teachers, and missionaries spread from the west through the Indo-Greek kingdoms to Indian cities such as Taxila in the north, or in southern India the trading port of Cranganore and the Roman settlement of Arikamedu, now Pondicherry. The similarities of culture would have made the Indo-Greek communities places where Greek and Syrian Christian

All early Buddhist art in China is modeled on the fusion of Greek and Buddhist styles. These two Bodhisattvas from the sixth century at the Yungang caves, Shaanxi Province, clearly show the togas, the Greek style of body posture, and the sunburst halos derived from the sun god Apollo. (© Tjalling Halbertsma/CIRCA)

missionaries felt quite at home. As we saw earlier, these cultural similarities are still strongly evident in the *Milindapanha*, the Buddhist teaching on which *The Sutra of Cause, Effect, and Salvation* (which was written nearby) was based.

Bishoprics were established in some of the Afghan cities by at least the early fifth century, and by 585 so many bishoprics and clergy were to be found in the area that the bishop of Herat (in present-day Afghanistan) was made an archbishop. Further north was also the powerful archishopric of Merv, center for missions to the Turkic tribes and Central Asia. By now the Church of the East was well established and powerful, yet we are only today, after centuries of obscurity, rediscovering its history.

From sites in Bactria and Sogdian, in present-day Afghanistan, Tajikistan, Uzbekistan, and Turkmenistan, have come beautiful Christian artifacts. In the Hermitage Museum of St. Petersburg, Russia, are examples of silver vessels with depictions of the Crucifixion and the burial and ascension of Jesus and an incense burner with the scene of the Last Supper. Coins have even been found near Tashkent with the cross engraved on them, as well as odd scraps of pottery with bits of Syriac on them.

✍ ST. THOMAS AND ✍ THE CHURCH IN INDIA

One of the first Christians to visit Gandhara, according to Thomarist Christian legend, was the Apostle Thomas, who preached to the first-century Indian king of Gandhara, Gundephar. The Thomarist Christians trace their Church from the Apostle and have existed in India as a distinct community from at least the fourth century. They bear witness to the belief that St. Thomas preached in India and even, according to their tradition, in China.

On the west coast of India, in the town of Cranganore, Thomas is supposed to have founded his first church in 52, making this one of the oldest churches in the world, before going on to found another six churches along that coast. In ancient times, the traveler from the Roman Empire came to India not by land but by sea. The trade winds and monsoon winds that make it possible to sail from the Persian Gulf or the Red Sea had been known to the Greeks since the fourth to third century B.C., and regular trade between Alexandria and India helped to make the fortunes of that great city. Thomarist Christian legend, possibly based on reality, says that St. Thomas, the Doubter, came along these trade routes to India in the early to middle decades of the first century. Indeed, Cranganore was a Greek and Roman trading port, and

considerable archaeological evidence of this trade has been exca-
vated there. Roman coins from Alexandria are almost as common
there as in the great city itself.

St. Thomas first appears in the written records in the Gospel
of John as one of the most ardent of the twelve special disciples of
Jesus. He declared himself willing to die for Jesus, but, with the
other disciples, abandoned Jesus at his time of need and later refused to believe that Jesus had risen from the dead: "Unless I see
the holes that the nails made in his hands and can put my finger
into the holes they made, and unless I can put my hand into his
side, I refuse to believe" (John 20:25). When Jesus appeared to
him and invited him to touch his wounds, Thomas was overwhelmed with emotion and declared his belief that Jesus was God.

Since his conversion, Doubting Thomas has stood for those
Christians who want to test faith for themselves. His later life as a
missionary has also been the subject of speculation. It is now accepted by all but the most timid scholars that Thomas did indeed
end up preaching in India, where he was martyred. The evidence
of the extensive trade routes between the Roman Empire and India plus the testimony of the Thomarist Christians who have existed in India as a distinct community for seventeen centuries
confirm this. Western Church tradition says Thomas was appointed to take the Gospel to the Persians, which he did and then
moved on to India. The third-century *Acts of Thomas*, which is
found in Greek, Latin, and Syriac versions and was known and
revered by Churches East and West, tells of his adventures: his de-
bates with Indian rulers, struggles with the Brahmins who tried to
silence him, and journeys beyond India. Even a book published in
1713 on the lives of the Apostles has Thomas preaching in Persia,
Ethiopia, India, the East Indies, and China.[26]

Although mostly the stuff of legend, *Acts of Thomas* does reflect actual historical events. One of the most delightful stories
concerns Thomas and King Gundephar (a historical king who did
live at the time of Thomas). It is said that the king asked Thomas

to build him a new palace and gave him immense wealth with which to do it. After some time the king wanted to know how the palace was progressing and was told that, instead of building a palace, Thomas was distributing the funds to the poor. The king asked Thomas whether he had built the palace. Thomas replied that he had. But when the king asked to see it Thomas answered, "Yes, but not now. You will see it when you die."

Having converted King Gundephar, Thomas traveled farther south in India to the Chola kingdom on the east coast in the region of present-day Madras. There he achieved remarkable success in converting the people, but was martyred. *Acts of Thomas* elaborated his martyrdom into a parallel with Jesus' death, involving a plot by the Chola king and an execution by four soldiers, but the truth is probably more prosaic. South Indian tradition has it that his work aroused the enmity of local Brahmin priests. In the course of a riot he was pierced with a lance and died.[27] It is said that he died with the same words on his lips as those with which he greeted the Risen Christ when he appeared to him in Jerusalem: "My Lord and my God."

Although *Acts of Thomas* is often dismissed as a Christian romantic fiction, oral tradition in India holds to a story that should not be lightly dismissed. Oral traditions in India have often preserved the ideas of written materials that have disappeared from history but have been verified later by archaeological discoveries, a good example of which is the life of Ashoka, the great Indian emperor of the third century B.C. who converted to Buddhism. Stories of his life have been recounted in India since his time. Yet Westerners, encountering these stories in the eighteenth and early nineteenth centuries, dismissed them as wishful thinking. However, when archaeological discoveries of documents and edicts of his reign established the historical existence of Emperor Ashoka, it became clear that his exploits were even more significant and diverse than the legends told. So the oral tradition on which the details of the *Acts of Thomas* were based could be historically true.[28]

Certainly, the persistence of oral tradition indicates some likelihood of this, as do discoveries about kings such as Gunaphar and the extent of trade from the West to India exactly in the places that Thomas is supposed to have visited.

Toward the end of the second century A.D., a new mission was sent from Alexandria to India to assist the churches in the Bombay area, now called Mumbai, headed by a great scholar named Pantaenus. From Pantaenus's report, we know that the Church in India used Syriac for its services, as it still does today. After the Church of the East arose, the Church in India looked for leadership to replace the compromised Church of Alexandria and the Church of the West. The Church of the East counted the Church of India as one of its oldest associate Churches, and materials from this Indian Church almost certainly influenced the writings of the Jesus Sutras, as we found in our translations of *The Sutra of Jesus Christ*.

✍ THE TEACHING OF NONVIOLENCE ✍

Another faith active in these traditional lands of the Indian Church was the Jain religion, which arose at almost the same time as Buddhism, around 500 B.C. Jains believe that their great teacher, Mahavira, was the latest in a long line of great teachers, called Tirthankaras, who over the ages came to teach the true principles of life. Central to Jainism is the principle of *ahimsa*: total nonviolence. Jain monks and nuns gently brush the ground before them as they walk, lest by accident they crush an insect. Jains are also strict vegetarians and have always sought to work in ways that do not harm living things. Unlike Buddhism, Jainism never became a missionary faith but has remained centered in India.

The Jain teaching of nonviolence also seems to have had an indirect influence on the Jesus Sutras through the agency of the Indian Church, for the Taoist Christians of Da Qin were themselves vegetarian, peaceful, and against the widespread practice of slavery. Other Hindu, that is, mainstream Vedic traditions in India, also practiced nonviolence; however, the Jains remain the most distinctive such group.

ᴄᴧᴓ THE CHURCH IN TIBET ᴄᴧᴓ

The final destination on this journey through the territories of the Church of the East, and perhaps the most unexpected, is Tibet. It is unclear exactly when Christianity reached Tibet, but it seems likely that it had arrived there by the sixth century. The ancient territory of the Tibetans stretched farther west and north than present-day Tibet, and they had many links with the Turkic and Mongolian tribes of Central Asia. To this day, Tibetan Buddhism is the form practiced in Mongolia. It seems likely that Christians first entered the Tibetan world around 549, the time of a remarkable conversion to Christianity of the White Huns. These greatly feared nomadic warriors of the region, who had extensive links with the Tibetans, sent a delegation to the patriarch of the Church of the East in 549 asking for a bishop because they had been converted. No one, then or now, is quite sure how they were converted or by whom, but the Church sent a bishop and the White Huns formed one of the most loyal Christian communities for many centuries.

Tibet in the sixth to eighth centuries A.D. was not Buddhist but Shamanic. The ancient folk religion of Bon dominated and continued to be the major popular expression of Tibetan religion into the fourteenth and fifteenth centuries. Buddhism only begins to enter Tibet in the late eighth century, where for hundreds of years it was limited to the elite classes. Buddhism took hold more widely much later, in the first half of the second millennium.[29]

A strong Church existed in Tibet by the eighth century. Patriarch Timothy I (727–823), head of the Church of the East, wrote from Baghdad in ca. 794 of the need to appoint another bishop for the Tibetans, and in an earlier letter of 782 he mentions the Tibetans as one of the significant Christian communities of the Church.[30] The Church's bishopric is assumed to have been in Lhasa, where it is likely to have been active as late as the thirteenth century, prior to the popular extension of Buddhism.

THE CROSSES OF TIBET

Carved into a large boulder at Tankse, Ladakh, once part of Tibet but now in India, are three crosses and some inscriptions. The rock dominates the entrance to the pass at Drangste, one of the main ancient trade routes between Lhasa and Bactria, the old Indo-Greek kingdom. The crosses are clearly of the Church of the East, and one of the words, written in Sogdian, appears to be "Jesus." Another inscription in Sogdian reads, "In the year 210 came Nos-farn from Samarkand as emissary to the Khan of Tibet."

It is possible that the inscriptions were not related to the crosses, but even on their own the crosses bear testimony to the power and influence of Christianity in that area. Christianity was sufficiently accepted in the region to warrant carving the Christian symbol to protect travelers.

The extent, size, and diversity of the Church of the East is perhaps one of the best-kept secrets of Western Christian history, which has traditionally dismissed the Church of the East as Nestorian and therefore heretical. At its peak in the eighth century, this once mighty Church far outstripped the Church of the West in the size, scale, and range of cultures within which it operated. Unlike many of the missions of the Church of the West to the Germanic tribes and the Anglo-Saxons in England, for example, the Church of the East was dealing with ancient, highly literate, civilized cultures and peoples. It had to find its way in a world where theological writings, philosophical debate, and schools of education had been in existence for hundreds, even thousands of years. It was a remarkably different world from the world of the West, and it produced remarkably different churches and forms of Christianity. Perhaps one of its greatest achievements was the Taoist Christian culture and the writings of the Jesus Sutras.

5

The Multicultural World
of Seventh-Century China

Flying into Xian airport in northwestern China can be a hazardous business. One of the major cities of modern China, Xian has smog that often blankets all but the largest or tallest features of the landscape, such as the ancient cliff-top pagodas that overlook the River Wei and the huge grass-covered mounds of the imperial tombs. You can smell the smog from miles up and it catches at the back of your throat. But on a good day, when the rains and wind have cleared the air, a wonderful panorama opens up as the plane tilts and begins its run toward the airport. Below is a landscape marked by virtually all the major epochs of Chinese history, from the Neolithic village of Banpo and the Great Tomb of the First Emperor (221–210 B.C.) to the tombs of the rulers of the Han Dynasty (209 B.C.–A.D. 221) and on to the monuments of the greatest of all the dynasties, the Tang (A.D. 618–906), which dominate the landscape as if the dynasties still ruled and Chang-an, the ancient capital city of China on which Xian is built, were still the greatest city in the world.

From the end of the Han in 221 to the rise of the first Tang tomb in the 620s, however, virtually nothing remains—no great mound covering some emperor, no trace of a capital city of that period. The reason for this is simple and it is fundamental to understanding why the rise of the Tang Dynasty was so important. From 221 until the end of the sixth century, there were no emperors of the whole of China; Chang-an was not safe to use as a capital city as it had been for more than four hundred years. China was divided among feuding warlords for two hundred years, until 420. Then, for another 170 years, until 589, it was split into a northern and a southern kingdom. China as we know it and as antiquity had known it simply did not exist for more than three and a half centuries. This is why no mighty tombs or other memorials around Xian commemorate the so-called emperors of these years of chaos.

By 221 the Han Dynasty had run its course. It didn't so much fall as simply cease to be. Three warlords arose from the decay, and for fifty years China was wracked by civil wars that destroyed most of the structures and norms of the imperial system of the previous four hundred years.

The time of destruction and distress is perhaps best captured by one of the remarkable poets of the time, Cao Zhi (192–232), himself a general. His father, Cao Cao, was one of the three warlords and came to rule over most of north China. Cao Zhi was his third son and a great favorite until he made a disastrous mistake during one campaign, after which he was humiliated publicly. This poem, written ca. 230, laments the ruin of the great city of Lo Yang (Lo-yang):

> I climb to the ridge of Pei Mang Mountain
> And look down on the city of Lo-yang.
> In Lo-yang how still it is!
> Palaces and houses all burnt to ashes.
> Walls and fences all broken and gaping,
> Thorns and brambles shooting up to the sky.
> I do not see the old old-men

I only see the new young men.
I turn aside, for the straight road is lost.
The fields are overgrown and will never be
    Ploughed again.
I have been away such a long time
That I do not know which street is which.
How sad and ugly the empty moors are!
A thousand miles without the smoke of a chimney.
I think of the house I lived in all those years:
    I am heart-tied and cannot speak.[31]

These civil wars, known to history as the wars of the Three
Kingdoms, impoverished and weakened China. As a result, the
"barbarian" tribes, as the Chinese historians called them, the Mongolians and Turkic tribes from the steppes, began to eye the wealth
of northern China. By the end of the third century, northern
China had passed into the hands of a succession of tribal invaders.
From then until the end of the sixth century, the north was dominated by changing power blocs of invaders while the south was
held by feeble and short-lived "dynasties" that bought off the invaders in the north to maintain a semblance of control. It was a
time of petty kings, minor dynasties, and changing fortunes: "For
more than three centuries, one dynastic founder after another had
attempted to restore the great centralised empire of the Han, but
all had failed. No dynasty had been more than a mere shadow of
the old empire, perpetuating at most the conditions of ineffectual
central government and complete dominance by the great families
that had characterized the dying days of Han rule."[32]

Eventually, from this chaos and disarray there arose a short-
lived dynasty, the Sui (589–618), which managed to regain much
of the north and create at least the semblance of a united China
again. But the forces of feudalism—the vast private armies of the
noble families who had become petty kings in their own right,
and the surging tribes of the steppes—proved too much for this

dynasty and it fell to one of its own generals in 618. It is doubtful whether anyone in 618 could have foreseen that the new dynasty then declared, the Tang, was going to be any different from the many others that had come and gone in the previous 350 years, but it soon became clear that the Tang was different, because guiding the new dynasty was one of the most outstanding men ever to rule in China.

Li Shimin had been one of the generals of the Sui Dynasty. He rose in rebellion in 616 and by the following year had captured Chang-an and declared it the restored capital city of China. In 618 he formally declared the Tang Dynasty and placed his father on the throne. Li then set about wiping out all opposition to his rule, including every one of his several brothers. Once they were dead, he deposed his father, and in 626 became the second emperor of the Tang, taking the title Taizong. As Emperor Taizong he ruled until 650. By this time, Tang China had become the most powerful empire in the world and was on its way to being the greatest in scale and power that China has ever seen.

At its peak, Tang China ruled from North Korea to the Caspian Sea and from Mongolia down to present-day Vietnam. Beyond this, the states of Japan, Korea, and what is today Thailand and Laos accepted the suzerainty of China and each year sent tribute to the Imperial Court at Chang-an. Tibet was the only power in the region even remotely comparable to China, but it too realized its future lay with China and it formed strategic alliances, including dynastic marriages with the Tang. Together, Tibet and China even invaded northern India, bringing the Ganges Valley under their combined control for some fifty years.

From chaos, Taizong created a mighty empire. It was this empire and this ruler that the first mission to China of the Church of the East encountered in 635.

As the foundation of his new dynasty, Taizong reintroduced the Confucian idea of a bureaucracy whose members rose through the ranks by examination and scholarship. In theory, the Confucian education system could enable any bright boy to rise to be prime minister of China, no matter what was his background. This meritocracy meant that the old privileged position of the nobility was undermined. Through the creation of the scholar class, Taizong broke the power of the noble families and established a civil service loyal to the emperor and the empire, not to individual local warlords or rulers. With the restoration of a proper civil service, traders knew they could trade securely and fairly, and merchants began to travel the Silk Road to Chang-an as they had in the time of the Han. The Tang armies repulsed the "barbarians" and soon much of the trade route to the West was under Chinese control. Such order and security had been unknown in the region for centuries. Taizong had founded an empire with a future.

This restoration of order and due process is reflected in the poetry of Bo Juyi (772–846), arguably the greatest of the great Tang Dynasty poets. His description of Chang-an, of the busy nature of this heaving metropolis and the pressure of the civil service examinations, is beautifully captured in the poem "Escorting Candidates to the Examination Hall," written ca. 810:

> At dawn I rode to escort the Doctors of Art;
> In the eastern quarter the sky was still grey.
> I said to myself "You have started far too soon,"
> But horses and coaches already thronged the road.
> High and low the riders' torches bobbed;
> Muffled or loud, the watchman's drum beat.
>   Riders, when I see you prick
> To your early levee, pity fills my heart.
> When the sun rises, and the hot dust flies
> And the creatures of earth resume their great strife,
> You, with your striving, what shall you each seek?
> Profit and fame, for that is all your care.
> But I, you courtiers, rise from my bed at noon
> And live idly in the city of Ch'ang-an.

Spring is deep and my term of office spent;
Day by day my thoughts go back to the hills.[33]

This poem gives a hint of the spiritual and philosophical life of Tang China, which was composed of four main belief systems: Confucianism, Taoism, Buddhism, and Shamanism. Of these, Shamanism was so old and so much a part of the fabric of China that it was more an overall regional, cultural attitude and mind-set than an active faith, and Confucianism and Taoism were indigenous. Buddhism, however, as an international missionary faith with structured monasticism, broke the mold of indigenous religions in China. Its arrival in the first centuries B.C. and A.D. was a profound shock to Confucianism and one reason for the emergence of Taoism as a monastic order in the second and third centuries A.D. Thus, when Christianity arrived in the seventh century, its missionaries entered a culture where the appearance of new religions—Buddhism and Taoism—and experimentation with their ideas and practices were part of the cultural psyche. In other words, people's views and practice of religion had become more fluid and more subject to change. Yet, beneath this apparent openness ran deep currents of Confucian and later Taoist opposition to "foreign religions"—especially to Buddhism.

✌️ SHAMANISM ✌️

Shamanism was probably the original religion of ancient China, having come from lands to the north, especially Siberia, which was and to some extent still is the heartland of Shamanism. Shamanic elements appear in the earliest legends of China and Shamanic practices are recorded in artwork from ca. 2500 B.C. Shamanism essentially holds that there are two parallel worlds: the material world we inhabit and the far more powerful and significant spiritual world. Through trances, shamans can communicate between the worlds and are used by the spirit world's forces to inform the human and material world of events at a deep level. Thus, shamans will go into trances to find the cause of illness, troubles, and disasters or to receive directions for what a people or a ruler should do next.

Shamanism is the underlying worldview of the earliest Chinese books, such as the *I Ching*, from about 1200 B.C. onward. It is likely that some of the semilegendary emperors of Chinese prehistory were actually priest-kings whose power came from their being shamans. By the time of the Han, with the rise of the Confucians, Shamanism was viewed as a troublesome leftover of a primitive world, suppressed by the Confucians and driven underground.

The rise of Taoism as a religion in the second century A.D. was, in certain ways, the reemergence of Shamanic practices newly cloaked in religious teachings more in tune with the developing world of Chinese civilization. Nevertheless, the Shamanic mind-set and practices persist in China to this day. Although disapproved of by the authorities, they are effectively protected by the Taoists.

✌o CONFUCIANISM ଠୈ

The title Confucianism comes from the Latin version of the name of the founder philosopher, Kong Fuzi, who lived in the sixth century B.C. Kong's family had been powerful some seven hundred years previously but had been in decline ever since, due, in Kong's view, to immoral forces. Family tradition was, and to some extent still is, important in China. Kong saw the same decline in morality that affected his family affecting all China. He believed that in the old times China had been ruled according to the True Way, the true Tao. To many in the West, the word tao, meaning "way," is associated only with the religion named after it, but study of the meaning of the Tao is common to all Chinese philosophy, especially that which flourished in the extraordinary period of philosophical exploration from the sixth to third centuries B.C. The essence of Kong's political philosophy is that a natural hierarchy exists that, if followed, ensures a world properly governed, where the righteous are rewarded and where all is in balance.

In Kong's thinking, the Tao establishes the hierarchy. It is the natural order of things and applies to all levels of existence. For example, within the family, the young must obey and serve the old and the old must teach and guide the young; the women must be subservient to the men and the men must protect the women. In the state, the ordinary person must be subservient to the local authority or administrators and the authorities or administrators must protect the people. The authorities must be subservient to the emperor and the emperor must ensure that the country is ruled fairly. The emperor must be subservient to Heaven and Heaven will then protect the empire. Heaven itself is subservient to the natural way of the universe, the Tao; the Tao in return ensures that the universe continues to exist. Humanity can either follow this natural hierarchy or can rebel against it and pay the price: troubles, disorder, chaos. Kong encapsulates this in his writings: "When the Tao prevails in the world, the rites, music and punitive military expeditions are initiated by the Emperor (Son of Heaven). When the Tao does not prevail in the world, they are initiated by the lesser lords. . . . When the Tao prevails in the world, policy is not in the hands of the Counsellors. When the Tao prevails in the world, there is nothing for the ordinary people to argue about" (*Analects,* bk. 16,2).

Kong sees the performance of rites and rituals as essential to maintaining this order. By following exactly the order laid down by previous generations, humanity can do what is right ritually, and this will ensure that it does what is right morally. The rituals are encoded ways of behaving and the emperor is responsible for ensuring that everyone follows them. Kong further sees rituals as vital to instill in ordinary people a sense of the morally right. He sums it up thus: "Guide them by edicts, keep them in line with punishments, and the common people will stay out of trouble but will have no sense of shame. Guide them by virtue, keep them in line with rites, and they will not only have a sense of shame but will reform themselves" (*Analects,* bk. 2,3).

When Kong died in 479 B.C., he was to all intents and purposes a failure. None of the rulers of his time paid serious attention to him; the civil wars and chaos continued unabated. But over the next few hundred years his ideas were codified and, in the third century B.C., when a unified China rose again, Confucian philosophy and practice were fully developed and ready for widespread adoption. From 221 B.C. until A.D. 1911, Confucian norms underpinned the concept of good government and empire in China. Even today, the Confucian mind-set is still a powerful influence in China.

Kong himself was not interested in the spirit world. He once commented that he had nothing to say about that world because he had quite enough to do reforming this world. Yet, over time, Kong himself was elevated to the status of a god. In China this kind of ancestor worship was common, a cultural inheritance from the Shamanic peoples. For example, if a good judge died, people might petition the emperor to have him appointed as one of the judges in the many Courts of Hell or as protector deity for the city. The supernatural world of China always was in part a mirror image of the world of the Chinese empire, and the emperor had a say in both worlds.

It was the reintroduction of the proper merit-based Confucian system for the education of the bureaucracy that helped Taizong break the power of the nobles and establish law and order throughout the land.

✍ TAOISM ✎

Taoism, the religion of the Tao, is the only other indigenous belief system besides Confucianism to emerge from China. Although they share an emphasis on the Tao, the two religions could not be more different.

The reputed founder of Taoism is Lao Zi. In fact, Lao Zi didn't found anything. He lived at the same time as Kong, the sixth century B.C., and developed his own understanding of the Tao. The book associated with him in Chinese tradition and legend, the *Tao Te Ching*, was not actually written by him but probably does contain some of his teachings. In many ways, he agrees with Kong in seeing the Tao as a moral force of order. Indeed, the *Tao Te Ching* has been described as a handbook to statecraft. It says this, for example:

> The highest form of government
> Is what people hardly even realise is there.
> Next is that of the sage
> Who is seen, and loved, and respected.
> Next down is the dictatorship
> That thrives on oppression and terror—
> And last is that of those who lie
> And end up despised and rejected. (ch. 17)

Lao Zi would perhaps have been rather surprised to discover that he was credited with founding a religion. In fact, what happened was that in the second century A.D. a mystic shaman, Zhang Dao Lin, had a vision of Lao Zi, who bestowed on Zhang the powers and authority to found a faith.

To understand the spirit of Taoism at its best, one needs to turn to the second "founder" of Taoism, Chuang Tzu. This delightful and very funny philosopher lived in the fourth century B.C.

and went to the heart of Taoism, exploring illusion and reality: "Once upon a time, I, Chuang Tzu, dreamt that I was a butterfly flitting around and enjoying myself. I had no idea I was Chuang Tzu. Then suddenly I woke up and was Chuang Tzu again. But I could not tell, had I been Chuang Tzu dreaming I was a butterfly, or was I a butterfly dreaming I was Chuang Tzu? However there must be some sort of difference between Chuang Tzu and a butterfly. We call this the transformation of things."[34]

Taoism turned from the illusions of this world—power, control, Confucian ethics—and sought to unite mystically with the Tao. In Taoism the Tao refers to a spiritual path that has concrete elements—rituals, techniques, and books—as well as the unseen and unknowable. Taoist cosmology is rich with deities, forces, and a belief in the possibility of becoming an immortal. Perhaps the best summation of what Taoism seeks is the image of the immortal: someone who has lived on earth and who, through either alchemical skills or meditation, has managed to make his body and thus his soul immortal. The character for an immortal in Chinese combines the character for man with the character for a mountain, together symbolizing a man alone on a mountain.

人　　　　山　　　　仙

man　　　*mountain*　　　*immortal*

Consider this in contrast to the Confucian ideal of a man at the heart of government! The Taoists turn their back on power politics and instead concentrate on meditation and reflection, alone before the might of the Tao as found in untamed nature.

Again, Chuang Tzu captures this rejection of the material world of power:

> Chuang Tzu was one day fishing in the Pu river when the King of Chu despatched two senior officials to visit him with a message. The message said, "I would like to trouble you to administer my lands."
>
> Chuang Tzu kept a firm grip on his fishing rod and said, "I hear that in Chu there is a sacred tortoise which died three thousand years ago. The King keeps this in his ancestral temple, wrapped and enclosed. Tell me, would this tortoise have wanted to die and leave his shell to be venerated? Or would he rather have lived and continued to crawl about in the mud?"
>
> The two senior officials said, "It would rather have lived and continued to crawl about in the mud."
>
> So Chuang Tzu said, "Shove off then! I will continue to crawl about in the mud!"[35]

Taoism as a religion rather than a philosophy or way of life emerges in the second century A.D. Founded by a series of remarkable mystics, it offered to ordinary people an alternative to the hierarchy and order of Confucianism, while also offering discourse and contact with the supernatural. In many ways, it is a codified version of Shamanism that became a whole way of life. It offers an understanding of the world, the Tao, and humanity's place within it that is a very different vision from that of the Confucians. It is perhaps best summed up in the core creed of Taoism, captured in chapter 42 of the *Tao Te Ching*:

> The Tao gives birth to the One, the Origin.
> The One, the Origin, gives birth to the Two.
> The Two give birth to the Three.
> The Three give birth to every living thing.

All things are held in yin and carry yang:
And they are held together in the qi of teeming energy.

The Tao is before the origin of all. In this sense it is almost like the idea of God in Christian thought, except that the Tao has no personality, no emotions, no divinity. It simply is the ultimate principle of all and origin of the origin. The origin gives birth to the two cosmic forces—again, not deities, just forces: yin and yang. Yin is the female: the dark, damp, winter force of life; yang is the male: the hot, dry, summer force. Together these two forces are locked in perpetual combat seeking to overcome each other. But this is impossible, for each carries the seed of the other within it. Autumn and winter are yin; just when it seems winter will never end, spring inexorably begins. Spring and summer are yang; when it seems the heat of summer will never abate, the cool winds of autumn begin.

The Three are Heaven, Earth, and Humanity. Heaven is yang, Earth is yin, and humanity combines both in the pivotal position of the balancer and arbitrator between yin and yang. Human error, pride, and foolishness disturb this balance. But at our best, humanity, through the rituals of Taoism, can ensure that yin and yang remain balanced and the world spins on.

Qi is the life breath that every living thing has and is an active expression of Tao. Life begins when qi enters the body; it is never added to but is steadily used up over the course of one's life. Death comes when the store of qi has been fully exhausted. The quest for health, healing, and even immortality in certain schools of Taoism consists of trying to hold on to qi and never use it up.

Before the Tang Dynasty, Taoism was viewed by the emperors as something of a problem religion. Although it was popular with many ordinary folk, who periodically made demands for justice and occasionally led Taoist-inspired revolts in certain provinces, it mocked and denied the ideals of Confucianism and thus often went against the principles of the empire. Taoism was thus not considered suitable for imperial patronage. But Emperor Taizong reversed this position. While developing the Confucian hierarchy, Taizong also gave huge support to the Taoists because, as noted earlier, to overcome the fact that he was more Turkic than Chinese he claimed to be a direct descendent of Lao Zi. Thus, during Taizong's reign and for a few decades afterwards, Taoism was the most favored religion and expanded greatly. This is especially significant for us because of the development of the Lou Guan Tai temple compound as a major intellectual and monastic center of Taoism under the patronage of the emperors in the seventh and eighth centuries A.D.

Let Bo Juyi the poet have the final word. His poem "In Early Summer Lodging in a Temple to Enjoy the Moonlight" captures the spirit of Tang Dynasty Taoism:

> In early summer, with two or three more
> That are seeking fame in the city of Ch'ang-an
> Whose low employ gave them less business
> Than even they had since first they left their homes,
> With these I wandered deep into the shrine of Tao,
> For the joy we sought was promised in this place.
> When we reached the gate, we sent our coaches back;
> We entered the yard with only cap and stick.
> Still and clear, the first weeks of May,
> When trees are green and bushes soft and wet;
> When the wind has stolen the shadows of new leaves
> And birds linger on the last boughs that bloom.
> Toward evening when the sky grew clearer yet
> And the South-east was still clothed in red,
> To the western cloister we carried our jar of wine;
> While we waited for the moon, our cups moved slow.
> Soon, how soon her golden ghost was born,
> Swiftly, as though she had waited for us to come.
> The beams of her light shone in every place,

On towers and halls dancing to and fro.
Till day broke we sat in her clear light
Laughing and singing, and yet never grew tired.
In Ch'ang-an, the place of profit and fame,
Such moods as this, how many men know?[36]

✌ BUDDHISM ⤫

To this day Buddhism is classified in China as a foreign religion. It arrived somewhere between the first century B.C. and the first century A.D., coming originally from India but through the Indo-Greek areas of Afghanistan. Although not a generally accepted theory, it is thus possible that Greek Buddhist missionaries first brought Buddhism to China.

Buddhism takes its name from the Buddha, meaning the Enlightened One. The historical Buddha of this era was born in a royal family in the sixth century B.C. at Lumbini in present-day Nepal. As a young prince he was pampered and protected from the realities of the world, but one day, when he was already the father of a young son, he ventured outside his palace home. He saw suffering, sickness, death, and old age for the first time, and he also encountered a mendicant. He immediately abandoned his young family and his wealth and took to the forests to seek peace and enlightenment. After five years he achieved enlightenment, then spent the remainder of his eighty years teaching. By his death he had created the teaching, Dharma, and the community to continue the teachings, the Sangha, or community of monks.

When Buddhism reached China, its first appeal was to the intellectual classes. Taoism was only just beginning to arise and was too closely associated with Shamanism and commoners for the comfort of the ruling elite. Buddhism offered a highly literate and ordered worldview, but it struggled with certain aspects of Confucianism. In Confucian thought, for instance, every son had a duty to have children to continue the family name, whereas Buddhism taught that monasticism was the highest level of human existence. This gave Buddhism problems for centuries, as it was open to attack by Confucians for being against family life.

This early form of Buddhism in China was Theravada. The historical Buddha seems to have taught a way of personal struggle and discovery that could last many lifetimes before enlightenment could be achieved. Theravada Buddhism stressed this arduous work, over many lifetimes, of getting rid of karma, the sum of the multiple consequences of all one's actions from all one's incarnations. In China this austere struggle was felt to be too long and complex, and Theravada Buddhism had only a limited appeal to the masses. For them, life was hard enough without having to try to solve everything by their own efforts.

Thus, during the chaos following the collapse of the Han Dynasty, a different form of Buddhism entered China. This was Mahayana Buddhism, and by the time of the Tang it had become the dominant form. Mahayana stressed that the individual seeking release from the threat of rebirth and the power of karma can call on divine assistance. With this form of salvationary Buddhism, the faith really became popular.

The central figures in Mahayana Buddhism are the Bodhisattvas. These beings, through countless lives of exemplary virtue and self-sacrifice, have rid themselves of all bad karma and thus will never be reborn. They have also sought to build up unimaginable quantities of good karma, which they dedicate to helping save all suffering beings. This compassionate Bodhisattva worldview is beautifully summed up in a famous text from the *Lotus Sutra*, one of the most popular of all Buddhist sutras in China from the fourth century A.D. to today. It describes what the Bodhisattva offers to tormented beings who long to escape the pains of karma and rebirth:

Every evil state of existence,
hells and ghosts and animals,
Sorrows of birth, age, disease, death,
All will thus be ended for him.
True Regard, serene Regard,
Far-reaching, wise Regard,
Regard of pity, Regard compassionate,
Ever longed for, ever looked for
in radiance ever pure and serene!
Wisdom's sun, destroying darkness,
Subduer of woes, of storm, of fire,
Illuminator of the world!
Law of pity, thunder quivering,
Compassion wondrous as a great cloud,
Pouring spiritual rain like nectar,
Quenching all the flames of distress.[37]

This is a wonderful picture of compassion that still has much to offer those seeking help. The teachings of Mahayana Buddhism rose to their full power during the Tang Dynasty and created a world that looked for supernatural assistance to overcome the difficulties and problems of karma and rebirth. The Tang was one of the most dynamic periods of Buddhist thought in China, and the quest for salvation is the predominant theme of this era.

It was also the high point of intellectual Buddhism, which was to be broken once and for all by the Great Persecution of A.D. 845, when the empire suppressed all "foreign" religions. A taste of this intellectual approach is the story of the famous competition set by the Fifth Patriarch of Chan Buddhism. He called for a verse to be written by his disciples that would reveal deep understanding of the faith. He promised that whoever wrote such a verse would become his successor, the Sixth Patriarch. His most favored disciple wrote the following:

Our body is the Tree of Perfect Wisdom,
And our mind is a clear mirror.
Faithfully clean them at all times
To free them from dust.

The Fifth Patriarch was quite impressed, but soon discovered that he had an even wiser pupil, Hui Neng, a recent addition to his group. Hui wrote the following two verses in which he not only dismissed the other poem but, to the Fifth Patriarch's delight, showed deep understanding:

The tree of Perfect wisdom is not actually a tree.
The clear mirror has no structure.
Buddha-nature is eternally clear and pure,
So where does the dust come from?

The mind is the Tree of Perfect Wisdom.
The body is the clear mirror.
This clear mirror is of its nature clear and pure,
So how can it be troubled by dust?[38]

The exploration of reality and nonreality in Tang Buddhism ran side by side with the more pietistic and salvationary Buddhism of the Boddhisattvas. But it was to be the salvationary Buddhism that survived the collapse of Tang Dynasty Buddhism in A.D. 845, that to this day shapes Chinese Buddhism, and that prepared the people's attitudes, hearts, and minds for the hopeful story of Jesus' spiritual power.

It was into this complex and multilayered world that Christianity came in the seventh century. A world in which the older traditions of what death meant had become confused and mixed with the introduction of Buddhist beliefs. A world where the concerns about reincarnation were met by claims of savior deities and Bodhisattvas who could save the virtuous and the repentant. A world in which the old indigenous religion of Taoism was trying to keep in balance its philosophical background, its popularist traditions, and its hold on the people in the face of Buddhist missionary activity. A world, too, where the state philosophy of Confucianism was struggling to keep its hold on the intelligentsia against the philosophies and lifestyle of Buddhism. And a world where the shrines, temples, books, and teachers in the capital city would have been as diverse and pluralist as the religions to be found today in London or New York. This was a world of changing values and many possibilities.

It was also a supremely confident world. The Chinese Empire was expanding and nothing stood in its way. After centuries of chaos, the Chinese were once again proud of their empire and rediscovering its cultural and philosophical depths. Never again would China and its vast metropolis of Chang-an be so open to other traditions as in those early years of the Tang Dynasty.

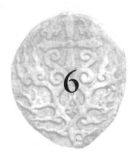

The Early Church in China

As the mission to China carried on translating the books it had brought with it, it also engaged more and more deeply with the faiths of China. The process of adoption of Chinese metaphor and images that started with the first sutra, *The Sutra of the Teachings of the World-Honored One*, continued apace, as is clearly seen in the other three earliest Sutras.

The teaching of *The Sutra of Cause, Effect, and Salvation*, the second Sutra, offers the clearest evidence that the Church was drawing on books that had been influenced in their presentation of spiritual concepts by teachings and cultures encountered in other mission fields. This Sutra was translated into Chinese sometime in the 640s in China, but originated in the Indo-Greek area of present-day Afghanistan or Pakistan, probably between the third and fifth centuries. It has no formal title in its Chinese version, but a codicil at the end says "First Part of the Discourse on the Oneness of Heaven." It is one of the texts found in antiques shops in the 1920s and is now in a private collection in Japan.

The Sutra assumes a Greek style of debate and discussion,

opening with a classic question-and-answer model. It goes on to use the four elements of classic Greek thought—earth, water, fire, and wind—first established by the Greek philosopher Anaximander around 560 B.C. Thus, the Sutra opens:

> **The question is asked: What is the cause of human beings?**
> **The answer is: Humanity is created both by that which can be seen and that which cannot.**
> **What causes the visible and the invisible?**
> **Everything under heaven consists of the Four Elements: earth, water, fire, and wind. All brought about by the Sacred Spirit. (1:1–5)**

This Sutra could not have been a Chinese book originally for the simple reason that in Chinese philosophy there are five elements—earth, water, air, fire, and metal—as first enumerated by Tsou Yen in the fourth century B.C.[39] Later Sutras of the Church in China always refer to the five elements, yet classical Buddhist philosophy, like Greek, assumes four elements rather than five—another indication that it originates in a non-Chinese but Buddhist environment.

After an opening discussion of the four elements, the Sutra discusses the nature of being human and characterizes our being in terms of an idea common to both Greek and Buddhist philosophy, namely, that we possess a body and a "soul." In classic Buddhist thought, the soul is the sum total of karmic actions of previous lives housed in the physical manifestations known as the Five Skandas: form, consciousness, mind, sensation, and desire. Variations on them are common in Buddhist Sutras. The second Jesus Sutra, *The Sutra of Cause, Effect, and Salvation*, states that there is an ultimate Power behind the four elements, then discusses the Five Skandas in classical Buddhist terminology and imagery, very similar to that used, for example, in book 2, chapter 3 of the *Milindapanha*. This seems to me unique in a Christian book and shows that this

Christian Sutra was created to debate Buddhist ideas outside the culture of China, in a place where classical Christian, Greek, and Buddhist thought met and debated.

✍ THE ENCOUNTER WITH ✌ BUDDHISM: KARMA AND REINCARNATION

The second Sutra also explores the consequences of karma and dwells on the issue of reincarnation. Karma and reincarnation fundamentally affected the nature of Christianity as it developed in China. This Sutra, which is one of the earliest Christian Sutras so far found in China, takes reincarnation very seriously, just as the *Milindapanha* does. Indeed, there are points where they seem to echo each other.

Karma and reincarnation had become key issues in the developing world of Chinese Buddhism in the seventh century. Reincarnation, the prospect of which provided no release from constant suffering, death, and rebirth, was feared. It seemed invincible and inevitable. Buddhism set out to break the power of reincarnation, to free people from the fear of rebirth.

In the early Theravada Buddhism, karma is the cause-and-effect force that drives reincarnation. Whatever you do has an effect. Your actions, whether motivated by greed, envy, jealousy, and violence or charity, love, and compassion, all yield consequences that, when you die, are unfulfilled. You therefore have to be reborn to continue working through the effects of past actions. The only way to escape this is to become so perfect that nothing you do causes any bad effects. This perfection comes from awakening or becoming enlightened. Only such enlightened people will have nothing left to work off when they die and so will not be reborn. This is the early Buddhist approach, as reported by his disciples to have been taught by the Buddha himself.

In this second Jesus Sutra, as in others, Christianity seriously addresses the threat of rebirth and the issue of karma. Jesus is rather charmingly described as "the Visitor" who offers his salvationary powers as a way of breaking the cycle of cause and effect, of birth, suffering, death, and rebirth. In their dialogue with the Buddhists, probably in the old Indo-Greek kingdoms, the Christians had moved radically in their thinking from classical Western nonreincarnational beliefs to seeing Jesus as the solution to the existential issues of rebirth and karma. In China this difference was to be developed even further.

Because the Chinese of this Sutra is at times awkward, we know it to be an early effort at cross-cultural communication. Whoever was translating didn't always understand Chinese, or was Chinese and didn't always understand the original language in which it was written or the concepts he or she was translating. Yet it is a most extraordinary document for what it reveals of an early dialogue between Christianity and Buddhism in lands far from China: Afghanistan and the northern areas of India and Pakistan today. It is significant because it takes Christianity away from the theological arguments of the West and into a direct and full encounter with classical Buddhism.

Although the Chinese translation is not skillful, the Sutra's mature integration of Greek, Buddhist, and Christian insights into one document is effective. It uses no classical Christian terminology or imagery, but weaves a Christian message through Greek and Buddhist philosophy. The original book must have been treasured to have been included in the bundle brought to China in the mission of 635. The Church probably felt it to be intelligible to Buddhists and so of use in China. As the missionaries would discover, however, Chinese Buddhism was somewhat different from what they had encountered before, so the Sutra doesn't quite connect with Chinese philosophy. This explains something of the difficulty the translator faced. Nevertheless, the Church in China was to follow the lead of this unique book and produce its own Christian/Buddhist and Chinese Sutras.

Although we may never be able to trace conclusively this early Sutra to its original language in dialogue between Christians and Buddhists or home in northern India and Afghanistan, it remains the only extant example of such an encounter. Here, then, is this unique document. (Please note that ellipses denote lost text.)

ᴄ⁄ᴐ THE SECOND SUTRA: ᴄᴐ⁄
THE SUTRA OF CAUSE, EFFECT, AND SALVATION

CHAPTER ONE

[1]The question is asked: What is the cause of human beings?

[2]The answer is: Humanity is created both by that which can be seen and that which can not.

[3]What causes the visible and the invisible?

[4]Everything under Heaven consists of Four Elements: earth, water, fire, and wind.[5]All brought about by the Sacred Spirit.

[6]The question is asked: Of what are the Four Elements made?

[7]The answer is given: There is not one thing under heaven which has not been created, and there is not a single creation which was not made by the One Sacred Spirit.[8]Without the Sacred Spirit, nothing would have been brought into existence.[9]It is like building a house: the very first thing needed is a place to build.[10]In this way the One Sacred Spirit caused existence to inhabit a space.[11]It happened because the One Sacred Spirit looked with compassion on all life.

CHAPTER TWO

[1]The One Sacred Spirit clearly distinguishes the visible and the invisible—Heaven and Earth.[2]In causing existence, the Sacred Spirit

is like the wind: being a spirit, nothing can be touched, nothing can be seen.³But you can see the effects of the One Sacred Spirit; you can see everything it brings into existence.⁴Nothing else can do this.

⁵The One Sacred Spirit made a vast multitude of beings.⁶Everything under Heaven is filled with this Sacred Spirit.⁷Creatures such as the worm or the deer cannot understand speech and do not know their origin.⁸There are multitudes, but no two or three are alike.

⁹Not everything under Heaven is visible.¹⁰People sincerely believe that the invisible is the gracious action of the spirits.¹¹But it is important to distinguish the multitude of living things because no spirit could create such diversity.¹²So many millions of beings, visible and invisible, each containing two characteristics created by the One Sacred Spirit.¹³All people have these two aspects.¹⁴The first has no understanding of the teaching; the other does.¹⁵If they were one, would there be any understanding?¹⁶Without there being the two, how could the Sacred Spirit create human beings?¹⁷No one knows.¹⁸Everything under heaven has these two qualities created by the Sacred Spirit.¹⁹The One Sacred Spirit made the Two.²⁰Everything under Heaven has two natures, and everything is united under Heaven.²¹The two natures are body and sacred spirit.²²These two reside in all existence under heaven.²³It is not only heavenly spirit; it is body as well.²⁴But the body only lives for a short time whilst the heavenly soul lives on in the power of the One Sacred Spirit and never decays.²⁵It is this power of the One Sacred Spirit which animates all people.

CHAPTER THREE

¹The soul has Five Skandas.²These are form, perception, consciousness, action, and knowledge.³Everyone can see, hear, and speak.⁴Without eyes you cannot see, without hands you cannot act, without feet you cannot walk.⁵Just as one and two are united, so is

everything mutually dependent.[6]The sun and fire are two united in one.[7]Fire emerges from the sun.[8]They share one nature, but without the sun there is no fire.[9]They are of the same whole yet are different for the sun never dies whilst the fire needs wood to keep burning.[10]It has no inherent light of its own.[11]Fire is not self-generating.[12]Yet the sun is; it is different from fire.[13]The power of the One Sacred Spirit is like this.[14]Different but the same.[15]The same but different.[16]Thus the Sacred Spirit is different from human existence.

[17]The soul of a human being can only exist because of the Five Skandas.[18]Without the Five Skandas, there is no soul.[19]No other Sacred Spirit can do this.[20]Only by being clothed in the physicality of the Five Skandas can the soul savor the beauties and wonders of existence.[21]The soul needs to be physically clothed.[22]The soul dwelling in the body is like the wheat seeds from which spring not just wheat but more wheat seeds.[23]The earth is like the Five Skandas.[24]The grain is put into the ground and is thus able to grow.[25]It produces more seed.[26]This is natural and requires neither manure nor water, just a gentle breeze.[27]This is like the soul and the body.[28]It does not require food, drink, or clothes.

[29]Heaven and Earth will pass away and the ghosts of the dead will come back to life.[30]The souls of the dead will once again be clothed by the Five Skandas.[31]But this time the Five Skandas will be perfected, needing no food to sustain them nor clothing to cover them.[32]The souls will exist in complete happiness, untouched by physical needs.[33]It will be similar to the existence and happiness of a flying immortal, or like having the knowledge to speak with powers.[34]Everything under Heaven feels happy if body and soul are happy.[35]Such a union of body and soul creates happiness.

CHAPTER FOUR

[1]A Visitor came to this world uniting body and soul: He was happy in this world without troubling His spirit.[2]The union of body and

soul was made by the sacred spirit of God.³Just as flavor creates food, so the qi [life breath] creates the body and soul.⁴All this comes from God.⁵Venerate God and all will be as it should be and will become clear to you.⁶Whatever you do in life will have its karmic impact upon your soul and will affect the physical life of the soul.⁷The Visitor brought the Five Skandas and the soul together and dwelt in our world.

⁸No matter how poor or inadequate the Five Skandas, they will be enhanced if the soul is rich with karma.⁹There can be no doubt that the Five Skandas are dependent on the bounty or otherwise of the soul's karma.¹⁰The Five Skandas are like modeling clay while the soul is the sculptor.¹¹This is why soul and body together make one being.

¹²To know the Sacred Spirit is true knowledge.¹³But the world does not understand this.¹⁴This is not surprising because both knowledge and soul were created before the world began—they are eternal, and the world is not.¹⁵Knowledge and soul are as they were in the past, are now, and ever will be.

¹⁶So it was that He existed before existing in His mother's womb.¹⁷But to change your karma, you must exist in this physical world.¹⁸A person can only change his karma residue by being born again into this world.¹⁹Do good and you will live to be in the world beyond this world.²⁰The other world can be found by doing acts of karma in this life, by living properly in this world.²¹This world is like a mother's womb in which you are shaped for the world to come.²²All creatures should know that the karmic consequences of what is done in this life will shape the next life.²³All under Heaven must understand this clearly.²⁴It is clear in this world: all eyes can see and can see clearly.²⁵All manner of sounds can be heard by those alert enough to do so.²⁶All kinds of fragrant smells can be smelled by those determined to do so and all sorts of food can be enjoyed by those whose mouths can savor the tastes.²⁷Anything can be undertaken by those with hands.²⁸But in the next world, none of this is relevant.²⁹It is only relevant to the world you enter physi-

cally through your mother's womb and the Five Skandas can only be formed in a mother's womb.³⁰This world is the only place to decide your next birth.³¹There is no other way forward—do good in this world to enter the next.³²It cannot be done elsewhere.

CHAPTER FIVE

¹Do not worship ghosts.²Virtue can only be practiced in this world.³The One Sacred Spirit controls everything and you should do as the Spirit demands: good deeds in this life.⁴This is the only world in which you can perform good karma.⁵Don't think about any other world.⁶All acts of merit and benevolence must be performed in this world, not the next.⁷Be charitable here because in the other world you can't be.⁸So being aware of this, become openhanded and not tight-fisted and narrow.⁹You can only be charitable and generous in this world, not the next.

¹⁰So rid yourself of the evil and poison in your heart and abandon all your bad thoughts and jealousy.¹¹You can only do it in this world, not the next.¹²With peace of mind, worship God in this world, for it won't be possible in the next.¹³Worship God with all your heart and your sins will be forgiven.¹⁴You can do this now, but not in the next world.

¹⁵You will reap the consequences of this life in the next world, but can do nothing once you are there.¹⁶This will bring happiness— it is how the One Sacred Spirit designed things and left it for us to choose.¹⁷There was no other way to free us from sins but for Him to enter this world.¹⁸So He came and suffered a life of rejection and pain before returning.¹⁹To know this is to know who He was, to know that the One Sacred Spirit became incarnate in the Holy Sacred Spirit.²⁰Knowing this, you should do as is commanded: follow these teachings and worship the One Sacred Spirit.²¹A benevolent act done in the knowledge of this suffering is the only truly benevolent act, acceptable only by these teachings and none other.

²²It is like building a house.²³The house needs firm foundations

or it will be useless.²⁴If people wish to be virtuous, they should follow the commands of the One and Only Sacred Spirit.²⁵Understand that the One Sacred Spirit presides over all existence to be venerated; strive to do what is right and be grateful for the grace you have received.

²⁶To sing praises, to chant and worship and encourage others to do so is highly virtuous.²⁷Always do good and keep your heart pure.²⁸Remain true to God.²⁹Unless you realize this, all your virtuous acts will fail just as the house without firm foundations will fall.³⁰As soon as the wind blows, the house is gone.³¹But built on firm foundations, not even the strongest wind can conquer.³²Thus a virtuous deed done without understanding of God fails.³³In order to see the One Sacred Spirit people must keep themselves pure in heart and, as an act of grace, all will become clear.

³⁴The Five Skandas are all different.³⁵Yet the Five Skandas with body and soul are all as one; they all become strong and worship the One Sacred Spirit for their creation and for the image they have been made in.³⁶Pray and worship for eternity.

³⁷All plants have a time of growth and harvest according to the seasons.³⁸Spring and autumn, winter and summer all follow one another and the four seasons shape the year.³⁹Day and night form the cycle of twelve days of the twelve characters cycle. [This refers to the traditional Chinese system of using the twelve animal signs as names for the days in twelve-day or -year cycles.]⁴⁰This happens through the benevolence of the One Sacred Spirit who is holy.⁴¹The wisdom of God is without origin, it is changeless and immutable.⁴²This is naturally so.

CHAPTER SIX

¹The Law and teachings of the One Sacred Spirit are better than any from our earthly rulers who call themselves Sons of Heaven.²Ordinary people and those of Jewish faith know about opponents.³Evil

The Stone Sutra is carved on the stele at left in the first hall of the Forest of Stone Steles Museum, Xian. (© Xia Ju Xian/CIRCA)

(Above) The Moon Gate at Lou Guan Tai temple. The inscription above the gate says, "Look out from here and you will see clearly." Legend has it that this is where the watchman saw the sage Lao Zi traveling west, stopped him, and asked him to write down his wisdom. This work became the classic Tao Te Ching.
(© Tjalling Halbertsma/ CIRCA)

(Right) The main entrance and terrace of Lou Guan Tai, from which the author spotted the Da Qin pagoda.
(© Tjalling Halbertsma/ CIRCA)

Da Qin pagoda and terrace. (© Xia Ju Xian/CIRCA)

Tang Dynasty pagoda of Da Qin with eighteenth-century Buddhist temple.
(© Xia Ju Xian/CIRCA)

View from the top floor of the Da Qin pagoda, looking back at the small hill of Lou Guan Tai, which appears in the center of the photo. (© Xia Ju Xian/ CIRCA)

The Yuan Dynasty stele (1383) commemorating the founding of a Christian monastery in that year. The cross on the book jacket surmounts this stele, held by four dragons (two are on the reverse side of the stele). (© Tjalling Halbertsma/CIRCA)

(Above) The interweaving of Christian and Chinese styles produces this extraordinary cross of 1383, reminiscent of the fusion created in the statues of the Da Qin pagoda six hundred years earlier. (© Tjalling Halbertsma/CIRCA)

(Left) The inscription states that this stone marks the site of the Monastery of the Cross. (© Tjalling Halbertsma/CIRCA)

Statue of Lao Zi on his ox, marking the spot where he stopped and dismounted before climbing to Lou Guan Tai to write the Tao Te Ching. (© Tjalling Halbertsma / CIRCA)

Ceremonial gate and statue of Lao Zi at the place where he stopped before climbing to Lou Guan Tai to write the **Tao Te Ching** *before disappearing forever into the West. (© Tjalling Halbertsma/CIRCA)*

ghostly spirits try to lead people away from the true course; they make them unable to hear or see the truth.[4]People thought they knew what to do from the teachings of other spirits and deities.[5]They did what seemed right, but they were easily confused and drawn into evil by bad spirits.[6]They did not know how to find the true center.[7]It is like someone who copies the good actions of other people but has no understanding of what or why he is doing it.[8]So it is with those who do not know the Sacred Spirit.[9]They can never have good fortune.[10]They are like animals on all fours and their hearts are no better than such a beast's.[11]Thus they cannot comprehend and because there is no true discernment or understanding they can find no chance of the Compassion of release.[12]Knowing this, one can see why animals cannot comprehend and do not worship the One Sacred Spirit.[13]They do not make sacrifices.

[14]Evil spirits cause evil deeds.[15]These evil spirits are truly evil.[16]There are none better at leading foolish people astray than the evil spirits, who entice them from the true path.[17]Some foolish people carve wood or stone and call it a sacred spirit, and this is why the evil spirits are called the enemies of humanity.[18]If people know good from evil they will be safe, but if not, the evil spirits will trap them.[19]Bad deeds come from the evil spirits, but if anyone could calm these spirits and bring them to understand the truth, then they could be enlightened and all would be as happy as flying immortals.

[20]The evil ones turn to the path of evil.[21]Then there are the foolish ones who, despite knowing what is right, do evil acts.[22]Such people are no better than the enemies of humanity and are foes of the One Sacred Spirit and the people.[23]By such actions they are cast out; they lose their true home and are sent to the region where evil dwells.[24]Thrown out of the Three Places, they dwell with the spirits.[25]The leader of these is the one known as the Cruel Evil Ghost [Satan] which is the name foreigners give to the most powerful of evil spirits.[26]The effect of the Evil Ghost Spirit's force is to turn people from the true way.[27]Those who follow the ways of the spirits

are called scions of the ghosts—they are like malignant spirits who turn people to the evil way.[28]Thus they are cast out from Heaven.[29]Evil forces blow across the world threatening all.[30]People fall under the influence of these spirits and these evil forces oppose their good nature and stay in their homes to trap them forever.[31]The worst of these is called San nu [Satan].[32]Foreigners have described this being as a ghost—it constantly strives to trap humanity.

[33]All these evil ghosts and spirits were cast from Heaven's light and went down the evil path.

[34]The evil spirits hate it when people do the right things.[35]So they never cease their attacks on those who worship the One.[36]They work endlessly to do evil and through evil to make people follow the evil way.[37]Many foolish people are thus seduced to stop worshiping and following the One Sacred Spirit with all their heart.[38]Their words become wicked.[39]Such a way leads to the central of three evil paths, guided by the evil spirits.[40]They are doomed to be reborn into the world with a worse position in life, trapped in the 10,000 kalpas [ages] from which there is no escape from rebirth.[41]The evil spirits concentrate on evil and only see evil and think evil.

[42]Over and against this, in the Four Quarters under Heaven, there is the One who encourages good.[43]Yet in the Four Quarters under Heaven there are also evil doers.[44]They try to trick people into following the evil way, the work of evil spirits.[45]Therefore, turn to the One Sacred Spirit and find true holiness in your actions.

[46]The First Treatise on the Oneness of Heaven.

◈ THE THIRD SUTRA: ◈ THE SUTRA OF ORIGINS

The next Sutra from this earliest collection, *The Sutra of Origins,* is an odd book nowhere near as sophisticated as *The Sutra of Cause, Effect, and Salvation*, with its deep philosophical basis, but much more dogmatic and simplistic. It too probably came from the Dunhuang caves, was purchased in China in the 1920s, and is now in a private collection in Japan. Yet it also tries to integrate some core Chinese ideas, including the fundamental Taoist notion of *wu wei*—actionless action or no action—which is first used here in connection with Christianity. This is developed fully in *The Sutra of Returning to Your Original Nature,* written probably 120 or 130 years later.

The Sutra of Origins illustrates the need that Christianity had to try to answer core questions by drawing, moderately successfully, on key terms gleaned from the culture around the Church. Its earnestness seems to speak of a worthy text prepared for a critical emperor.

CHAPTER ONE

[1]Every living thing comes from the One Sacred Spirit.[2]Everything originates in the One Sacred Spirit.[3]All that can be seen is created by the One Sacred Spirit.[4]So it is that we know all is created by One Sacred Spirit.[5]Everything visible and invisible is caused by the One Sacred Spirit.[6]From this we can see that all that exists has its origin quite clearly in the One Sacred Spirit.[7]Because of this, Heaven and Earth are stable and nothing changes.[8]Heaven has no need of support to stop it falling down.[9]If it wasn't for the One Sacred Spirit, how could it stand?[10]If the One Sacred Spirit was not, what would keep Heaven and Earth firm?[11]This shows how the One Sacred Spirit has truly mysterious powers.[12]No tent pole holds up Heaven yet Heaven cannot remain where it is by itself.[13]It does so because of the One Sacred Spirit's power.[14]Were we to see the tent pole supporting Heaven we would believe in the One Sacred Spirit's powers.[15]In fact, it is the One Sacred Spirit at work.

CHAPTER TWO

¹Humanity is seen as dwelling between Heaven and Earth. ²Yet humanity is restless—indeed the world is a restless place. ³Trying to find security in this world is like looking for calm waters, but where can such calm waters be found? ⁴When the wind is still and the earth doesn't shake or fall, we can see nothing moving. ⁵Yet the One Sacred Spirit is at work.

⁶It is like an archer. ⁷We see the arrow fly and fall but cannot see the archer himself. ⁸Even though we cannot see the archer, the flying arrow tells us there must be one. ⁹It is the same with the One Sacred Spirit. ¹⁰Because we see Heaven and Earth stand secure and firm we know that the One Sacred Spirit exists. ¹¹We cannot see the One who holds up Heaven and Earth but we know that such a One must exist. ¹²An arrow falls to the ground once it has used up the force it was given by the archer. ¹³Likewise by seeing that Heaven and Earth remain stable and do not fall we know the power of the One Sacred Spirit is still at work in all life. ¹⁴Heaven and Earth exist because of the One Sacred Spirit. ¹⁵This is not the work of any other spirit.

¹⁶No one can see the Sacred Spirit but there are two aspects. ¹⁷These can be compared to having hands and feet: one on the right, one on the left; two up, two down, with no difference between them. ¹⁸That is what it is like with the two aspects. ¹⁹From the One Sacred Spirit the other spirit came but with nothing to differentiate it from the One Sacred Spirit—like hands and feet. ²⁰The One Sacred Spirit contains all. ²¹There is no second or third. ²²Uncreated, unborn: it is impossible to see the One who holds up Heaven and Earth but we can see that the One Sacred Spirit feeds and sustains all life. ²³As there is one master in the house, so there is one heavenly soul in each body. ²⁴More than one master in a house is not good. ²⁵Likewise each person only has one heavenly soul in their body. ²⁶It is not possible to survive if one has two or three. ²⁷One master per house, not two or three.

CHAPTER THREE

[1]So it is that there is One Sacred Spirit to sustain Heaven and Earth, not two or three.[2]One Sacred Spirit to contain Heaven and Earth, invisible as the heavenly soul in the body.[3]No one can see the heavenly soul in the body though everyone would like to see the heavenly soul.[4]The Great Holy Intelligence is as the Void: emptiness and thus invisible.[5]The One Sacred Spirit itself is as all-pervasive as the heavenly soul is all-pervasive through the body.[6]All below Heaven have but One Sacred Spirit, whose palace is Heaven and who is intangible.[7]The One Sacred Spirit is not confined to one place, is not to be found in two or three places.[8]The One Sacred Spirit is everywhere, between one moment and another in two places at once as if here and Persia or between Persia and Bethlehem.[9]The being and actions of the One Sacred Spirit are everywhere, no beginning and no end.[10]Creation is like this also—no beginning and no end.[11]This power is without boundaries—arising from wu wei—actionless action and from creationless creation—there being no stage one and stage two.[12]So the One Sacred Spirit is the embodiment of wu wei, originless origin, and nonsubstantial substance.

[13]Therefore do not ask whether all that is is also partaker of this wu wei, this beginningless beginning, this absence of sense, timeless in time.[14]The One Sacred Spirit simply is, existing in wu wei, being in beinglessness and beyond touch.[15]Existing in nonexistence never extinguished into nonbeing.[16]All that exists does so as the manifestation of the beingness of the One Sacred Spirit.[17]The One Sacred Spirit exists and moves in perpetuity.[18]The One Sacred Spirit is uncreated and is the essence of all existence and can never be emptied.

[19]All under Heaven can see this though some claim not to just as some can discern the heavenly soul.[20]Some have this understanding, others do not.[21]Those who understand can see the two aspects, the two seeds of being: the heavenly soul and the sacred spirit.[22]The human being and the Spirit come from one root.[23]The

Spirit and heavenly soul create the true human being.[24]No body, no human being; no heavenly soul, no human being; no Sacred Spirit, no human being.[25]Nothing to be seen under Heaven exists of itself. This is the meaning of two aspects, one root.[26]The visible world is one aspect, the invisible One Sacred Spirit is the other aspect.[27]There is no existence without the nonexisting, unending Spirit.[28]All that lives does so by the One Sacred Spirit.[29]Untold numbers.[30]And all go back to the Four Elements. . . .

✍ GATHERING MANY STRANDS ✍

China at the time of the Tang Dynasty was as much Shamanic/ Taoist as Buddhist or Confucian. Travelers would have spoken of it as a culture that in part would have been familiar to the Church from its work among the Bon people in Tibet and the White Huns.

We believe that the last book in this collection of the four earliest Jesus Sutras, which is named in Chinese *The Sutra of Jesus Christ*, is a compilation of texts created in China sometime after the mission had arrived there. Found in an antiques shop in Beijing in the 1920s and now in Japan, it shows some degree of familiarity with Chinese thought. For example, it talks of Yama, the Judge of the Dead, who resides as supreme judge over those who have died and decides what their next life will be. The Sutra draws Yama into the cosmology of the Church not as Satan but as the unattractive alternative of rebirth after judgment in the Earth Prisons of Hell. The Earth Prisons are not the same as the Christian concept of Hell. In Taoist and Chinese Buddhist thought, there are either ten or eighteen such hells where the most awful tortures take place. Each hell deals with a particular set of sins; for example, the Second Hell is for those who have led astray the young, those who practice medicine without being qualified, those who deliberately hurt another creature, and those who know a marriage is doomed before it begins but fail to warn one of the partners.

The punishments are horrific: being hacked to pieces, put together again, and then hacked apart again, for years; being stretched on a rack; being dunked in boiling water time and time again; being forced to climb trees whose leaves are as sharp as swords; being constantly gnawed by wolves. However, the torments do end when you move on to the next hell until you eventually have served your time in all of them and can now be reborn into whatever form your accumulated karma dictates. The Sutra contrasts the prospects of salvation—being taken to the world of God—with being left to the mercies of Yama and rebirth.

The Sutra also shows familiarity with the hierarchical nature of China and contains a long piece about Confucian loyalty to parents and emperor. Clearly it is trying to help Chinese Christians reconcile Confucian ethics with Christian insights. It presents the Ten Commandments as Ten Covenants, for instance; thus, the first three Covenants are Honor God, Honor the emperor, Honor your parents.

The Sutra is an anthology of bits and pieces, a kind of primer, designed to help someone understand the Christian faith. It opens with sections that resemble other Christian Buddhist dialogues, but it lacks the Greek philosophical rigor of the Gandharan/ Bactrian *Sutra of Cause, Effect, and Salvation*. It discusses the Buddha as part of the Christian cosmology as it discusses Yama, god and judge of the Underworld and of reincarnation, as also part of this cosmology. It draws on fairly standard Christian apologetics in its use of the image of the Wind that cannot be seen but also uses material that can have been drawn only from a Christian Tibetan book early on in the anthology, as I discuss below. These references occur even before a section on Yama and the Ten Covenants, which clearly belongs to another source document.

THE TIBETAN INFLUENCE

The Tibetan Christian section of the Sutra, with its highly distinctive terminology and concepts, occurs after the brief discussion of the spirit of God as the Wind. The key text is as follows:

> **All that has life, know in your hearts that this is so, and by grace understand how to do that which is good. Everything that is born must die. Everything that lives exists only because the Winds give it life. When it is time for life to end, the Winds depart from the body. A person's heart and mind are not their own, but are created by the Winds. The Winds' departure is a time of great distress, but nobody can see the Winds at that time. Nobody can see them because they have no form, no color, not red nor green or any other. The Winds are invisible. The path is unknown. (2:1–9)**

At first this might seem to be a muddled version of the Chinese concept of qi, or energy, the Breath with which we are all born, the preservation of which ensures immortality. In Chinese classical thought, we have a finite store of qi or breath; once we use it up, we die. Earlier in the Sutra however, qi appears quite explicitly to differentiate it from the Winds. Qi is essentially passive, existing for and within each life, but it does not create the body or enter into it as a creative force. It simply is part of every body.

My colleague Eva Wong, who worked with me on the translations of these texts, thinks this distinct, perplexing section, which continues for a number of paragraphs, may in fact be part of a large section taken from a Tibetan Christian book that constitutes a fair proportion of this Sutra. Much more work needs to be done to ascertain this. The text quoted above does not correspond to any Chinese philosophical idea, nor is it a Greek idea, or Christian, in which tradition God puts his breath into Adam at creation, but the breath does not create in and of itself. It is not a Buddhist theory either, at least not of that time. It does appear much later in Tibetan Buddhist thought, but via the influence of the Bon religion. The only theory of the creative force of Winds in human life comes from Tibet. The following excerpt, taken from *Clear Light of Bliss: Mahamudra in Vajrayana Buddhism*, echoes the Jesus Sutra:

> You must know the ten doors through which the winds can enter the central channel because it is impossible to generate simultaneous great bliss without channeling these winds. These ten are the only doors through which the winds can enter.
>
> Normally, except at the time of death and during sleep, the winds will not enter this channel unless one engages in appropriate meditative practices. Therefore the secret mantra practitioner generates simultaneous great bliss—for use in meditating upon emptiness—by intentionally bringing the winds into the central channel through any of the ten doors by force of single-pointed concentration. . . .
>
> According to secret mantra these three [channels, winds, white and red drops] constitute what is called the vajra body [Vajra means tantric wisdom].[40]

In other words, the wind or winds (in Chinese, it is often impossible to tell whether the character is singular or plural) are a creative force that operates independent of the body but brings the body to life and sustains it at will. This is different in nature to the qi of Chinese thought. The teaching about these channels, winds, and drops seems to be a part of Tibetan dogma that has been lost.

From this reading it seems that sections of a Tibetan Christian book drawing on Bon Tibetan cosmology and philosophy were incorporated into a Chinese Christian Sutra. It is possible that it originally formed a key book that provides the basis for this whole Sutra, and that was later edited and improved by incorporating more Chinese-orientated material. It may be an anthology in the way that, for example, the Book of Common Prayer is in Anglicanism. This book has been the basis of worship for the Church of England for four hundred fifty years and contains prayers written over a hundred-year period and material from even earlier prayer books, which often reflect very different worldviews and priorities. The Book of Common Prayer includes, for example, the Athanasian Creed (see Chapter 3) of the fourth century, Psalms compiled between 1000 and 400 B.C., and this magnificent prayer of Archbishop Thomas Cranmer, written ca. 1549:

> Oh God,
> The source of all good desires,
> All right judgments and all just works,
> give to your servants that peace
>   which the world cannot give;
> that our hearts may be set to obey
>   your commandments,
> and that freed from fear of our enemies
> we may pass our time in rest and quietness
> through Jesus Christ our Lord: Amen.

Only one other tiny fragment is left of the Christian mission in Tibet. In the cave at Dunhuang a Tibetan book of divination, written in Tibetan, was found. This unnamed book mentions Jesus the Messiah and a judge who sits on the right hand of God. However, as some scholars point out, Manichaeism was strong in Tibet as well and this oracle might owe its origins to that faith, which combined Christian, Zoroastrian, and Buddhist beliefs.[41]

THE TEN COVENANTS

The remainder of *The Sutra of Jesus Christ* is a collection of teachings organized around the theme of the Ten Commandments, which have been much transformed by the writers. The Chinese translation makes it clear that the first three Covenants are volitional acts of agreement between God and humanity, not commands: Honor God, Honor the emperor, Honor your parents. Covenants 4 and 5 are about not harming and not killing and extend to all living creatures, not just fellow human beings. From the text on the Stone of the Church of the East, we know that the Taoist Christians were vegetarian and nonviolent.

The Church of the East in China also treated men and women as equals and its members did not own slaves. In contrast, Buddhist monasteries in China ran on slave labor on a huge scale. When those monasteries were closed by the emperor in 845 in the Great Persecution of all "foreign" religions, more than 150,000 slaves, property of the Buddhist monasteries, were released. Monasteries of the Church of the East were also closed at that time; three thousands monks were turned out, but no slaves were listed for the Taoist Christians had none.

The Sutra's interpretations of the Commandments do not seem to have come from the Church in Persia, which had not developed such a broad reading in its own books. Perhaps, again, this book was collected from another mission. Such a broad, nonviolent view might have come from contact with Jainism, the only extant creed at the time of these texts that primarily taught a philosophy of not harming any living creature. Buddhism is not inherently a nonviolent creed, nor does it usually encourage vegetarianism. In fact, the only Buddhist school that was formally vegetarian was found in China from A.D. 550. Elsewhere and within other schools of Buddhism in China, meat eating was permitted if the meat came as a gift from the faithful.

Jainism arose at the same time as Buddhism, around 500 B.C. It never achieved the international scope of Buddhism but remained rooted in the area of its origin, western and northern India, to the north of where the Thomarist Christians were. There was considerable trade and travel between the Jain and Thomarist communities, but we have no idea whether books emerged from dialogue with this profound, ancient tradition. Nor do we know if there was any contact in India with Vaishnavism, the Hindu tradition of devotion to Vishnu, which also taught strict vegetarianism.

Whatever the origin of this remarkable reworking of the Ten Commandments, it shaped the actual life of the Church in China by banning slaves and banning the taking of any life. It resulted in the only officially vegetarian branch of the Christian Church ever to have existed.

The remaining Covenants are fairly faithful versions of the original Commandments, namely, prohibiting adultery, stealing, coveting your neighbor's belongings, and bearing false witness. Compare the list with the original Ten Commandments found in Exodus and the second version in Deuteronomy. The list of Covenants ends with what can be seen as further expansions of the traditional last Commandment, which was followed by a collection of Jesus' sayings simplified for preaching and that reiterate the ban on the taking of life.

The final text incorporated in this anthology is a version of the story of Jesus that resembles the fuller version given in *The Sutra of the Teachings of The World-Honored One*. We can tell we have moved to another text because a different name is used for the Holy Spirit: Cool Breeze. This looks to be a version taken from the *Teachings of the Apostles*, the compilation of the life and teachings of Jesus described in chapter 2.

This composite Sutra pulls together a variety of materials as a handbook or guidebook, an anthology of insights for use in the mission field of China. We know it is a composite by its lack of internal editing and the inconsistency in its terms. It offers a profound insight into a Church that was gaining in confidence and influence and is perhaps the most important collection we have of fragments of older Christian texts from Tibet and India. The text breaks off, due to damage to the only copy extant, in the midst of the extract from the *Teachings*.

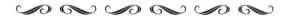

THE TEN COMMANDMENTS
IN EXODUS (20:1–17)

You shall have no gods except me.

You shall not make yourself a carved image or any likeness of anything in heaven or on earth beneath or in the waters under the earth; you shall not bow down to them or serve them. For I, Yahweh your God, am a jealous God and I punish the father's fault in the sons, the grandsons, and the great-grandsons of those who hate me; but I show kindness to thousands of those who love me and keep my commandments.

You shall not utter the name of Yahweh your God to misuse it, for Yahweh will not leave unpunished the man who utters his name to misuse it.

Remember the sabbath day and keep it holy. For six days you shall labour and do all your work, but the seventh day is a sabbath for Yahweh your God. You shall do no work that day, neither you nor your son nor your daughter nor your servants, men or women, nor your animals nor the stranger who lives with you. For in six days Yahweh made the heavens and the earth and the sea and all that these hold, but on the seventh day he rested; that is why Yahweh has blessed the sabbath day and made it sacred.

Honour your father and your mother so that you may have a long life in the land that Yahweh has given to you.

You shall not kill.

You shall not commit adultery.

You shall not steal.

You shall not bear false witness against your neighbour.

You shall not covet your neighbour's house. You shall not covet your neighbour's wife, or his servant, man or woman, or his ox, or his donkey, or anything that is his.

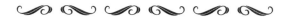

THE TEN COMMANDMENTS IN DEUTERONOMY (5:1–21)

You shall have no gods except me.

You shall not make yourself a carved image or any likeness of anything in heaven or on earth beneath or in the waters under the earth; you shall not bow down to them or serve them. For I, Yahweh your God, am a jealous God and I punish the father's fault in the sons, the grandsons, and the great-grandsons of those who hate me; but I show kindness to thousands, to those who love me and keep my commandments.

You shall not utter the name of Yahweh your God to misuse it, for Yahweh will not leave unpunished the man who utters his name to misuse it.

Observe the sabbath day and keep it holy, as Yahweh your God has commanded you. For six days you shall labour and do all your work, but the seventh day is a sabbath for Yahweh your God. You shall do no work that day, neither you nor your son nor your daughter nor your servants, men or women, nor your ox nor your donkey nor any of your animals, nor the stranger who lives with you. Thus your servant, man or woman, shall rest as you do. Remember that you were a servant in the land of Egypt, and that Yahweh your God brought you out from there with mighty hand

and outstretched arm; because of this, Yahweh your God has commanded you to keep the sabbath day.

Honour your father and your mother, as Yahweh your God has commanded you, so that you may have long life and may prosper in the land that Yahweh your God gives to you.

You shall not kill.

You shall not commit adultery.

You shall not steal.

You shall not bear false witness against your neighbour.

You shall not covet your neighbour's wife, you shall not set your heart on his house, his field, his servant—man or woman—his ox, his donkey, or anything that is his.

THE FOURTH SUTRA:
THE SUTRA OF JESUS CHRIST

CHAPTER ONE

[1]At this time the Messiah taught the laws of God, of Yahweh.[2]He said: There are many different views as to the real meaning of the Sutras, and on where God is, and what God is, and how God was revealed.

[3]The Messiah was orbited by the Buddhas and arhats [disciples of the Buddha who have attained semidivine status].[4]Looking down he saw the suffering of all that is born, and so he began to teach.

[5]Nobody has seen God.[6]Nobody has the ability to see God.[7]Truly, God is like the wind.[8]Who can see the wind?[9]God is not still but

moves on the earth at all times.[10]He is in everything and every-where.[11]Humanity lives only because it is filled with God's life-giving breath.[12]Peace comes only when you can rest secure in your own place, when your heart and mind rest in God.[13]Day in, day out there you exist in contentment, open to where you may be led.[14]God leads the believer to that place of contentment and great bliss.

[15]All great teachers such as the Buddhas are moved by this Wind and there is nowhere in the world where this Wind does not reach and move.[16]God's Palace is in this place of peace and happi-ness yet he knows the suffering and actions of the whole world.

[17]Everyone in the world knows how the Wind blows.[18]We can hear it but not see its shadow.[19]Nobody knows what it really looks like, whether it is pleasing to look upon or not, nor whether it is yellow, white, or even blue.[20]Nobody knows where the Wind dwells.

[21]God's sacred spirit force allows him to be in one place, but where it is nobody knows, or how to get there.[22]God is beyond the cycle of death and birth, beyond being called male or female.[23]God made both Heaven and Earth.[24]God's sacred spirit force has never been fully manifested.[25]This power can grant longevity and lead to immortality.

[26]When people are afraid they call upon Buddha's name.[27]Many folk are sadly ignorant.[28]God is a sacred spirit force.[29]God is al-ways beside the believer.[30]There are the Sutras.[31]People say they know who God is but they do not.[32]It is in Buddha's nature to be-stow grace, and with this grace comes also a deep, clear under-standing that lifts us above folly.[33]This way anybody can attain Heaven, even if he is not a scholar.[34]The sacred spirit power of God works in everybody, bringing all to fullness.[35]All existence is an act of grace, every physical form is created, God has brought every-thing into being.[36]Everything is born, dies, and decays, returning into the earth and continued suffering.

CHAPTER TWO

[1]All that has life, know in your hearts that this is so and by grace understand how to do that which is good.[2]Everything that is born must die.[3]Everything that lives exists only because the Winds give it life.[4]When it is time for life to end, the Winds depart from the body.[5]A person's heart and mind are not their own, but are created by the Winds.[6]The Winds' departure is a time of great distress, but nobody can see the Winds at that time.[7]Nobody can see them because they have no form, no color, not red or green or any other.[8]The Winds of Life are invisible.[9]The path is unknown.[10]Similarly, people want to know where God is.[11]The path is unknown, and so it is impossible to see God.

[12]Only the virtuous can enter into the presence of God, can see God.[13]It is not possible for everyone to see God.[14]Those who are blessed and fortunate can feel God close by, but those who do evil will remain sunk in evil.[15]People must first understand that God cannot be seen, and never has been seen.[16]So the question arises: How can anyone practice the correct way to be blessed?[17]If they avoid the Way of Earth, of Hell, they can attain the Way of Heaven.[18]However, even if they do attain the Way of Heaven, it is still easy for them to sink into the Way of Evil again.

[19]If what they do does not show wisdom, then they are not following the Way of Heaven. All that lives, regard this grace well.[20]There is a great, a very great, distance between Heaven and Earth.[21]Some lives are shaped by evil.[22]Those who put their souls into serving the nation receive much wealth as a reward, but those who live wicked lives, not doing what is ordered by the Power of Heaven, will never achieve success or a good post.[23]Instead they will be exiled, to die in ignominy. Is this not the Power of Heaven?[24]All such evil stems from the first beings, and the disobedience in the fruitful garden.[25]All that lives is affected by the karma of previous lives.[26]God suffered terrible woes so that all should be freed from karma, for nobody is beyond the reach of this Buddha

principle.²⁷Those who do good will be blessed and fortunate, but those who do evil will suffer.

CHAPTER THREE

¹Foolish people make wooden statues of camels, cows, horses, and so on.²They may make them seem very lifelike and worship them, but this does not really bring them to life.³If you can understand all this, then understand the process of karma's cause and effect.⁴This is a gift unique to human beings.⁵In today's world there are so many who create images of people, of scholars and gurus.⁶They think this makes them like God, but they cannot give life to their creations.⁷They really are confused!⁸They make gold, silver, or bronze statues of spirits, then venerate them.⁹They even make wooden statues of the spirits, people, and animals.¹⁰But no matter how much the human statue looks like a human, or the horse statue like a horse, or the cow statue like a cow, or the donkey statue like a donkey, they cannot walk, they cannot speak, they cannot eat or drink.¹¹They have no real flesh, or skin, or organs, or bones.¹²Even though these statues cannot talk, everybody today wants to talk to them.¹³If you eat something, you should know by its taste and smell whether it is good or bad.

¹⁴Only somebody who truly worships God can teach the Sutras and expound the texts.¹⁵Someone who fears punishment does what is right, and tells others to do likewise.¹⁶God loves such a one, and they are known as one who follows God's Law.¹⁷However, somebody who knows in their heart the right way to follow, but does not do good and encourages others not to do good, is unacceptable to God.¹⁸Such people are trapped by luxuries and illusions, too preoccupied with appearances, too attracted to life's pleasures, and they are following the wrong path.¹⁹Such people will end up in the hands of King Yama, God of Judgment and Rebirth.²⁰But even those who accept the teachings of God, who often say "I obey God," who teach others to obey God, should fear God.²¹Be watchful

every day of slipping.²²Remember all life depends on God.²³Everybody should seek the right relationship by resolving their bad actions.²⁴Life and death are controlled by the sacred spirit, and everyone should fear God.

²⁵This fear is like the fear of the Emperor.²⁶The Emperor is who he is because of his previous lives which have led to his being placed in this fortunate position.²⁷He is chosen by God, so cannot call himself God, because he has been appointed by God to do what is expected.²⁸This is why the people obey the Emperor, and this is right and proper.²⁹Everyone should obey the Commands.³⁰If anybody disobeys then they are punished.³¹Wise people understand this and teach others to act likewise.³²Those are the people who live by the Precepts.³³If you do not fear God, even if you live by the Law of the Buddha, you will not be saved.³⁴Indeed, you will be counted among the traitors.

³⁵The third aspect is to fear your parents.³⁶You should honor your parents just as you honor God and the Emperor.³⁷If you honor the Emperor and not your parents then God will not bless you with good fortune.

CHAPTER FOUR

¹Of these three aspects, the first and most important is to honor God.²The second is to honor the Emperor.³The third is to honor your parents.⁴The whole of Heaven and Earth follows this way.⁵Everything follows this way of respecting parents; throughout the world everything owes its existence to parents.⁶The sacred spirits have ordained that the Emperor is born as the Emperor.⁷We should fear God, the Sacred One, and the Emperor.⁸Also, fear your parents and do good.⁹If you understand the Law and Precepts, do not disobey, but instead teach all people true religion.¹⁰Buddha creates Buddha's own bitterness and suffering.¹¹Heaven and Earth have been made to show clearly the causes of creation.¹²The Emperor should be the embodiment of enlightenment.¹³He does what is naturally

right to do.[14]The first covenant of God is that anything that exists and does evil will be punished, especially if they do not respect the elderly.

[15]The second covenant is to honor and care for elderly parents.[16]Those who do this will be true followers of Heaven's Way.

[17]The third covenant is to acknowledge we have been brought into existence through our parents.[18]Nothing exists without parents.

[19]The fourth covenant is that anybody who understands the precepts should know to be kind and considerate to everything, and to do no evil to anything that lives.

[20]The fifth covenant is that any living being should not only not take the life of another living being, but should also teach others to do likewise.

[21]The sixth covenant is that nobody should commit adultery, or persuade anyone else to do so.

[22]The seventh covenant is not to steal.

[23]The eighth covenant is that nobody should covet a living man's wife, or his lands, or his palace, or his servants.

[24]The ninth covenant is not to let your envy of somebody's good wife, or son, or house or gold, lead you to bear false witness against them.

[25]The tenth covenant is to offer to God only that which is yours to give.

[26]But there is much more than this.

[27]Do not bully those weaker than you.[28]Do not despise those more powerful than you.[29]If someone is hungry, even if he is your enemy, care for him, forgive and forget.[30]If someone is hardworking, help and support him.[31]Clothe the naked.[32]Do not abuse or try to deceive your workers, especially if you have no real work for them.[33]To do so, and thus fail to pay them, brings suffering to their families.[34]If you see someone abusing their workers like this, know that the sacred spirit will severely punish them.

[35]If a poor person begs for money, give generously.[36]If you have

no money, have the courtesy to explain why you can give only a little help.[37]If someone is seriously ill or handicapped do not mock, because this is the result of karma and not to be ridiculed.[38]Do not laugh at poor people in rags and tatters.[39]Do not obtain anything by deception or force. If someone is arrested tell only the truth.[40]Never try to use false means to achieve anything.[41]If someone who is alone, or a widow, or orphan, brings a complaint against anyone, their quest for justice should not be hindered.[42]Do not boast or brag.[43]Do not cause dissent and strife by picking quarrels, arguments, or fights, and do not side with one party against another.

[44]Someone who has power and authority should not abuse it to make things go his way, so do not use your influence with authority to win a case.[45]Keep quiet.[46]Those who follow the precepts should be charitable and humble.[47]Turn away from evil to good.[48]Doing good will save you from tribulation, so do good to all.[49]Those that do so, and follow the covenants, are those who know the precepts.[50]If while studying the Sutras you come to believe, then you have received the precepts.

[51]If you study, but do not believe, then you have not received the precepts.[52]All rests ultimately with God.[53]Our saintly ancestors, both great and small, will stand before us and judge us in the end.[54]The first thing is to obey God.[55]God protects all that lives; everything that lives does so as a result of this.[56]It is forbidden to take a life even for a sacrifice, for these teachings forbid taking any life.[57]All sacrifice and slaying of the lamb is to be offered for the sacred spirits' blessing and forgiveness.[58]If any living being does not follow this, does not do good or sets out to do evil in secret, God will track them down.[59]God will not look with compassion on such behavior, but God does look with compassion on those who turn away from rejecting God and doing evil.[60]God responded by coming to promote good deeds and replace the former law.

CHAPTER FIVE

[1]So God caused the Cool Breeze to come upon a chosen young woman called Mo Yan, who had no husband, and she became pregnant.[2]The whole world saw this, and understood what God had wrought.[3]The power of God is such that it can create a bodily spirit and lead to the clear, pure path of compassion.[4]Mo Yan gave birth to a boy and called him Ye Su, who is the Messiah and whose father is the Cool Breeze.[5]Some people claimed they could not understand how this was possible, and said that if the Cool Breeze had made Mo Yan conceive, then such a child must have been created at the bottom of the world.

[6]If the Emperor sends a command, all loyal citizens must obey it.[7]God looks down in compassion from Heaven, and controls everything in Heaven and Earth.[8]When Ye Su the Messiah was born, the whole world saw a bright mystery in the Heavens.[9]Everybody saw from their homes a star as big as a wagon wheel.[10]This mysterious light shone over the place where God was to be found, for at this time the One was born in the city of Wen-li-shih-ken [Jerusalem] in the orchard of But Lam [Bethlehem].[11]After five years had passed the Messiah began to talk.[12]He did many miraculous and good things while teaching the Law.[13]When he was twelve he assumed the Holy Word and began teaching.

[14]He came to a place of running water called Shu-Nan [Jordan] so that he might be given a name.[15]Thus he came to one called the Brother who dwelt in the wilderness and who, from his birth, had never eaten meat or drunk wine, but instead lived on vegetables and honey gathered from the wilderness.

[16]At that time many people came to the Messiah, bringing gifts, and worshiped him.[17]These people were deeply troubled.[18]The Messiah went to them, bringing the precepts.[19]When he emerged from the waters the Cool Breeze visited him from Heaven and a voice proclaimed "This is my son, obey him."

[20]The Messiah showed everyone that the way of God is the way

of Heaven.[21]He spoke the words of the sacred spirit, telling people to renounce evil and talking about doing good.[22]This began when he was twelve and he preached until he was thirty-two.[23]He found people who were living evil lives and brought them back to the way of goodness, the True Way.[24]He instructed his followers, especially his twelve disciples, and traveled the land teaching and healing.[25]Those departed from this world were restored to life.[26]The blind were able to see.[27]The crippled and sick were restored and able to walk.[28]Those troubled by ghosts had them cast out.[29]Some of the sick were healed simply by asking, others by holding on to his gown—but all were healed.

[30]Those who do evil, and do not recognize the True Way or the words teaching of God's religion, as well as the unclean ones, can never be truly saved, not today or even in this generation.[31]The scholars, fearing the Messiah, attacked and denounced him, but the people believed his holy teachings, so he could not be taken.

[32]The evil ones schemed together, pretending to be speakers of truth and purity.[33]They tried to slander him, but could not trap him, so they went to the great king Pilate, wanting him to kill the Messiah.[34]The Messiah ignored all this and continued teaching the people about true religion and how to do good.[35]He became famous.

[36]When he was thirty-two the evil men came before the great king Pilate and were able to state their case, saying that the Messiah must die.[37]The great king said that he would not kill him, as there seemed to be no clear case against him.[38]The seekers of evil in this affair argued that he must die, because otherwise what would become of us?

[39]The great king Pilate ordered water brought and washed his hands, showing the evil ones he washed his hands clean of the case.[40]The evil ones continued to press their case until he had no option but to kill the Messiah.

[41]The Messiah gave up his body to the wicked ones for the sake of all living beings.[42]Through this the whole world knows that all

life is as precarious as a candle flame.[43]In his compassion he gave up his life.

[44]The evil ones brought the Messiah to a place set apart, and after washing his hair led him to the place of execution called Chi-Chu [Golgotha].[45]They hung him high upon a wooden scaffold, with two criminals, one on either side of him.[46]He hung there for five hours.[47]That was on the sixth cleansing, vegetarian day.[48]Early that morning there was bright sunlight, but as the sun went West, darkness came over the world, the earth quaked, the mountains trembled, the tombs opened and the dead walked.[49]Those who saw this believed that he was who he said he was.[50]How can anyone not believe?[51]Those who take these words to heart are true disciples of the Messiah.[52]As a result . . . [here the text breaks off].

The four earliest Jesus Sutras show a remarkable ability by the Christians to learn to use material from other mission fields and Churches to integrate the faith into a Chinese context. If, as I believe, *The Sutra of Jesus Christ* was compiled in about 650, then we have a gap of seventy years or so before the next Jesus Sutra was written. From these later writings it is clear that during those seven decades the Church built on its first twenty years with extraordinary success. These final Sutras of the Church in China are among the finest pieces of religious writing ever to have been produced in China.

The Fruits of the Church:
The Great Liturgical Sutras

The four great liturgical Sutras are the jewels of the mature Church of the East in China. Through them we can hear, for the first time in more than a thousand years, the voices of the Taoist Christians and their radical practices. We can stand with them in their worship and listen with them to the teachings of Jesus as they expressed them—perhaps more startlingly and even more beautifully than almost anything else being written by Christians elsewhere in the world at that time.

✑ HOW THE CHURCH OF ✎
THE EAST IN CHINA WORSHIPED

The liturgical Sutras represent the mature faith and language, imagery and skills of this most unusual form of Christianity. We know that these Sutras were treasured because they had been carefully hidden and preserved in the caves at Dunhuang. They seem to have formed a prayer book or prayer collection and convey a sense of how the Chinese Christians worshiped. We have no idea

The tentative restoration of the original painting discovered in the cave of Dunhuang in 1908, which is now in the British Museum.

what music they used, though the Sutras themselves talk about the people chanting and singing in praise of the Messiah.

From two fascinating illustrations that have survived from the Church of the East in China we can make an educated guess about how the people worshiped. Long before we had found the ruined monastery at Da Qin and its ancient statues of the Nativity, my team and I began to wonder how these ancient Taoist Christians worshiped. This prompted us to look at the first and most extraordinary illustration, housed in the British Museum in London. Although it is rarely displayed due to its fragile state, I have had the privilege of seeing it once.

THE SILK PAINTING OF A
CHRISTIAN DHARMA KING

Along with the seventh-century scrolls in the cave of Dunhuang was found a frail silk painting on a banner. It is badly damaged but enough remains for us to see that it is of a holy person. Initially, one might think this a classical Chinese painting of a Bodhisattva from the ninth century, but then one notices three crosses. One is on the end of a staff held across the body, one on his headdress, and one, at least, on the collar. This is meant to be a saint. And, despite looking very Chinese, the figure has a small, thin red moustache— most un-Chinese.

The position of the hands is particularly fascinating. Many classical Christian paintings from the West and from the Orthodox Churches depict saints' hands pointing at the most important person in the painting, or praying, or holding identifying objects. The only figure who does not do this is Christ. In Orthodox paintings Christ's hands signify teaching. The hands of the figure in the silk painting are teaching hands. They are depicted exactly as are the hands in Buddhist paintings and on statues, in a *mudra* or position that symbolizes deep spiritual insight. In any set of three statues of Buddhas in a Chinese Buddhist temple representing the Buddha of the Past, the Buddha of the Present, and the Buddha of the Future, the hand positions tell you which they are and what they taught. Thus, the Buddha of the Past has his hands resting together on his lap, to show completion; his teaching is over. The Buddha of the Present has one hand raised in the position of teaching and the other touches the Earth, calling on the Earth to bear witness to the truth of what is being taught. The Buddha of the Future has his hands raised in the position ready to teach, for his time is coming.

The mudra of the Dunhuang silk painting is visible only in the right hand; the majority of the left hand has gone, although it seems to have been meant to hold the staff. Given that the hand position on the banner shows the mudra of debate, of teaching, and that this is the only hand mudra also used in the Orthodox Church but solely for Christ, it is possible that this figure is Jesus. If so, then we have an image of Jesus from the Church in China. But whether or not it is Jesus, the painting is clearly of a Christian teacher, priest, or saint and is all the more wonderful for having survived at all.

The Church of the East in China obviously ascribed meaning to the hand positions of the figure, so it is safe to assume that worshipers would also have used their hands in the services of the Church in China.

THE OASIS PAINTING OF THE MASS

The second painting is from the ruined walls of a church found in the deserted town of Koqo in the Turfan oasis in what was one of the most western provinces of Tang Dynasty China. Probably dating from between the ninth and eleventh centuries, it lies a little outside the geographical areas we are primarily considering, but offers a portrait, the only one found so far, of a Chinese Christian at worship.

The scene is simply painted and scholars dispute the import of what is going on. A priest is holding a chalice and appears to be preaching.[42] Facing him are three members of his congregation holding what look like palm leaves. The scene resembles a celebration of Palm Sunday, though some think it may be a baptism ceremony. Of the three figures, the front two are clearly Uighurs, members of a powerful tribe from Outer Mongolia who were dominant in the region in the eighth to tenth centuries. Their Uighur identity is confirmed by their head gear, but the third figure is equally clearly a Chinese woman. As such, she is the only early Christian Chinese worshiper of whom we have a picture.

This scene is set inside a church depicting a service in which the participants are standing. It is very reminiscent of Christians worshiping in a magnificent fourth-century Roman fresco from the Lullingstone villa in England. There the worshipers are standing and their hands and arms are raised at either side, palms turned upward in invocational prayer. Similar positions of worship would have been adopted by members of the Church of the East. The invention of pews is very late; most if not all early Christian services were conducted with all participants standing, and today this is still the case in Orthodox churches. The English have a reminder of this in a common phrase, "The weak go to the wall," which comes from the time when churches had only standing room and the weak moved to lean against the wall during the long services.

So we can picture members of the Church in China standing, arms raised, using mudra hand gestures to signify different aspects of the service or meaning in the liturgy. We know they chanted and sang and that they listened to readings, joined in prayers, and celebrated the mysteries of Christianity. The Koqo painting makes it clear that communion was celebrated there. The Church of the East Stone appears to talk of communion, using the beautiful phrase **"Every seven days we have an audience with heaven."** Curiously, none of the Sutras tells the story of the Last Supper, at which Christ created the Communion service, the Mass. The answer to whether this was a significant part of the Church of the East in China may become clear when we excavate at the Da Qin monastery.

By the date of the next Jesus Sutra, some 130 years or more had passed since Aluoben had arrived with his books and icons. With one magnificent exception, the late Sutras are not translations of other cultures' and Churches' teachings. They are instead original Sutras composed in Chinese, by Chinese, for Chinese. The Church had made the great leap—which it has so often failed to do in the more recent past—from missionary Church to truly indigenous Church, a process that was inestimably assisted by the emperor giving land within the sacred precincts of the Taoist Imperial Ancestral Shrine of Lou Guan Tai. The building of the Da Qin monastery at Lou Guan pushed the Church into a serious engagement with Taoism, and consequently with Buddhism and Confucianism. These great liturgical Sutras bear witness to the success of that engagement by their creation of a Christian vision and belief system that moves with ease through the conceptual worlds of eighth-century China.

These later Sutras, primarily from the end of the eighth century (though one comes from 720), were all found at Dunhuang. The *Let Us Praise* Sutra, found in 1908 by Professor Paul Pelliot, is now in the Bibliothèque Nationale in Paris (Collection Pelliot 3847). The others were obtained in either 1908 or 1909 by a Chinese collector, Li Shengduo, who sold them to the Japanese collector, Yashushi Kojiima, who maintains them in a private collection.

These four later Sutras reinterpret the meaning and significance of the Resurrection, drop all mention of original sin, and present a thorough understanding of the pressing existential issues confronting the Chinese. These are the Sutras that provide the means as well as the theories of the Taoist Christians, for they contain not only teachings but actual liturgies for breaking the cycle of reincarnation.

Instead of doing what many missionaries have tried to do—namely, make people adapt to a Western mind-set of original sin and the classic death-resurrection model—these teachings take seriously the spiritual concerns of China and offer Jesus and his teachings as a solution to these issues. These Sutras enter directly into the challenge of the Chinese worldview, bringing salvation to the people rather than trying to reconfigure their entire worldview.

Many contemporary Christians who read these Sutras will find them too radical. Yet in them the Church of the East achieved one of the most remarkable retellings of the significance of Jesus, one faithful to the Gospel message of redemption and liberation from our failures and weaknesses (karma) and a message of hope—hope that the inevitability of rebirth could be broken and each believer freed to live in eternal bliss in the presence of God.

ORIGINAL NATURE, NOT ORIGINAL SIN

One core concept that shapes all the liturgical Sutras is that of original nature. This is radically at variance with traditional Christian thought, which has tended to emphasize the defects of humanity: the fault of Original Sin. In China, the tables are dramatically turned. The Church of the East broke away from the West just in time to avoid the magnificence and the curse of St. Augustine of Hippo, who took the basic notion of original sin and built it into the destructive force it was to become. In looking at the theology of the Church of the East, we can see what Christianity without St. Augustine might have been like.

St. Augustine saw humanity as almost irredeemably wicked and perverse, rejecting any idea of some innate goodness. To him, salvation is an entirely undeserved act of grace that plucks us from our filthy state of evil. Augustine was opposed in his time by the first British theologian on record, a monk named Pelagius, who argued the opposite, that human nature was basically good but had been corrupted and misguided by human weakness. The theology of Augustine triumphed in the West, but it was a theology similar to Pelagius's that triumphed in China.[43]

The term "original nature," or "innate nature," occurs in both Taoist and Buddhist thought. It signifies that all life is innately good but becomes corrupt or loses its way through the compromises of life and existence. A wonderful example of what this means is given in the writings of Zhuang Zi, the Taoist philosopher and wit of the fourth century B.C.: "Horses have hooves so that their feet can grip on frost and snow, and hair so that they can withstand the wind and cold. They eat grass and drink water, they buck and gallop, for this is the innate nature of horses. Even if they had great towers and magnificent halls, they would not be interested in them. However, when Po Lo [renowned as the first and greatest trainer of horses] came on the scene, he said, 'I know how to train horses.' He branded them, cut their hair and their hooves, put halters on their heads, bridled them, hobbled them and shut them up in stables. Out of ten horses, at least two or three die. . . . The people have a true nature, they weave their cloth, they farm to produce food. This is their basic Virtue."[44] Zhuang shows how people have been corrupted by those who wished to control them, just as the poor horses were destroyed and damaged by the actions of Po Lo.

This idea of original nature could not be further from the concept of original sin. So the later Sutras adapted to the Chinese view that human nature was essentially good but could be distorted. In these Christian Sutras from China is the shape or outline of a post-Augustinian theology that the West itself needs in order to become free from the burden of original sin and thus reconfigure or rediscover Christianity. Given that original sin was unknown as a central theme of Christian thought before the early fifth century, it is possible to agree with Pelagius that true Christianity holds a notion of original goodness. In a post-Augustinian Christian world, this rediscovery, embodied in the actual books and thoughts of a major ancient Church, may well be a version of Christianity that can speak to spiritual seekers today.

All these liturgical Sutras celebrate freedom from karma, reincarnation, and the power of death, and the possibility of spiritual freedom from these forces on earth as well as in heaven. As Jesus said when asked by the Pharisees when the kingdom of God was to come, "The coming of the Kingdom of God does not admit of observation and there will be no one to say 'Look here! Look there!' For you must know, the kingdom of God is among you" (Luke 18:20–21). These Sutras celebrate the inherent reality of that spiritual liberation.

⸎ THE FIRST LITURGICAL SUTRA: ⸎ TAKING REFUGE IN THE TRINITY

The first liturgical Sutra is the earliest of the mature Sutras. It is dated by its own record as having been written in 720. This places it some seventy years after the bulk of the books brought by Aluoben and his team had been translated. It shows a remarkable depth of understanding of Chinese culture and language and tells of yet another center of Christian activity at a monastery in Shachou (present-day Dunhuang) in Gansu Province, northwest China. This Sutra is titled *Da Qin Christian Liturgy of Taking Refuge in the Three*. We have titled it *Taking Refuge in the Trinity*.

"Taking refuge" is a classical Buddhist term and reinforces the comforting, compassionate imagery used for God and the Trinity throughout these Jesus Sutras. The nearest comparisons in the West are some of the ancient Celtic Christian or Anglo-Saxon texts. For example, from the Celtic Church comes this prayer, dating from sometime in the fifth to ninth centuries:

In name of Father,
In name of Son,

In name of Spirit,
   Three in One:

Father cherish me,
Son cherish me,
Spirit cherish me,
   Three all-kindly.

God make me holy,
Christ make me holy,
Spirit make me holy,
   Three all-holy.

Three aid my hope,
Three aid my love,
Three aid mine eye,
And my knee from stumbling,
My knee from stumbling.

Be the eye of God dwelling with you,
The foot of Christ in guidance with you,
The shower of the Spirit pouring on you,
Richly and generously.[45]

From the *Dream of the Rood* (meaning the tree on which Christ was crucified) comes this powerful piece, a magnificent Anglo-Saxon account of the Crucifixion:

Then the young warrior, God Almighty Himself,
Stripped and stood firm and without flinching.
Bravely before the multitude He climbed upon the Cross
To save the world.
I shivered when the hero clung to me. . . .

On that hill I saw and endured so much.
I saw the God of Hosts stretched on the rack.
I saw darkness cover the lifeless body of the Ruler with
    clouds.
Against His shining radiance
Shadows swept across the land,
Strange powers moved under the clouds.
All creation wept,
Weeping and moaning for the death of the King.
For Christ was on the cross.[46]

The *Taking Refuge* Sutra uses terms that show how sophisticated the Church had become in less than ninety years after its arrival. In comparison with the centuries that Buddhism needed to
develop a truly indigenous theology and terminology, the Eastern
Christians' achievement is remarkable. For instance, this Sutra
contains phrases such as **"Jade-faced One, exalted as the sun and
moon,"** a wonderful image. In Chinese imagery and context, jade
is the most highly prized material, even more loved than gold. It is
imperishable and incorruptible and thus stands as the supreme
metaphor for purity and eternity. An emblem of immortality, jade
is occasionally used in connection with the Bodhisattva Avalokitesvara (Kuan Yin in Chinese), the goddess of compassion, who
is generally accepted by cultural archaeologists and mythologists to
derive much of her imagery and iconography from Mary, the
mother of Jesus. In this particular phrase, the Church confidently
and poetically employs powerful symbols and gives them a distinctive but intelligible Christian significance for the Chinese. Another
phrase used in the Sutra, **"the hundred Ways,"** refers to the many
different schools of thought active at the time and is a very posi-
tive image in old China, where diversity of ideas was valued. The
use of the Buddhist term Dharma Kings or Lords captures the idea
that these saints, who are listed in the Sutra, taught the Law that

Triumphs, the teaching that saves. Dharma means "teaching" in San-skrit, showing their importance as truth bearers.

This Sutra avers that the endless cycle of rebirth is broken and remade into a new cycle that reunites one with God. No longer do you need to fear the horrors of the Earth Prisons and reincar-nation. Because this is clearly a liturgical Sutra, I have taken the liberty of breaking it up as I think it might have been used in a service. The terms "Priest" and "Congregation" do not appear in the original Chinese.

¹**Da Qin/Syrian Christian liturgy of taking Refuge in the Three**

²**All reverence to the Great Holy Compassionate Father of All**
    Things—Allaha!
³**Priest: Oh radiant Jade-faced One**
Exalted as the sun and moon
Your virtues are greater than those
Of all the Holy Ones and Dharma Lords—

⁴**Congregation: The laws of Compassion save us all!**
⁵**Echoing through the world like a tolling golden bell. . . .**

⁶**Priest: Great Holy Law Giver**
You bring us back to our original nature.
⁷**And the souls that are saved are countless:**
Divine compassion lifts them up from the dust
Redeeming them from the saddened realm of ghosts

⁸**Congregation: The hundred Ways bring us clarity and kind-**
    hearted mercy. . . .
⁹**Priest: Now I draw close to our Holy Compassionate Father**
The One who creates salvation—
See the angelic spirits crossing the Ocean of Dharma!

[10]We know to practice peace in our hearts through You.

[11]This whole gathering unites in singing to You, Honored One:

[12]All: The Great Law is now the Heavenly Wheel
Of returning—to You.

[13]Worship the Dharma Kings. Begin with the Sutra of Dharma King John. Then continue with the Sutra of the Psalms and the Path of Grace Sutra.

[14]On the 2nd day in the 5th month of Hai Yun [720], Su Yun of the Da Qin Religion of Light in the Great Holy Oneness of the Dharma, a monk of the Da Qin monastery at Shachou [Qansu], wrote this faithfully for the faithful.

✑ A GREAT CHINESE SAINT ✑
AND SCHOLAR

The three remaining Sutras are almost certainly the work of one man, Jingjing, one of the greatest treasures the Church ever produced. His name means Luminous Purity: one purified by the Religion of Light teachings. Clearly a religious name, it seems to denote someone converted, hence the "purified" description. The taking of a specific religious name is common in all monastic religious traditions. The Stone of the Church of the East (see chapter 8) contains a reference that indicates Jingjing was Chinese, and indeed, the outstanding quality of his writing proves this.

Jingjing was a monk, and is identified on the Stone as a priest of the Da Qin monastery. If, as we believe, the Stone was established to celebrate the completion of the restoration of the monastery and the building of its pagoda in 781, then we can reasonably suggest that Jingjing was a monk of that very monastery. It seems likely that he composed his Sutras there. Given the extraordinary degree of familiarity with Taoism and in particular the *Tao Te Ching* shown in his Sutras and texts, Jingjing becomes the very embodiment of why the Church built a major monastery right beside the Taoist monastery and academy dedicated to the *Tao Te Ching*.

Jingjing did translate some significant teachings and is honored in one of the Sutras for this, but he wrote his own surviving Sutras in Chinese. It is clear that his Sutras, which were among documents found at Dunhuang, are from a continuing church that treasured the works of their greatest writer. More than two hundred years after he wrote his liturgies and Sutras, Jingjing was still revered and praised for his work. The codicil on the liturgical Sutra *Let Us Praise*, below, speaks of two key historical figures in the life of the Church: Aluoben and then Jingjing.

Jingjing should be recognized as a Dharma King: a saint. One of the most outstanding Christians ever produced by China, he is also, to the best of our limited knowledge, the greatest product of the Tang Dynasty Church in China. He wrote works that are masterpieces of world spirituality in his ability to interpret to a Chinese world the significance of Jesus' human incarnation. He deserves to be recovered from obscurity and recognized by contemporary spiritual seekers with the same admiration and affection that his own Church clearly had for him.

◁ THE SECOND LITURGICAL SUTRA: ▷ LET US PRAISE

The first of Jingjing's liturgical Sutras is the *Invocation of the Dharma Kings and Sacred Sutras*, which we have titled *Let Us Praise*.

With *Let Us Praise*, the long list of Sutras indicates the breadth of material the Church then had available in its more established years. It is likely that one or two mentioned in the list are ones we have translated under different names. For example, *The Sutra of*

Subtle Peace and Happiness may well be the Sutra I have called *The Sutra of Returning to Your Original Nature*, and *The Sutra of the Origin of Life* may be *The Sutra of Cause, Effect, and Salvation*. Others are clearly books from the Bible, such as the Book of Psalms and the Acts of the Apostles. Others are tantalizing hints of Sutras that have not yet been found, for example, *The Sutra of Charity and the Origin of the Soul* and *The Sutra of Broad Teaching and of the Three Levels*. The titles alone show us that the Church in China had undertaken the development of a Gospel for the Chinese cultural world.

The term "Mar," used as a suffix to various names in the Sutra, is a religious title meaning either "Holy" or "Father," as, for example, in association with a bishop or patriarch. Some of the names (e.g., King Gur, King Henana) refer to people of whom we know nothing. It is possible King Henana refers to the head of the Theological College of Nisibis ca. 610. Mar Barsauma was the great fifth-century saint who built the foundations of autonomy for the Church of the East in Persia, and Mar Sergius may be the Bishop of Elam, sent to the Turkic tribes by Patriarch Timothy ca. 780.

The text at the end offers a fascinating insight into the work of the Church and confirms that Jingjing is almost certainly the author of all three of these Sutras. It also shows that, although Syriac was the "language of the priests" and the majority of the books (530) remained in Syriac, thirty-four books were translated into or written in Chinese. That the document was written by a Chinese is clear from the rather regretful note that because most of the books were still in Syriac, the insights "remain untranslated, still tied up."

[1]Invocation of the Dharma Kings and Sacred Sutras

[2]Let us praise Allaha—Great Father and Mysterious One
[3]Let us praise the Messiah—his Supreme Son
[4]Let us praise the Holy Spirit, who witnesses divinity

⁵These Three Beings creating as One.

⁶Let us praise the Dharma:

⁷Dharma King John, Dharma King Luke
⁸Dharma King Mark, Dharma King Matthew
⁹Dharma King Moses, Dharma King David,
¹⁰Dharma King of Easter, Dharma King Paul,
¹¹Dharma King of the Thousand Peacock Eyes
¹²Dharma King Simeon, Dharma King Mar Sergius,
¹³Dharma King George, Dharma King Mar Barsauma,
¹⁴Dharma King Simon, and the Twenty Four—
¹⁵Dharma King Henana, Dharma King Hosea
¹⁶Dharma King Michael, Dharma King Silas
¹⁷Dharma King Gur, Dharma King Announcing
    Teachings—John

¹⁸Let us praise:

¹⁹The Constantly Bright Supreme Happiness Sutra
²⁰The Sutra of Origins
²¹The Sutra of Subtle Peace and Happiness
²²The Sutra of Heavenly Treasures
²³The Sutra of Psalms
²⁴The Sutra of the Message of Grace
²⁵The Sutra of the Origin of Life
²⁶The Sutra of Understanding Truth

²⁷The Sutra of Precious Brilliance, and of Revealed Teaching
²⁸The Sutra of Charity and the Origin of the Soul
²⁹The Sutra of Broad Teaching and of the Three Levels
³⁰The Sutra of Discipline, the Sutra of Grace

³¹The Sutra of Proclamation
³²The Acts of the Apostles according to Luke

³³The Sutra of Paul's Dharma, and of Zakarias
³⁴The Sutra of George the Monk, and of Anichilia
³⁵The Sutra of Ceremonies, and in Praise of the Three Powers

³⁶The Sutra of the Laws of Moses, and of Elijah
³⁷The Sutra of Bethlehem, and the Announcing Dharma King
³⁸The Sutra of the Messiah—Creator of Heaven and Earth
³⁹The Sutra of the Four Gates, and of Revelation

⁴⁰The Sutra of Mar Sergius, and of The Cross, and of Hymns

⁴¹Let us praise them

[Followed by this note:]

⁴²We have examined these sutras and we know that in all there are 530 belonging to the Da Qin rooted religion.⁴³They are written in the priests' language.

⁴⁴In the 9th year of the Zhenguan era in the reign of the Emperor Taizong of the Tang, priest Aluoben, Bishop of the West, came to China and offered a petition to the imperial throne in his own language.

⁴⁵Fang Xuanling and Wei Zheng translated the liturgy and presented it.⁴⁶Then the Emperor ordered priest Aluoben (Jingjing) to translate the 30 sutras above.

⁴⁷However most of the sutras remain untranslated, still tied up.⁴⁷

ꙮ THE THIRD LITURGICAL SUTRA: ꙮ
THE SUTRA OF RETURNING
TO YOUR ORIGINAL NATURE

In what is the most beautiful of the Jesus Sutras, *The Sutra of Returning to Your Original Nature,* we are taken step by step through

This nineteenth-century woodblock depicts the Buddha preaching to a universal gathering. The Sutra of Returning to Your Original Nature describes Christ in just such a cosmic setting. (© Martin Palmer/CIRCA)

a salvationary journey to freedom from karma, past lives, and rebirth. In a fusion of uniquely Christian imagery, Taoist teachings, and Buddhist philosophy, Jingjing weaves a masterful narrative. This Sutra and the one that follows it are dated ca. 780–790. Both are in private collections in Japan.

The start of the Sutra has been lost except for a few words, but after a few damaged lines, we enter a text modeled on the classic Buddhist Sutra style of Buddha in discourse with his followers.

The Sutra is wonderfully rich in imagery. Its basic outline is a discourse between the Messiah, his disciple Simon, and the adoring throng of **"all who had escaped from the Realm of Desire,"** that is, the physical world, and come to **"the Great Preaching Place of Purity and Clarity."** This could be a figurative image of the Sermon on the Mount, or a Christian version of Vulture Peak, where, in Buddhist Sutras of the Chinese tradition, the Buddha taught of the cosmos. The core notion of ending the wheel of karma is introduced immediately, when the Messiah says all must **"clear their minds, and set aside all wanting and doing."** Desire and action generate karma, its cause and effects. For what you do now, you pay or reap the rewards later. By practicing wu wei, the Taoist term meaning actionless action, you do not create bad karma.

The Sutra explains the nature of the Messiah and God and leads to the Messiah promising that because of who he is, he can rescue all creatures, and **"it is this which will enable you to transcend rebirth."** The Messiah then introduces what could be called the Tao of Jesus. The heart of it is summed up in four terse phrases that are then explored for the rest of the Sutra: **"No wanting, no doing, no piousness, no truth"** (2:35). The Sutra then says that being a Christian is the fulfillment of good deeds in past lives: **"From goodness in past lives, people come to this religion and through the faith they find Happiness. . . . Simon, know this: You ask me about the Triumphant Law. What your ancestors have done bears fruit in you, their karma finds its outcome in you"** (3:18, 20–21).

This is followed by my favorite image in all the Sutras, that of Jesus scaling ladders and steps cut into the mountain to enable the faithful to be brought to the place of Peace and Happiness. This image may be original or may be derived from Hindu or Buddhist imagery; for instance, the game of snakes and ladders has its origins in Hindu imagery of karma and rebirth and salvation. Here, the Incarnation has become a means by which God rescues those unable to move from this world of cause and effect, rebirth and desire, to the Pure Land of God. It does not dwell on the Crucifixion or Resurrection because, in this context, what is important about the Messiah is that he can save you from the hopelessness of existence in this world.

Then follow the Ten Ways of observing the world, a Christian guide to living and understanding, containing some of the most interesting metaphors to be found in the Jesus Sutras. As we translated it, we all agreed this wisdom is even more pertinent today than it was in the eighth century! Following this we come to the fullest exploration of the Four Laws, the Tao of Jesus, a remarkable Christian insight. Finally, we end with some wonderful images. Two are biblical: the image of putting on armor from St. Paul's Epistle to the Ephesians (6:10–17), and the image of a fire on a hilltop derived from Matthew (5:14–16). The others are Chinese images of the meaning and significance of being a Christian. Central to these is the image of being carried by Christ to salvation. This refers to one of the oldest images of Jesus, which he used to describe himself: the Good Shepherd who carries his lamb to safety. In Jesus' words: "What man among you with a hundred sheep, losing one, would not leave the ninety-nine in the wilderness and go after the missing one till he found it? And when he found it, would he not joyfully take it on his shoulders and then when he got home, call together his friends and neighbors? 'Rejoice with me,' he would say, 'I have found my sheep that was lost.' In the same way I tell you, there will be more rejoicing in heaven over one repentant sinner than over ninety-nine virtuous men who have no need of repentance" (Luke 15:4–7). In the earliest images of Christ, carved in the catacombs of Rome and on gravestones dating from the second century, Jesus is depicted as the one who carries the sinner to safety. In this Sutra, the image is given a Buddhist element, but the basic idea remains faithful to the images Christ himself used.

In this outstanding Sutra, designed to be chanted, as the Sutra itself says, we have the fullest expression of the Dharma Law of God, the Tao of Jesus, a magnificent fusion of the best of all the worlds in which the Chinese Christians of the age found themselves.

CHAPTER ONE

¹A transcript of the teaching given when the Eternal One [Jesus] taught in the Great Preaching Place of Purity and Clarity, addressing all who had escaped from the Realm of Desire.²To his left and right and all around Him, people sat listening with deep reverence.³They wanted to hear the words that would save them. . . .

⁴Simon spoke up and said: "We didn't know the truth—and we
  need salvation."
⁵The Messiah replied: "So, good.⁶Everything that exists needs
  the True Law,
And every kind of person can find what's just below the
  surface—
Buried deeper than our eyes.

⁷The truth is like looking at the white of the moon in water.
⁸If the water is cloudy, you can't see it clearly.
⁹It's like burning straw in a fire—
If the straw is wet, the fire can't burn brightly.
¹⁰Spiritual life can be hidden and dampened like this.

¹¹So, Simon, if anyone wants to follow the Way of Triumph
They must clear their minds, and set aside all wanting and
doing.
¹²To be pure and still means to be open to purity and stillness—
As a result you can intuit the truth.
¹³This means that the light can shine
Revealing the workings of cause and effect
And leading to the place of Peace and Happiness.
¹⁴Simon, know this.¹⁵I carry myself in strangeness
In words that can reach out north, south, east, and west.

¹⁶And if I am everywhere in the world, then I don't know how
I am—
If I am truly in my words, then I don't know what I signify.
¹⁷If a person has a made-up name, no one really knows who
he is.
¹⁸Trying to know and to see are irrelevant.¹⁹Why is this?
²⁰People struggle trying to figure it all out.
²¹This struggle creates the desire to do something.
²²Doing creates movement which results in anxiety:
Then it is impossible to find Rest and Contentment.
²³This is why I teach no wanting and doing without doing
It stops you thinking about things which disturb you
Then you can enter into the source of pure empty being.

²⁴Detach yourself from what disturbs and distracts you,
And be as pure as one who breathes in purity and emptiness.
²⁵This state is the gateway to enlightenment—
It is the Way to Peace and Happiness."

CHAPTER TWO

¹"Simon, know this.²I can be found throughout Heaven and
Earth

³I am the Way to the Spirits, I can be seen among the
   people.
⁴I can embody forms beyond knowledge—
I protect everyone regardless of who they may be.
⁵I have come to help those who have gone wrong.
⁶This has never been seen before—
This pure effortless emptiness has never been known.
⁷Why is this?⁸Those who act piously soon achieve a name
But fame makes people behave differently
They become driven by worldly ambitions.
⁹This makes them inflated and defined by what they do.
¹⁰People like this can never achieve Peace and Happiness.

¹¹The All-Knowing Essence speaks through me, and what it
   says is:
Those who don't act piously and don't seek a name
Trust in their own heart's guidance.
¹²They can go beyond wanting, and trust
In direct spiritual communication.
¹³Understanding what is true, they know
That this is the way to Peace and Happiness.

¹⁴Simon, you should know this. ¹⁵I see the Law.
¹⁶I see the reality without the distraction of form.
¹⁷I hear the Law.¹⁸I am not distracted by sounds.
¹⁹I smell the Law, and I know how to ignore smell.
²⁰I taste the Law—and I am not distracted by flavors.
²¹I embody the Law, and I can sense it in my body.
²²My heart is the Law, so I can feel it all.
²³These six principles lead to the highest awakening:
Through the light of this teaching everyone can be saved.

²⁴This Teaching has existed in Heaven from the beginning,
And it brings great blessing as well as good fortune.

²⁵It brings fortune for everyone as great as the sheerest
    mountain,
And there is nothing to compare with it.
²⁶So gather all you good people together, pray and sing!
²⁷The light will come and enlighten you
You will discover the all-embracing knowing, the mystery
Which will lead you to Peace and Happiness.
²⁸And it is this which will enable you to transcend rebirth:
Simon, know this.²⁹It is a place of incredible blessing
Beyond all conceivable imagining.³⁰And it is for everyone.

³¹I study this myself—and yet there's no way to prove it.
³²Why is it like this?³³Because it cannot be proved.
³⁴How can you define what is beyond definition?
³⁵This is why I say: no wanting, no doing, no piousness, no
    truth.
³⁶These are the Four Essential Laws.
³⁷They cannot teach you in themselves
But follow them and you will be free
From trying to sort out what to believe.
³⁸Feel compassion, and be compassionate over and again
Without trying to show it off to anyone.
³⁹Everyone will be freed this way—
And this is called the Way to Peace and Happiness."

⁴⁰And then everyone got to their feet, bowed, and then sang:

⁴¹"All Praise to the Limitless One
Great is the Supreme Highest One—
You teach us the Triumphant Law as it is
In its depth and mystery, beyond imagining."

⁴²And though I don't pretend to understand
I will go on studying until the end. . . .

CHAPTER THREE

¹"Master, you said that no wanting, no doing, no piousness,
    and no truth
Are the Four Laws which are called the Way to Peace and
    Happiness.
²But if there is no existence, how can there be happiness?"
³And the Honored One replied: "That is a wonderful question.

⁴Now listen carefully while I say this again:
Peace and Happiness like this can only exist
Where nothing else exists.
⁵Think of your question.⁶And imagine for a moment
A distant bare mountain ringed with forests and glades
Plenty of places of shelter and rest—
Animals of all kinds are naturally drawn to it.
⁷Or imagine a great ocean which is vast and fathomless:
You don't have to worry how its creatures will survive,
They gravitate there, and find all they need.

⁸And you, what do you do?⁹You gravitate
Naturally to these teachings, and through them
You will come to live in Peace and Happiness.
¹⁰Animals practice true faith and live by these laws
So they are already there, in that realm,
And so you will come to be in a place
Where nothing else exists or is needed."

¹¹And everyone said "Yes!" to this, and "Amen!"

¹²Then he spoke to the assembled crowd and said:
"This Sutra is profound and unimaginable.
¹³All the gods and gurus agree on this, and acknowledge
This Way that is the essence of connection and return.

¹⁴To move you need light to see by—this teaching provides it
Just as the sun slants out, so you can see what is in front
    of you
This Sutra offers understanding, and by its light
You can know the Way of Peace and Happiness in your heart.
¹⁵All the holy ones know that this teaching
Is at the root of all that is true.

¹⁶If anyone wants to share these teachings with friends or
    family
Of course they can.¹⁷Honor them, sing and pray together—
And this will bless you and your family into the next
    generation.
¹⁸Every generation is united in this communion—
From goodness in past lives, people come to this religion
And through the faith they have they find Happiness.
¹⁹It's like the spring rain which refreshes everything—
If you have roots, you will flourish in its coming
But if you have none, it is impossible to rise.

²⁰Simon, know this: You ask me about the Triumphant Law.
²¹What your ancestors have done bears fruit in you,
Their karma finds its outcome in you."

²²Everyone stood in quiet respect. Then they praised the Eternal One again:

²³"What mercy, what amazing compassion
There is no one higher than You, Great One:
Be present in Your Love and protect us, guide us!
²⁴You have watched over us for generations
Saving our fathers and forefathers, and daily
Bringing people to share in Peace and Happiness.
But some of us are lost and need to be led back. . . ."

25And the Messiah said: "What you say is true—
It is like a precious mountain.26Its translucent jade forests
And fragrant pearl fruits are food for those who thirst for
      healing.

27I will tell you a story.28There was a sick man
Who heard people talk about this precious mountain.
29Day and night he longed to reach it—the thought never
      left him.
30But the mountain was high and miles away and he was
      very crippled.
31He longed to realize his dream, but he couldn't.
32But he had a close relative who was wise and resourceful.
33And this man had scaling ladders brought and steps cut
And with some friends he levered and pushed the sick man up
Until he reached the summit.34And there, he was healed.

35Simon, know this: people coming to this mountain
Were confused and unhappy because of their worldly desires.
36They had heard the truth.37They knew it could lead them to
      the Way.
38So they tried to scale this mountain, but in vain—
Love and faith had all but died in them.

39Then the Compassionate Knowing One came like the close
      relative
And taught them with skill and sincerity so they knew
That He is the scaling ladder and the steps cut in stone
By which they can find the true Way, freed of their weight
      forever."

CHAPTER FOUR

¹"There are Ten Laws for observing the world, and they are all
   useful.
²What are they?

³The first way of observing the world
Is to notice how people grow old and sick.
⁴No one escapes this.⁵It's like being a traveler—
He will stay wherever he can lie down for a night.
⁶He doesn't care too much whether the bed and food are
   the best
And so it is between us and our bodies.
⁷Once we go we leave all this behind—
No one here gets out alive.

⁸The second way of observing the world is to see
That the family we love we will also have to leave,
Just as the leaves of a tree fall in autumn.
⁹Nothing can stop this, and no leaf survives.
¹⁰The wind takes them all in its swirling breath.

¹¹The third way of observing the world is this:
Some are great and powerful—for others, life is brief and
   glorious!
¹²And with both, nothing lasts forever.
¹³It's like the magical light of the moon shining
   everywhere
All it takes is a cloud to drift across it
And the light is dimmed or eclipsed altogether.

¹⁴The fourth way of observing the world is this:
Some are bullish, provoking everyone they meet—
While others exploit those who are weaker than they are.

15And in the end both can be killed in an instant:
They are like moths drawn to the flame
They fly straight at it thinking this is it
And then they suffer.

16The fifth way of observing the world is this:
There are misers who do nothing but accumulate
        wealth.
17They wear themselves out with no end of pain
And they can't take any of it with them.
18They are like little clay bottles filled with sea water:
How can you hope to catch the vastness of the sea
In something so tiny?

19The sixth way is this: the sex-obsessed,
Fantasizing about having it all the time—
Even though they're left frustrated and depressed.
20They're like a tree invaded by termites
Being eaten away until the wood is so rotten
It collapses, threatening anyone in sight.

21The seventh way is to drink and party,
Sleeping around in such a mixed-up state
That you don't know what is real, and what is a dream.
22You're like a pool of water that has been churned up;
Once it has become so unclear
It is impossible to see anything else in it.

23The eighth way is this: people see life as a drama
As a game in which they are here to entertain themselves.
24This wastes the body and depletes the spirit.
25It's like an idiot climbing a stem to see a flower
Or fighting to bend down a branch
Exhausting himself for no purpose.

²⁶The ninth way is this—to wander from religion to religion
Seeking enlightenment, but ending up in confusion.
²⁷It's like someone who makes plaster casts of cattle:
No matter how life-like they seem
Take them out to the fields, and they can't do a thing!

²⁸And the tenth way is this: there are some who believe
They know it, and who appear to everyone as if they do.
²⁹But in reality they don't share anything and the truth dies
    with them.
³⁰They are like oysters with pearls grown in them—
The pearl is no use to the oyster, and the oyster no use
Until it is caught and prized open.

³¹Think about these ten ways and hold them in you
In your mind, your feelings and your body.
³²This is one way of really understanding the Triumphant
    Law."

CHAPTER FIVE

¹"Now, what are the Four Essential Laws of the Dharma?

²The first is no wanting. ³If your heart is obsessed with
    something
It manifests in all kinds of distorted ways.
⁴Distorted thoughts are the root of negative behavior.
⁵It's like a plant: if the roots, however deep, are damaged
Then this will come out on its leaves and how it grows.
⁶And so it is with people—if there is wanting
It will come out in your body and everything you do.
⁷And all the body's openings will become clouded,
Losing their energy and brightness.⁸This is the Law of No
    Desire.

[9]The second is no doing. [10]Don't put on a mask
And pretend to be what you're not. [11]Be your most natural,
And don't run after fantasies and illusions!
[12]It's as if you are in a boat on the broad ocean—
The wind drives you this way and that, you have no control,
And all the time you're scared of drowning so there's no rest.
[13]In fact there's no peace at all! [14]This is just like people—
That which appears on the outside is not the truth.
[15]The effort needed to hold a direction is abandoned—
And there is simply action and reaction. [16]So walk the Way of
    No Action.

[17]The third is no piousness. [18]And what that means
Is not wanting to have your good deeds broadcast to the
    nation.
[19]Do what's right to bring people to the truth
But not for your own reputation's sake.
[20]It is like the great Earth herself
Giving food to each according to their needs:
The blessings that are given are countless.
[21]So anyone who teaches the Triumphant Law
Practicing the Way of Light to bring life to the truth
Will know Peace and Happiness in company.
[22]But don't talk it away—this is the Way of No Virtue.

[23]The fourth is no truth. [24]Don't try to control everything,
Don't take sides in arguments about right and wrong.
[25]Treat everyone equally, and live from day to day.
[26]It's like a clear mirror which reflects everything anyway
Green or yellow or in any combination—
It shows everything as well as the smallest of details.
[27]What does the mirror do? [28]It reflects without judgment.
[29]And you—you should do likewise.
[30]Then true Peace and Happiness will flow from your heart,

And others will join you in the quest for the True Way
While you will not claim credit for being virtuous.³¹This is No
　　Truth."

CHAPTER SIX

¹The Messiah continued: "If someone joins an army
He needs armor to protect himself.²And it must be strong
　　enough
To help him defend himself and survive being attacked.
³The Luminous Religion and its Laws are the best armor!
⁴All of life can be protected by them.
⁵If someone wants to sail across the great ocean
He needs a well-made boat to carry him through the storms.
⁶And yet no matter how good the vessel is
There's no guarantee of getting to the other side.
⁷But the Way of Light and its laws
Can carry all of us across the ocean of life and death
To reach the shores of the Land of Peace and Happiness.

⁸If someone is dying in a horrible plague
And they smell the balm of mysterious power
They can be revived.⁹Its scent restores their qi.
¹⁰And well, the laws of this Light are the best balm there is
Because they guide us through the pain and hardships of life
And by facing them, you come back to the true knowing.

¹¹All of you should chant this day and night
Because it brings back clear seeing, and each of you will
　　return
To your own original nature, your ultimately true beingness,
Free from all falsehood and illusion.¹²And you will see
These teachings are inexhaustible.

¹³Anyone, even if he has only a little love
Can walk the Bright Path, and he will suffer no harm.
¹⁴This is the way that leads to Peace and Happiness—
And he can come to this even from the darkest of darks.
¹⁵If you really follow the Sutras, imagine how easy this
    could be!

¹⁶Now go and make friends of this teaching from everyone—
It's like a royal person defending against assault
Or like a beacon lit on a hillside—everyone can see it,
And the Princely One is like this.¹⁷He's like a high mountain
The Sutras shine out, like a great burning fire:
If you follow the teaching, you will be a light to the world."

¹⁸Then the crowd sang praises, wanting more.¹⁹But the Mes-
    siah said:
"It is enough now—even though we cannot stop the Word.
²⁰It is like a good well that never runs dry.
²¹When you've been saved from your sickness in body
    and soul
There's no need to go on drinking.²²So it is with my teaching
Which is only the beginning of you touching your own
True original nature.²³Too much would not be right."

²⁴The crowd all agreed, thanked him warmly, and began to
    disperse.

²⁵This is the end of the Sutra of the Pure Land of Peace and
    Happiness, and of Returning to Our True Original Nature.

⌇ THE FOURTH LITURGICAL SUTRA: ⌇
THE SUPREME

This last Sutra is titled *The Christian Liturgy in Praise of the Three Sacred Powers*. It is in fact either a beautiful translation into superb Chinese of the classic Christian hymn "Gloria in Excelsis," or an original Chinese composition inspired by that hymn.

This Sutra, also found in the cave at Dunhuang and now in Paris, shows the maturity associated with Jingjing's Sutras. It is clearly designed to be sung and chanted. Along with the two other clearly liturgical documents and *The Sutra of Returning to Your Original Nature*, these texts provide a window into the devotional life of the Church.

Rooted deeply in transcendent Christian imagery, the Sutra talks about **"the Enlightened,"** about how **"countless of the Suffering are saved from the Realm of Suffering,"** how the **"Compassionate Joyous Lamb"** will **"free us of the karma of our lives, bring us back to our original nature."** The worshipers pray that God will **"hear our prayers, send Your raft of salvation to save us from the burning streams."** It also uses a classic Buddhist image of the compassionate benevolence of the Bodhisattva (see quote from the *Lotus Sutra* in chapter 5), of **"sweet healing"** coming down to save all life and revive the true essence of all.

¹Christian liturgy in praise of the Three Sacred Powers

²The highest skies are in love with You.
³The great Earth opens its palms in peace.
⁴Our truest being is anchored in Your Purity.
⁵You are Allaha: Compassionate Father of the Three.

⁶Everything praises you, sounding its true note.
⁷All the Enlightened chant praises—

Every being takes its refuge in You
And the light of Your Holy Compassion frees us all.

[8]Beyond knowing, beyond words
You are the truth, steadfast for all time.
[9]Compassionate Father, Radiant Son,
Pure Wind King—three in one.

[10]In the midst of kings and emperors, You are supreme
Among the World Famous, You are Lord of
    Everything.

[11]You live perpetually in light
The light which enters every sphere.
[12]Yet you have never been seen
No eye can see Your Form
Or Your Unclouded Nature.

[13]Among all spirits You alone are unchanging
Making all that is good, beyond reckoning.
[14]The root and essence—the thing itself!

[15]Today I reflect on Your Compassion and Grace,
I delight in Your Delight which covers our land
Messiah, Great Holy Son of the Honored One
As countless of the Suffering are saved—

[16]Supreme King, Will of Ages,
Compassionate Joyous Lamb
Loving all who suffer
Fearless as You strive for us
Free us of the karma of our lives,
Bring us back to our original nature
Delivered from all danger.

¹⁷Divine Son invited
To stand on the right of the Father
This Altar exceeds all others—
Great Messiah: hear our prayers
Send Your raft of salvation
To save us from the burning streams!

¹⁸Great Teacher, I stand in awe of the Father.
¹⁹Great Teacher, I am awed by the Holy Lord.
²⁰Great Teacher, I am speechless before the King of Dharma.
²¹Great Teacher, I am dazzled by the Enlightened Mind—
Great Teacher, You who do everything to save us.

²²Everything looks to You, without thinking.
²³Shower us with Your Healing Rain!
²⁴Help us to overcome, give life to what has withered,
And water the roots of kindness in us.
²⁵Great Holy World-Honored One,
Messiah, as we love Our Father,
Boundless Sea of Compassion
And the Clean Pure Wind
Whose clarity cleanses through the Law
Reaching beyond all grace

²⁶Da Qin Religion of Light Sutra of Praise to the Three Powers
(Father, Messiah/Son, and Holy Spirit).

These Sutras deserve to be better known. They are classics of
the most radical fusion of Western and Eastern spirituality as well
as classics of Tang Dynasty poetry. I hope that by bringing them to
life again through translation they can join the corpus of great
works of spirituality. After a thousand years of silence, they sing
out again.

By the time the Da Qin monastery had built its pagoda, it would have had these magnificent Sutras to house. In a remarkably short time the Church of the East had become fully Chinese and produced masterpieces of Chinese spirituality. The future looked assured and good. The light of the Dharma King Christ had never shone so brightly and the sound of praise and singing was to be heard in many places. Great teachers such as Jingjing had emerged. It was time for the Church to take stock. And this was exactly what it did.

8

The Way of Light:
The Stone's Teaching

The ancient Confucian temple of Xian is a magnificent set of buildings. It is fronted by a huge wall, designed to prevent evil spirits—who apparently can travel only in straight lines—from entering this holy place. Should this wall be breached, another line of defense is in front of the main gate itself, a series of beautiful carved marble bridges over small pools. Evil spirits cannot cross water.

Once inside the main gate, a vista opens up, some one hundred yards long, leading to the middle gate, a delicate wonder of wood, gently rising upward. Along the path to the middle gate are hitching posts where the officials who came to worship here tied their horses. The pillars, cut from white marble, are alive with creatures carved on them. Beyond the middle gate lies a series of pavilions where scholars could sit and think and in which are housed important edicts of the emperors. After this stretch are the main compounds of the temple, in which one of the world's most extraordinary museums, the Museum of Stone Inscriptions, is located. Most of the steles in the beautifully named Forest of Steles are more than six feet high; some are more than a millennium and a half old; all are astonishing.

Gathered here under a series of roofs is the largest collection of steles in the world. It is, in effect, a stone library. The ancient Chinese wanted to ensure that their greatest books were preserved, so they inscribed them on the longest-lasting material they could find. These stone books now line the walls and crowd the floors of the ancient temple. In the first hall, for example, you can find the complete text of the *I Ching*, engraved more than fifteen hundred years ago and legible to this day. Here you can also consult the definitive text of the *Classic of Filial Piety*, the greatest of the Confucian teachings and the foundation of Confucian hierarchy.

And here in the second hall is the Stone of the Church of the East that launched my search for the Taoist Christians.

The Stone was originally erected in 781, when the Da Qin monastery added its pagoda. Such stones were commonly erected to coincide with major building projects, and the Stone actually talks of a rebuilding of the churches at the time. It also recounts most of the history of the Church in China up to 781, and contains a succinct version of the teachings of the Church that confirms beliefs and events in the translated Jesus Sutras. As discussed in chapter 7, the text was written by Jingjing, and the first portion of the Stone describes the basic teachings of the Luminous Religion. The Stone is steeped in Taoist and Buddhist imagery and language and has many echoes of the greatest of Taoist texts, the *Tao Te Ching*.

✒ THE TAOIST-CHRISTIAN CREATION ✑

Under the Stone's topmost carving of the cross and dragons are nine large characters, beautifully carved. They spell out: **"Da Qin Religion of Light Record of its Transmission throughout China"**— best put into contemporary English as "The Record of the Transmission of the Religion of Light of the West in China." These are the nine characters on the cover of this book.

The first section of the Stone's text covers the origin of all the universe and can be compared to the best of Taoist writings. In classic language it tells of the utter beingness of existence, which is the origin before origins: **"In the beginning was the natural constant, the true stillness of the Origin, and the primordial void of the Most High. Then the spirit of the void emerged as the Most High Lord, moving in mysterious ways to enlighten the holy ones"** **(2:1–2)**. This can be compared to the Taoist creed as set out in the *Tao Te Ching* (see chapter 5): "The Tao gives birth to the One" (ch. 42). The Stone continues: **"He is Joshua, my True Lord of the Void, who embodies the three subtle and wondrous bodies, and who was condemned to the cross so that the people of the four directions can be saved" (2:3)**. This description of the Trinity is very similar to Celtic understandings of the Trinity, for example, in this prayer by St. Patrick:

> I breathe in strength as I stand today:
> Calling on the Father, Son and Holy Spirit
> Believing in the Threeness,
> Witnessing the Oneness,
> On my way to meet You face to face.[48]

The Stone goes on to describe how the Most High Lord creates the twin forces of yin and yang. Again this follows the cosmology of the creed of chapter 42 of the *Tao Te Ching*: "The One gives birth to the Two." The Stone spells out the Chinese belief that when yin and yang were created, the lighter vapors of yang rose to form Heaven and the sun, and the heavier vapors of yin sank to form Earth and the moon. The yang sun creates day and the yin moon creates night. All this is spelled out by the Stone. Then the Stone describes the creation of "myriad things," meaning all life, and in particular "the first people." / gain, these parts of the text reflect the final section of the Taoist creed: "The Two give birth to the Three; And the Three give birth to every living thing. All things are held in yin and carry yang: and they are held together in the qi of teeming energy." Thus we have a classic Taoist vision of creation and origins, but reinterpreted to be the actions of the Trinity.

✐ ORIGINAL NATURE ✑

The Stone then begins its extraordinary journey into the distinctive theology of the Church in China, where original sin had become original goodness—original nature—and where karma and reincarnation were the context of theological exploration. The Stone describes God giving to the first people the original nature of goodness, which is simply the true state of existence of humanity, as is made clear by further comments that present the first people thus: **"Their minds were empty; they were content; and their hearts were simple and innocent. Originally they had no desire"** **(2:8–9).** This is a classic Taoist description of human nature at its purest, most faithful to the Tao. It is the original or innate nature of all living things that Chuang Tzu, the fourth-century B.C. Taoist philosopher, describes. Although innate goodness can become overlaid by negative emotions, it is always there to be recovered. As Chuang wrote:

> The mean person desires wealth,
> The nobleman desires fame.
> In the ways in which they affect their true form,
> and change their innate natures,
> they are different.
> But as they cast aside what they have
> in pursuit of something they don't have,
> they are identical.
>
> So it is said,
> Do not be a mean person,

Turn again and desire the heavenly within.
Do not be a nobleman,
Pursue the path of Heaven within.
Whether bent or true,
See all in the light of Heaven.
Learn to face all four directions,
And flow with the tides of the season.[49]

The Stone says that original goodness becomes obscured by the traps of Satan. This is the only place where the Syriac version of the Hebrew name Satan occurs in any of the Jesus Sutras. Elsewhere, the term Yama King of the Earth Prisons is used, or a more generic term such as the Great Evil Ghost. Satan in Hebrew means the Accuser, the one who tests people to see if they really will do good. The language of the Stone means something similar. Again, we need to turn to Taoist texts to understand what is meant here when the Stone says **"under the influence of Satan, they abandoned their pure and simple goodness for the glitter and the gold" (2:9)**. The *Tao Te Ching* offers us a vision of this same problem. In chapter 3 it says:

If the sage refuses to be proud
The people won't compete for his attention:
If the sage does not buy treasures
Then people won't want to steal them. . . .

The sage always makes sure
that the people don't know what he's done,
so they never want to take control—
and are never driven by ambition.

He keeps them in truth like this
acting invisibly.

You see, if there is nothing to fight for
then there is nothing that can break the flow.

Greed, seeking "glitter and the gold," are base distractions from just being and as such are the Taoist equivalent of sin, but not the totally corrosive sin of so much Western theology. It is possible to escape this affliction of greed. As the last lines say, if there is no greed, then there is nothing to disturb the natural flow. The Four Laws of the Tao of Jesus in *The Sutra of Returning to Your Original Nature* spells this out: "**No wanting, no doing, no piousness, no truth.**" In this context, Satan is simply a manifestation of the general tendency in humanity to want more and more. The power of Satan that the Stone presents is the power to disrupt and divert from true existence. As such, Satan here is not the all-demonic, all-powerful creature of Western mythology, but much more a descriptive and pictorial expression of what Zhuang Zi and the *Tao Te Ching* see as the emergence of a false sense of what is important, an illusion that distorts the original goodness of humanity.

ぐ⃝ GUARDIANS, NOT MASTERS, ⃝ゝ OF CREATION

An interesting line here deserves commentary. In the description of the first people we are told "**He gave to them the original nature of goodness and appointed them as the guardians of all creation**" **(2:7)**. This is quite a different slant on the verses in Genesis, which have so often been translated as humanity being given dominance, lordship, over creation: "God blessed them, saying to them, 'Be fruitful, multiply, fill the earth and conquer it. Be masters of the fish of the seas, the birds of heaven and all living animals on the earth' " (Genesis 1:28).

The Stone emphasizes protecting and guarding the rest of

creation. This vision manifests itself in the dramatic reworking of the Ten Commandments in *The Sutra of Jesus Christ* that prohibits killing any living being in all creation. It also reflects chapter 32 of the *Tao Te Ching*:

> At the beginning of time
> The sage gave names to everything—seen and unseen.
> A ruler who walks the Way
> Is like a river reaching the seas
> Gathering the waters of the streams
> into himself as he goes.

✌ THE WHEEL OF SUFFERING ᕊ AND KARMA

The next part of the Stone talks of the confusion that results from following the base way of greed and refers to 365 forms of sin— that is, a sin for every day. Then Jingjing brings us back to the core problem: through actions of sinfulness, greed, and ego, we spin a web of cause and effect—karma—that leaves us trapped in the worlds of consequence, doomed to wander from life to life until we can be rid of this "retribution." We are caught in the ever-turning wheel of fire, the wheel of samsara, of suffering, which prevents us from returning to our state of original goodness and thus to union with the Godhead.

✌ THE INCARNATION ᕊ

The next section of the Stone outlines in the most succinct way the Incarnation, revealing its Persian theological roots. Because people's innate good nature had become confused and obscured, God had to come to Earth as Ye Su, **"the One emanating in three**

subtle bodies" (2:17), and become human. It describes the Nativity and adds that the Persians saw a bright light, which they followed to bring the Child gifts. This one mention of the Magi of Persia is important, because it is a reminder that the Church of the East had grown up in a culture where it was always in the minority and had long ago found how helpful it was to find some feature of the dominant culture to relate to the Christ story.

The text next speaks of the twenty-four holy ones, writers of the Old Testament (bearing in mind that tradition held that Moses wrote the first five books, the Torah). Then Jingjing writes, **"Heaven has decreed that the new religion of the 'Three in One Purity that cannot be spoken of' should be proclaimed"** (2:20). This is a direct echo of the opening lines of the *Tao Te Ching*: "The Tao that can be talked about is not the true Tao. The name that can be named is not the eternal Name."

The Stone then uses Taoist and Buddhist terminology to express the significance of the Incarnation and the teachings of the Religion of Light. This part of the text is frankly unclear and has defeated many, and I offer only one possible interpretation. It is probably derived from one of the Buddhist categories of eight—the eightfold path, for example:

Right Views;
Right Thoughts;
Right Speech;
Right Action;
Right Livelihood;
Right Effort;
Right Mindfulness;
Right Concentration.

A similar confusion has hung over the phrase that follows: **"Reveal the gate of the three constants, lead us to life, and destroy death"** (2:21). However, here Taoism is the key to understanding the reference. I believe that the text means the three constants in Taoism: yin, yang, and qi. Yin and yang are the core building blocks of the cosmos, the Two that originate in the One. They are also seen as, respectively, the moon and sun, constants in that they are always there. Qi is the original breath with which we are all born and have to sustain ourselves if we wish to avoid death. When the qi, the original breath within us, has been used up, we die.

In the context of "**Lead us to life and destroy death,**" it is quite clear that this is what the three constants represent, to which the Christians give added emphasis by an implicit link to the Trinity. Yin, yang, and qi are the fundamental and potentially eternal elements of each person's existence: a core Taoist concept put in a new light by the Incarnation and Gospel.

⤖ THE BUDDHA CHRIST, ⤖ THE JESUS BODHISATTVA

The next part of the Stone text uses classical Buddhist terminology. Jesus is described as the one who rows or launches "**the raft of salvation and compassion**" **(2:23)** that ferries the souls across the great divide and away from reincarnation. This is one of the oldest images of the salvationary activities of the Buddhas and Bodhisattvas.

Jesus, like the saving Bodhisattvas, carries the soul away from falsehood and greed, karma and rebirth to the Pure Land, where there is no karma, no rebirth. This image also appears in Jingjing's *Sutra of Returning to Your Original Nature*, and the links to the Good Shepherd are echoed again here. *The Sutra of Returning to Your Original Nature* speaks explicitly at one point about a Pure Land of Peace and Happiness, which is also a Buddhist phrase signifying the Palace of Amida Buddha, the future Buddha who rules over the Pure Land. There is some speculation among scholars of early Mahayana Buddhism as to whether the Bodhisattva idea and the Pure Land emerge from contact in Afghanistan with Christianity. In this instance, Christianity clearly feels very comfortable with Buddhist Bodhisattva and Pure Land imagery.

✷ THE IMMORTAL ✷

The Stone goes on to describe Christ ascending to Heaven at the end of his time on Earth and leaving behind twenty-seven books of scripture. Interestingly, the Stone actually says Christ **"ascended to immortality" (2:24)**, an image tied to the three constants, the preservation of which, especially qi, is fundamental to the Taoist quest for immortality. The Christian Sutra, however, stresses the unusual nature of Jesus' ascension to immortality, which took place in broad daylight. Most Eastern immortals ascend secretly and are only discovered to be immortals when their coffins are lifted and found to be empty. By saying that Jesus ascended in broad daylight, the text emphasizes a very special form of immortality.

✷ CHINA'S BIBLE ✷

The twenty-seven books of scripture refer to the New Testament. Surprisingly, although the Western canon of the New Testament has twenty-seven books, the canon of the Syrian Church, which did not accept the four disputed Epistles (2 Peter, 2 and 3 John, and Jude) nor the Book of Revelation, had only twenty-two. This reference to the set of twenty-seven has long perplexed scholars. Perhaps the answer lies in a previously almost unnoticed contact between the Orthodox Church of the Byzantine Empire and the Tang Court at Chang'an. In 719 and again in 742, missions from the Byzantine Empire reached the Tang Court. Missions from one empire to the other were not rare, but these two are recorded in the Chinese records as being led by Dadeseng. This name literally means "Monk of Great Virtue" and means in this context archbishop.[50]

Archbishops would likely have brought copies of the Bible or at least the New Testament as gifts. The Church in China, as we have already seen, was more than happy to use whatever came to hand to help explore and proclaim the Christian faith as it came to understand it. Possibly, they welcomed the Orthodox Bible and rejoiced in its full range of books.

⌘ THE LIGHT ⌘ AS THE RESURRECTION

The practice of baptism is mentioned in the next section. It doesn't mention the Last Supper, which is surprising as communion is a key sacrament of the Church. Of the greatest mystery, the Crucifixion and Resurrection, there is only the line: **"The Religion of Light teachings are like the resplendent sun: they have the power to dissolve the dark realm and destroy evil forever" (2:22).** The Crucifixion and Resurrection, as traditionally understood, were played down in the Church in China. They were expressed as a light sent forth that vanquishes death and evil. This is similar in concept to the language and imagery that came to the lips of the Protestant martyr Latimer as he was burned at the stake in Oxford under the rule of Queen Mary in 1555. Turning to his fellow martyr and fellow bishop, Ridley, he said: "Be of good comfort, Master Ridley, and play the man. We shall this day light such a candle by God's grace in England as I trust shall never be put out." Sacrificial death has been interpreted as lighting a candle, bringing light into the darkness, and thus overcoming the darkness. This ties in to the line in *The Sutra of Jesus Christ* that every life is as precarious as a candle flame. The Church in China used the imagery of light, candle, or sunlight to convey salvation from the wheel of karma and rebirth.

ᗑᗇᗆ THE DAILY CYCLE OF THE MONKS ᗑᗇᗆ

The next section of the Stone presents a unique window into the everyday life of the churches in China at this time. The Stone describes the priests calling the people to worship by striking a piece of wood. To this day you can see and hear this call if you stay at an Orthodox monastery or nunnery in Greece: to summon the faithful to worship, a monk walks around the outside of the church striking a plank of wood with a wooden hammer. The rhythm is set, and it is highly likely that the same sound was also heard in the confines of the monastery we rediscovered at Da Qin or in the great monastery in Chang-an. Buddhist monasteries in China do the same.

The Stone then talks of the **"Eastern-facing rites" (2:28)**, the direction of prayer. All other worship in Chinese temples is either to north or south, so the eastern direction of the Church's prayers was sufficiently distinctive to warrant comment. It is why we believe Da Qin to be a Christian site, as it is orientated east-west, not north-south.

In China in the eighth century, the Church saw all people as equal and thus banned slavery. It also seems that women were treated with considerable equality; the text from *The Sutra of Jesus Christ* on the equality and protection of women is most telling on this. The Stone's description of the priests as **"those who choose to grow beards, shave their heads, travel on the open roads, renounce desire, have neither male nor female slaves, see all people as equal, and do not hoard material goods" (2:29)** gives us a delightful picture of the itinerant monks and priests of the Church at work.

The Stone text continues: **"We use abstinence to subdue thoughts of desire; and we use stillness to build our foundation" (2:30)**. This sounds as if we are hearing the true values of the monastic life direct from the heart of Jingjing. The Stone describes the practice of prayer seven times per day, a pattern similar to the West's. And, in the only reference in any of the Jesus Sutras or Chinese texts, there is this description of Holy Communion: **"Every seven days we have an audience with Heaven. We purify our hearts and return to the simple and natural way of the truth"** **(2:32–33).** The seven-day week was not the norm in China; the structure of the month in the traditional calendar focused on the waxing and waning of the moon.

The British Museum possesses one of the earliest printed books in the world, a copy of the Almanac Calendar for the year 877. It comes from the Dunhuang caves. Not only is this a fascinatingly early example of printing, but it is also possible evidence of use by either a Christian or a Manichaean worshiper. The days of the Chinese months have an annotation added to them in red ink. A tiny illegible character has been added by hand, marking off the Sundays of the months for the year 877. Someone turned the traditional Chinese almanac calendar into a helpful system to remind the user of the seventh day, the day Jingjing says was when **"we have an audience with Heaven."**

The Stone then returns to wider philosophical thought and again becomes very Taoist: **"This truth cannot be named but its function surpasses all expectations. When forced to give it a name, we call it the Religion of Light. As it is with the Way, that which is sacred is not sacred unless it is highly sacred, and that which is the Way is not the Way unless it is the Great Way"** **(2:34–36).** Here Jingjing makes direct reference to Taoism—Tao meaning, of course, the Way. He is drawing parallels between Taoism's teachings on what the true Way is and Christianity's understanding of the true nature of truth. The parallels with the first chapter of the *Tao Te Ching* are clear: "The Tao that can be talked about is not the true Tao. The name that can be named is not the eternal Name." A good example of Taoist development from this stark statement is the following, taken from the *Dao Di Lun, The Embodiment of the Tao,* written just a few decades before the Stone.

The author was a great favorite of the emperor and his writings would certainly have been known to Jingjing.

> Question: . . . Why then does the Scripture say that the nameless is at the root of the myriad beings? Why does it not say that it has a name?
> Answer: The Tao is an expression for that which pervades all life. When something pervades all life, there are bound to be outer manifestations. Once there are such manifestations, one can name them. Therefore one can attach names to the Tao, but none of these names will ever be truly permanent.[51]

✌ THE STORY OF THE CHURCH ✍

From this point on, with one or two exceptions, the Stone describes the history of the arrival and development of Christianity in China. Using classic Taoist imagery, it tells of Aluoben coming **"on azure clouds" (3:3)**. Azure was the sacred color of Heaven and was worn by the emperor when he went to worship Heaven. The symbolic significance of cloud colors was well developed in Chinese thought; for example, green clouds foretold plague, red foretold warfare, black foretold floods, and yellow foretold good fortune. The azure clouds therefore foretell the blessing of a Heavenly Message. In Taoism, the most ancient and holy of the deities are associated with azure clouds. Taoism's most sacred mountain, Tai Shan, has as its female deity the Princess of the Azure Clouds. She is in fact a Shamanic deity who, along with her husband, is credited with creating all life and of ruling over the entrance to the underworld and afterlife. To come on azure clouds was to be deemed very, very powerful spiritually.

The Stone describes the reception of Aluoben **"after a long and arduous journey" (3:3)** and of how Aluoben was welcomed to the palace and asked to translate the scriptures he had brought. **"When the Emperor heard the teachings, he realized deeply that they spoke the truth"**; as a result he issued this decree: **"The Way does not have a common name and the sacred does not have a common form. Proclaim the teachings everywhere for the salvation of the people. Aluoben, the man of great virtue from the Da Qin Empire, came from a far land and arrived at the capital to present the teachings and images of his religion. His message is mysterious and wonderful beyond our understanding. The teachings tell us about the origin of things and how they were created and nourished. The message is lucid and clear; the teachings will benefit all; and they shall be practiced throughout the land"** (3:6, 8–13). This imperial notice is the first evidence from China itself of the coming of Christianity and is found in official Tang Dynasty records and histories.

The Stone describes where in the capital the first monastery was built for twenty-one monks. An imperial text was written and set over the main doorway. This habit of emperors penning an often rather general statement of the worthiness of a holy place continued until the twentieth century, and many temples still exhibit these boards, with the handwriting of the particular emperor painted or carved on each. The one over the door of the first monastery read: **"Reveal the splendor and brightness of Heaven; glorify the Religion of Light saints; and let the benevolent teachings illuminate this realm of existence"** (3:16).

The location of the Da Qin lands is then described as a place where **"only the Religion of Light teachings are practiced"** (3:24). Was this wishful thinking by Aluoben? Having left Persia before the Arab Muslim invasion, it is possible that he thought Persia was indeed about to become a Christian state, or he may have simply been trying to score a diplomatic victory. Manichaeism and Zoroastrianism had both entered China earlier than Christianity and he may have been trying to show that these faiths had no real support or substance back home.

The Stone records that the teachings spread, and monasteries were built in hundreds of cities and many people were blessed. The evidence seems to argue that this is an exaggeration, though in fact the Church had a major impact in its short but eventful life. But then, until a hundred years ago, we knew virtually nothing of the Church in China except for that written on the Stone, and five hundred years ago we knew nothing whatsoever because the Stone had not yet been found. There is undoubtedly considerably more to be revealed and discovered about the Church in China.

ᐧᕫᐧ PERSECUTION AND RECOVERY ᕫᐧᕫ

The Stone proceeds to recount that persecution came, around 698, when a group of Buddhists and some rather disreputable people slandered the Church. The main priest, presumably the equivalent of a bishop, defended the Church by displaying what appears to have been special reliquaries and the main monks defended the teachings in debate. **"Thus, a disaster was averted,"** records the Stone **(3:32).**

The building of a specific church **"where the doctrine could be taught to more people in simple and straightforward ways" (3:33)** is described. This took place during the reign of Daozong (713–756).

In or around 742, the emperor ordered General Gao Lishi to attend the consecration of a church whose title we have preserved in the text: Acts of the Five Saints Church. Although we do not know who these five saints are, the Da Qin monastery is known to have been founded by "five brothers," or monks. Perhaps Da Qin is the church referred to in the Stone. The Stone also mentions treasures sent by the emperor—lavish but not unusually so for an imperial gift. Typical of what can be seen to this day in many temples is the gift of a commemorative tapestry on which is embroidered yet more imperial words of wisdom: **"The Dragon [emperor] may be far away, but the bow and sword can reach the**

corners of the sun to bring light and celestial music to the three realms" (3:37). This is a fairly typical example of imperial religious thought.

The Stone records that another monk, whose Chinese name is Jiehe and who is an astrologer or astronomer, had come from Persia to assist the Church. He is thought to be Bishop Giwargis (George). The Persian Church had received a very favorable report on the progress of the Church in China in 732, as recorded in the letter of Bishop Zhele to the patriarch, and it looks as if Jiehe was sent to assist and develop this success. The high standing of the Church is indicated by the fact that Jiehe and other priests, twenty of them in all, were invited to perform a high ceremony of prayer and offering in the palace.

The support of Emperor Suzong (756–762) is mentioned, for he established monasteries in Ling Wu and four other places. The town of Ling Wu in Gansu Province was significant, because for a brief period during the rebellion by An Lu Shan the Imperial Court took refuge there. The gift of a monastery to such an otherwise relatively unimportant town must have been one of gratitude. That an emperor should think to offer a church by way of thanks may indicate that the Church had stood by him in his hour of need, or that the role of the largely Christian Uighurs in suppressing the uprising led to Christianity being favored.

The next emperor was Daizong (763–779), and the text makes it clear he did nothing to hinder the Church but also little to further it. Hence the reference that he **"continued to promote the Sacred Way and follow the principles of wu-wei [no action]" (3:48).** However, we do get one brief and intriguing insight. On Christmas Day at some time in his reign, he honored the Church by sending incense to be offered and writing a plaque to be hung over the doorway. In it we have a direct reference to the Nativity and Incarnation: **"Due to your wonderful and meritorious works, many people have found salvation. Because the sacred took on human form, the poisons of the world can be stopped" (3:50–51).**

After a brief mention of the then reigning emperor, the Stone text offers a beautiful description of the Christian life: **"To penetrate the mysteries, to bless with a good conscience, to be great and yet empty, to return to stillness and be forgiving, to be compassionate and to deliver all people, to do good deeds and help people reach the other shore—these are the great benefits of our path of cultivation. To calm people in stormy times, to help them understand the nature of things, to maintain purity, to nourish all things, to respect all life, and to answer the needs of those whose beliefs come from the heart—these are the services the Religion of Light Church can offer" (3:54–55).** The Stone then sums up the Church's teachings: **"The True Lord of the Primordial Void, in absolute stillness and constant naturalness, crafted and nourished all things. He raised the earth and established the sky. He took on human form and His compassion was limitless. The sun rises; darkness is banished; and we are witnesses to the true wonder" (3:70–73).** The text ends with the following statement: **"This doctrine is great and its working powerful and mysterious. If forced to describe it, I would call them the work of the Three-in-one Lord. All this humble servant has done is to record on the monument what has happened and to glorify the Primordial Lord" (4:1–3).**

An inscription records that this stele was erected in the Second Year of Jianzhong (781) **"accompanied by the proper ceremonial music and rites" (4:4)**—the only clear evidence of the use of music in the Church.

The Stone of the Church of the East was obviously designed to impress everyone with the degree of support that the various emperors had given to the Church, by following standard Chinese practice, which had begun a hundred or so years before, of recording in stone the major books of China. The Tang Dynasty in particular developed this by sponsoring the carving of thirteen of the great classics on huge stone slabs. Preprinting cultures needed to preserve their greatest writings from the ravages of fire, flood, and other disasters that so swiftly destroy books of paper. In recording their key teachings on the Stone as well as recording how well received they had been—apart from the one period of trouble in 698—the Church was doing what Chinese culture generally was doing: ensuring the survival for later generations of its most important texts. The fact that we are discussing these teachings today bears witness to the wisdom of this action.

✌ THE STONE SUTRA ✍

PART ONE

[Across the top of the monument:]
**¹The Record of the Transmission
of the Religion of Light
of the West in China**

**²The Minister of the Administration of Monasteries bestows
the Purple Robe to Yeli,
the Chief Priest of the Monastery.**

[At the bottom of the monument:]
**³The erection of this monument is supervised by the monk
Gongdong
[with] monk Lingbao.**

[At top upper right:]
**⁴Monument commemorating the transmission of the Religion
of Light in China**

[At middle right:]
⁵Related by the monk Jingjing of the Da Qin Monastery

PART TWO

¹In the beginning was the natural constant, the true stillness of the Origin, and the primordial void of the Most High.²Then, the spirit of the void emerged as the Most High Lord, moving in mysterious ways to enlighten the holy ones.³He is Joshua, my True Lord of the Void, who embodies the three subtle and wondrous bodies, and who was condemned to the cross so that the people of the four directions can be saved.

⁴He beat up the primordial winds and the two vapors were created.⁵He differentiated the gray emptiness and opened up the sky and the earth.⁶He set the sun and moon on their course and day and night came into being.⁷He crafted the myriad things and created the first people.⁸He gave to them the original nature of goodness and appointed them as the guardians of all creation.⁹Their minds were empty; they were content; and their hearts were simple and innocent.¹⁰Originally they had no desire, but under the influence of Satan, they abandoned their pure and simple goodness for the glitter and the gold.¹¹Falling into the trap of death and lies, they became embroiled in the three hundred and sixty-five forms of sin.¹²In doing so, they have woven the web of retribution and have bound themselves inside it.¹³Some believe in the material origin of things; some have sunk into chaotic ways; some think that they can receive blessings simply by reciting prayers; and some have abandoned kindness for treachery.¹⁴Despite their intelligence and their passionate pleas, they have got nowhere.¹⁵Forced into the ever-turning wheel of fire, they are burned and obliterated.¹⁶Having lost their way for eons, they can no longer return.

¹⁷Therefore, my Lord Ye Su, the One emanating in three subtle bodies, hid his true power, became a human, and came on behalf of the Lord of Heaven to preach the good teachings.¹⁸A virgin gave birth to the sacred in a dwelling in the Da Qin Empire.¹⁹The message was given to the Persians who saw and followed the bright

light to offer Him gifts.[20]The twenty-four holy ones have given us the teachings, and heaven has decreed that the new religion of the "Three-In-One Purity that cannot be spoken of" should be proclaimed.[21]These teachings can restore goodness to sincere believers, deliver those living within the boundaries of the eight territories, refine the dust and transform it into truth, reveal the gate of the three constants, lead us to life, and destroy death.[22]The Religion of Light teachings are like the resplendent sun: they have the power to dissolve the dark realm and destroy evil forever.

[23]He set afloat the raft of salvation and compassion so that we can use it to ascend to the palace of light and be united with the spirit.[24]He carried out the work of deliverance, and when the task was completed, He ascended to immortality in broad daylight.[25]He left twenty-seven books of scriptures to inspire our spirit; He revealed the workings of the Origin; and He gave to us the method of purification by water.

[26]Borne on gentle winds and brilliant clouds of purity, the white seal carves the words, gathering the four radiances to be united with the void.[27]The sound of wood striking propagates the voice of virtue and benevolence:

[28]"The Eastern-facing Rites can give you the path of life.[29]Those who choose to grow beards, shave their heads, travel on the open roads, renounce desire, have neither male nor female slaves, see all people as equal, and do not hoard material goods, are followers of My rites of purification."

[30]We use abstinence to subdue thoughts of desire; and we use stillness to build our foundation.[31]At seven we gather for service to pray for the salvation of all.[32]Every seven days we have an audience with heaven.[33]We purify our hearts and return to the simple and natural way of the truth.[34]This truth cannot be named but its function surpasses all expectations.[35]When forced to give it a name, we call it the Religion of Light.[36]As it is with the Way, that which is sacred is not sacred unless it is highly sacred, and that which is the Way is not the Way unless it is the Great Way.

PART THREE

[1]The sacred doctrine that has brought light to the world came here during the reign of the Emperor Taizong.[2]The glorious teachings were carried by Aluoben, a man of high virtue from the Da Qin Empire.[3]He came on azure clouds bearing the true scriptures, and after a long and arduous journey, arrived in Chang-an during the ninth year of Zhenguan.[4]The emperor sent his minister Fang Xuanling to greet him at the western suburb.[5]The visitor was welcomed into the palace where he was asked to translate his scriptures.[6]When the emperor heard the teachings, he realized deeply that they spoke the truth.[7]He therefore asked that these teachings be taught, and in the seventh month in the autumn of the twelfth year of Zhenguan, he issued a decree:

[8]"The Way does not have a common name and the sacred does not have a common form.[9]Proclaim the teachings everywhere for the salvation of the people.[10]Aluoben, the man of great virtue from the Da Qin Empire, came from a far land and arrived at the capital to present the teachings and images of his religion.[11]His message is mysterious and wonderful beyond our understanding.[12]The teachings tell us about the origin of things and how they were created and nourished.[13]The message is lucid and clear; the teachings will benefit all; and they should be practiced throughout the land."

[14]On the street named Yining in the capital, the Da Qin Monastery was erected for twenty-one Religion of Light monks.[15]Through His great virtue and His ascension to the blue skies in the west, the light of the Way and the Religion of Light spirit has reached the Great Tang.[16]On the eastern gate of the monastery is an imperial declaration penned by the Emperor: "Reveal the splendor and brightness of heaven; glorify the Religion of Light saints; and let the benevolent teachings illuminate this realm of existence."

[17]According to the maps of the western territories and the records of the Han and Wei histories, the southern part of the Da Qin Empire touches the coral seas.[18]Northward it stretches toward

the Mountains of the Many Treasures.[19]Westward it overlooks the flowering woods of paradise.[20]Eastward it extends to lands where the wind never stops and the rivers are few.[21]From there came cotton-filling to make warm clothing, frankincense, shining pearls, and bright gemstones.[22]In that land there are no thieves.[23]People are happy and healthy.[24]Only the Religion of Light teachings are practiced, and nothing other than virtue is promoted.[25]The buildings are large and spacious, and the country is rich in culture and learning.

[26]The Emperor Gaozong praised his ancestor for recognizing the value of the true teachings and decreed the building of Religion of Light Monasteries in many provinces.[27]He conferred on Alouben the title "Lord Protector of the Great Teachings."[28]The teachings spread to the ten directions and the country prospered.[29]Monasteries were built in hundreds of cities and many people received blessings from the Religion of Light Church.

[30]In the following years, the Buddhist teachers from the eastern district spread vicious rumors and gathered a group of dishonorable people in the western suburb to slander [the Religion of Light Church].[31]The chief priest, the Honorable Lo-hsieh, brought out the golden religious objects, and the high monks defended the wondrous doctrine.[32]Thus, a disaster was averted.

[33]The pious Emperor Xuanzong ordered five princes from the dukedom of Ning to supervise the building of a church where the doctrine could be taught to more people in simple and straightforward ways.[34]Within a short time, many people were converted.

[35]In the early years of Tianbao, the emperor ordered General Gao Lishi to attend the consecration of the Acts of the Five Saints Church.[36]He also sent gifts of one hundred bolts of satin and a commemorative tapestry.[37]On the tapestry was embroidered: "The Dragon may be far away, but the bow and sword can reach the corners of the sun to bring light and celestial music to the three realms."[38]From the Da Qin Empire came the monk Jiehe, who ob-

served changes in the stars and gazed at the sun in an audience with the Lord.[39]The emperor also asked the Honorable Jiehe, Lexie, Bulun, and seventeen other monks to perform a high ceremony of prayer and offering at the Celebration Hall.[40]At the Tiandi Monastery there is a plaque written by the emperor.[41]Decorated with sparkling jade and suspended from a high rafter, it floats like a many-colored cloud from heaven.[42]On it is written:

[43]"As great as the Southern Mountains, as grand as the largest lakes, and as deep as the Eastern Seas, the Way can accomplish anything, and what it accomplishes must be described.[44]There is nothing that the holy ones cannot achieve, and what they have achieved will always be recorded."

[45]The enlightened Emperor Suzong established Religion of Light Monasteries in Ling-wu and four other provinces.[46]He supported charitable works and celebrated the great festivals.[47]Thus he was blessed, and his reign was prosperous.

[48]The scholar and military Emperor Daizong continued to promote the Sacred Way and follow the principles of wu-wei.[49]On the morning of the Holy Birthday, he offered incense and honored the Religion of Light Christians with an imperial declaration.[50]It read: "Due to your wonderful and meritorious works, many people have found salvation.[51]Because the sacred took on human form, the poisons of the world can be stopped."

[52]During the years of Jianzhong [of the Emperor Dezong], my pious emperor issued eight edicts and drove away the darkness.[53]He opened the nine realms and renewed the life of the Religion of Light Church.

[54]To penetrate the mysteries, to bless with a good conscience, to be great and yet empty, to return to stillness and be forgiving, to be compassionate and to deliver all people, to do good deeds and help people reach the other shore—these are the great benefits of our path of cultivation.[55]To calm people in stormy times, to help them understand the nature of things, to maintain purity, to nourish all

things, to respect all life, and to answer the needs of those whose beliefs come from the heart—these are the services the Religion of Light Church can offer.

[56]The Minister of Religious Affairs and the Assistant Provincial Governor of the tribute kingdoms bestowed the purple robe on the monk Yishi in the Examination Room on behalf of the emperor.[57]In a harmonious and benevolent way, this monk dedicated his life to spreading the teachings from the capital to the heart of the country.[58]His skill was impeccable and his learning was without peer.[59]In the beginning he befriended the Governor.[60]Later, he made himself known in the community of scribes.[61]Finally, he got Duke Guo of Hanyang to introduce the rites of abstinence in the tribute kingdoms.

[62]When the Emperor Suzong saw that his father was bedridden and unable to walk, he vowed that he would continue the policy of his ancestor.[63]He sent messages to his ministers and ordered them to distribute his wealth generously, and to send gifts of cloth and gold [to the Religion of Light].[64]He offered to renovate the older monasteries, rebuild the churches, and redecorate the halls and chambers.[65]He also asked the Luminous Religion Church to follow the principles of virtue and benevolence.[66]Every year, he invited the monks of the four monasteries to plan their charitable activities together with him.[67]He bid them to feed the crippled, give clothing to those suffering from cold, heal the sick, and bury the dead.[68]His devotion was so great that he asked a white-robed Religion of Light priest to write a plaque to glorify the luminous doctrine.[69]The text reads:

[70]"The True Lord of the Primordial Void, in absolute stillness and constant naturalness, crafted and nourished all things.[71]He raised the earth and established the sky.[72]He took on human form and His compassion was limitless.[73]The sun rises; darkness is banished; and we are witnesses to the true wonder."

[74]Throughout the reigns of the emperors there were records docu-

menting the history of the Religion of Light Church [in China].[75]They tell us that the Religion of Light teachings were brought into the Tang Empire, that the scriptures were translated, and that monasteries were built.[76]These teachings are like a raft, carrying salvation, blessings, and goodwill to the people of my country.

[77]Following the footsteps of his ancestors, the Emperor Gaozong built beautiful monasteries and churches throughout the land.[78]The True Way was proclaimed and the title "Lord Protector of the Great Teachings" was conferred.[79]The people were happy and there was prosperity everywhere.

[80]The Emperor Xuanzong promoted the sacred doctrine even further.[81]He followed the true teachings, penned declarations to endorse them, and issued imperial decrees to support them.[82]In simple and glorious words, he praised the deeds [of the Religion of Light] and deemed them worthy of celebration.

[83]The Emperor Suzong revived the Way of Heaven and observed the holy days.[84]Within one night, the fair winds swept away the impurities that have corrupted the palace.[85]The dust was cleared and the country was made whole again.

[86]The Emperor Daizong was filial and virtuous.[87]His piety was as great as heaven and earth.[88]He opened the imperial treasury and gave gifts of precious materials and jasmine incense.[89]To those who were virtuous, he rewarded them with gemstones that were as bright as the full moon.

[90]The reigning Emperor of Jianzhang [the Emperor Dezong] believed in the enlightened teachings.[91]During his time, the military and the generals kept peace in the four corners of land and the scholar officials were honest and upright.[92]He encouraged everyone to examine the nature of things with the hidden mirror.[93]People in the six directions were enlightened, and the hundred unruly tribes were brought under jurisdiction.

PART FOUR

[1]This doctrine is great and its workings are powerful and mysterious.[2]If forced to describe it, I would call them the work of the Three-in-one Lord.[3]All this humble servant has done is to record on the monument what has happened and to glorify the Primordial Lord.

[4]Erected in the second year of Jianzhang of the Great Tang, accompanied by the proper ceremonial music and rites, in the seventh month, on a day when the bright sun illuminated the forest.

[5]Attended by Chief Priest Ningshu and the followers of the Religion of Light teachings from the East.

[6]The calligrapher is the former military adviser of the Dai Province, the Honorable Imperial Appointee Lu Xiuyan.

9

The Fate of the Church

The Great Khan, having obtained this signal victory, returned with great pomp and triumph to the capital city of the Kanbalu [Beijing]. [During] the festival of Easter . . . he commanded all the Christians to attend him, and to bring with them their Book, which contains the four Gospels . . . he devoutly kissed it, and directed that the same should be done by all his nobles who were present.[52]

The demise of the radical Taoist-Christian Church is tragic and revealing of timeless political impulses. As demises often do, the fall comes after a golden age.

In the year 751 Chinese control over most of Central Asia collapsed, defeated by the armies of Arab Muslims, and Central Asia became a place of petty kingdoms and feuding families. After China's defeat, the Uighurs, a Turkic tribe from the steppes, moved into the power vacuum. They became important allies of China and helped maintain peace in the region. It is likely that a sizable minority of the Uighurs were Christians, with a majority of the tribe Manichaeans. Documents from Church of the East Patriarch Timothy indicate that from the mid–eighth century many of the kings of Central Asia were Christian. The fresco of the church service from Koqo described in chapter 7 comes from a Turkic city in Central Asia and illustrates not just a Chinese woman at prayer but two Uighur men also at prayer.

The Christianity of the Uighurs and their friendliness toward the Chinese gave the Church in China immense prestige. Duke Guo was advised by a Chinese Christian priest, Yi Shi, who assisted the duke in befriending and pacifying the Uighurs in the "tribute kingdoms" of Central Asia. As a result, the Church in China was patronized by the emperor and entered its golden age, achieving greater power and wealth than perhaps at any other time in its history.

All this is recorded in outline on the Stone of the Church of the East; in fact, the creation of the Stone and the building of the pagoda at Da Qin are the results of this imperial favor. The Stone tells the story of the rise of the Church in its own words. By 781, the Church was established and widespread, imperially supported, successful by its own standards, and producing Sutras of astonishing beauty. It had clearly integrated itself into Chinese society. The long list of clergy on the sides of the Stone indicates a well-ordered Church. This was the high point of the Church. But over the next hundred years or so, things started to go wrong.

Slowly, the Church began to lose ground to the forces of reaction within China. These forces were mainly directed to breaking the power of Buddhism. The Confucian bureaucracy and the Taoist hierarchy resented the growing power of the Buddhists, and other faiths, including Christianity, got caught up in the backlash that resulted.

The roots of this persecution lay in the extraordinary story of the Empress Wu Zetian, who had been brought up as a Buddhist. When she was married to Emperor Gaozong, she used her influence to increase imperial support for Buddhism. Gaozong was unwell for most of his reign (650–683), so the empress took more and more power into her hands. When the emperor died, she assumed full responsibility, exiling the new emperor and ruling in her own name. In 690 she even dropped the dynastic name Tang and substituted Zhou, claiming herself as the first ruler of this new dynasty.

Empress Wu firmly rooted her power in popular Buddhism. She was extravagantly generous to monasteries and temples and ignored all other religious communities in China. She claimed to be the manifestation of the Future Buddha Maitreya, whose coming had long been expected in China. Such claims gained her even more popular support while further alienating the traditional culture of China. Confucian culture had no place for a woman ruler, which was contrary to all its norms of hierarchy and order, but Confucians were powerless.

For ten years, from 695 to 705, Empress Wu had her way, and it is no coincidence that the Stone mentions persecution during this time. In 705 the empress was forced out and a new emperor restored the Tang Dynasty. By 711, reaction to the Buddhism of Wu was beginning to set in and Taoism was regaining its position. Confucian forces in the Court, rattled by this upsurge of Buddhism and female power, resolved to bring down the power of the Buddhists. Slowly but surely, they began to trim the power of the Buddhist monasteries.

✌ DISSOLUTION ∾
OF THE MONASTERIES

What probably tipped the balance for the emperor and his advisers was exactly what made King Henry VIII of England abolish the Christian monasteries in the 1530s: the wish to obtain the vast amounts of land, gold, and wealth they possessed.

From 841 onward, the Court turned against the Buddhists. At first it snubbed them at high and sacred moments in the ritual calendar. Then came the defrocking of nearly thirty-five hundred monks and nuns in the capital city in 843. At the same time, Manichaeism was also banned because of its links with rebellious tribes in Central Asia. In 845 a court order seized all gold, silver, and bronze statues, not just in temples but in private homes as well. A census of the Buddhist monasteries lists 260,000 monks and nuns, 4,600 temples, and 40,000 shrines. Describing Buddhism as "this insignificant Western religion," an imperial edict ordered the destruction of all temples and shrines, seized the 150,000 slaves owned by the Buddhists, and ordered all the monks and nuns to return to lay life. As an afterthought, the edict commanded, "3000 Religion of Light and Zoroastrian monks must return to lay life so they will not adulterate the customs of China."

Buddhism was permitted again within a very short time, but the blow it had suffered was massive and it never again regained its intellectual power or dynamism.

For the Christians in China proper it was almost the end. Probably during this period, the Da Qin monastery was destroyed, leaving little more than the pagoda standing. No evidence remains of any Church of the East monasteries still functioning in China proper after 845. The persecution seems to have stopped the Church in its tracks.

In 987 (377 A.H. in the Muslim calendar) an Arab writer met a Christian monk he had known previously. They encountered each other in the Christian quarter of Baghdad, "just behind the Church," as the writer Abu'l Faraj says in his book *Kitab al Fihrist*. The monk had been sent seven years earlier by the Catholicos to China with five other clergy "to set in order the affairs of the Christian Church." Abu'l Faraj asked him what he found and was told: "Christianity was extinct in China; the native Christians had perished in one way or another; the church which they had used had been destroyed, and there was only one Christian left in the land."[53]

By the mid–eleventh century, our Da Qin monastery was deserted, though people remembered it had once been a great and busy place. The following poem was written in 1062 by the poet Su Tung-po after he had visited the Da Qin monastery:

ON DA QIN TEMPLE

The rivers flow, bright, vast, smooth,
Flowing from the foothills of the green mountains.

In the distance I faintly see a pagoda
Lonely, standing stark against the mountain. . . .[54]

There is also this poem written in 1200 by General Yang Yong Yi, also about the Da Qin temple fifty miles from Chang'an:

DA QIN TEMPLE

The temple is in ruins,
the labor of those who built it,
now in vain.

The faithful no longer come,
and in its courts, only peace and quiet dwell.

The soft green moss covers every tile
And the colors of the roof are gone.

Yet, the pagoda stands
slender tower,
dazzling white in the evening light.

Clouds shroud the valley
A lone bird flies home
Home to the mountain.

The dusk covers the land,
turning smoke into silvery gray.

The days have gone,
the dream is over.

Now I must ponder on water, clean and pure.[55]

This poem could stand as a description of how we first saw the monastery and its pagoda. Little has changed. The changes all took place many, many centuries ago in 845.

A BROKEN CHURCH

The Church was now to all intents and purposes cut off from its Mother Church in Persia. The defeat of the Chinese by the Arabs in 752 at the Talas River in Central Asia had begun the closing of the door for any possible revival. Muslim control over much of Central Asia, combined with declining Chinese power in the same region, meant the old routes down which the Church in Persia sent its priests and monks had become much more hazardous—in some places impenetrable.

The rise of Islam broke not just the links between the Church of the East in Persia and its daughter Church in China, but ultimately the infrastructure of the Church itself. Life became more and more difficult under Muslim rule, and the attractions of belonging to the dominant religion became more and more persuasive. The Church of the East peaked in the eighth to ninth centuries, but all that is left today is a strong but small community in India, the Thomarist Christians, and a quarter of a million or so adherents in Iraq and Iran.

The collapse of the Tang Dynasty itself in 906 is seen by some as the primary cause of the disappearance of the Church: "Dependence on government is a dangerous and uncertain foundation for Christian survival. When a church writes 'Obey the Emperor' into its version of the Ten Commandments it is writing a recipe for its own destruction."[56]Although the Church of the East had learned to coexist with all manner of temporal powers, it was not in the same position as the Church of the West, which survived at least in part precisely because Constantine tied it to the state. If the persecution of 845 was the key blow to the Church, then this was one given by the Tang themselves.

Ultimately, we can only guess at the fate of China's Church. Faith can be a fragile thing. Churches that one generation produce outstanding religious figures can turn inward and fall spiritually dead the next. Anglo-Saxon England is an example. Its Church, contemporary with the Church of the East in China, was almost wiped out by invasions by the Vikings from 793 to the start of the eleventh century, and then by ignorance and indifference. Between its great luminary figures—Bede in the eighth century, Alfred in the ninth, and Dunstan in the tenth—it declined and almost disappeared each century, not least through the ignorance of the clergy and indifference of the people. It required charismatic figures such as Alfred and Dunstan to keep it going precisely because it was not integrally linked into a large, international Church, but was making do largely on its own.

❧ THE GODDESS OF ❧ THE SILK ROAD

The Great Persecution of 845 damaged Christianity in China—it would seem, at first glance, beyond repair. It is likely that it was around this time that the Da Qin monastery was vandalized, the statues literally defaced, and the site abandoned. It appears that Christianity went underground, but we have hints that it did better than just barely survive. The cache of Christian Sutras from Dunhuang and the silk painting show an active Christian community. And there are three other hints of the secret continuation of the Church from the persecutions of the ninth century to the liberalization of religious practice that the Mongol invasion of Genghis Khan brought in the thirteenth century.

First, in the late tenth century, a Buddhist historian, Zan Ning (919–1002), wrote that Christianity, Zoroastrianism, and Manichaeism were suppressed in 845: "Nevertheless the roots [of these perverse religions] were not completely eradicated and in due course they spread and became prolific."[57] The second clue comes from fragments of Syriac texts found in China. In 1905, Dr. A. von Le Coq discovered a few pages of Syriac at Gaochang near Turfan in Xinjiang Province. These proved to be pages from a Church of the East service book and a hymnal for Christmas Day. They have been dated to ca. ninth–eleventh century and probably were used by priests who served the Christian communities of this remote section of the Silk Road, a combination of Uighurs and Chinese.

But there is another Syriac book, found in the Imperial Library within the Forbidden City, Beijing, and now in Tokyo. This third clue dates from the thirteenth century and thus came to China as part of the return of the Church of the East under the Mongols in the thirteenth century, which is discussed below. Its significance for us is that it commemorates "the martyrs of China." It is clear from the text that the Church in China had suffered grievously at some time in the past and that memory of this suffering was preserved by the Church on the Silk Road and in Mongolia, where it seems likely that this was written. The text reads: "Faithful is the Lord. Your labors are not rejected, ye martyrs, King Christ has not passed by whom ye have loved in the land of Sin [China]. Your bones which are illustrious in the

Book of Life, your names, Lovers of the Son. Righteous is all. (Psalm. XLV.17). Not on account of the riches of the world have we loved, say the martyrs, affirming in confidence, but because we know the truth that Thy Kingdom and Thy Godhead are imperishable."[58]

Are these martyrs the martyrs of 845 onward? It seems likely, but without further corroboration from Chinese sources the true fate of the Church will remain lost in time. I believe it continued and that Polo, as we shall see later, found the church still alive but underground. We await more discoveries.

These clues are fascinating, but perhaps the legacy of the early Church in China is to be found in more unusual ways than this, ways still powerfully at work today in the figure of Guanyin.

In the wilder regions of China, especially in the northwest along the Silk Road, one of the most remarkable contributions of Christianity to China and world spiritual life was made. The Silk Road was one of the earliest conduits of Christianity to China, the very road by which so many monks and priests would travel to and from China. The extensive remains of churches, monasteries, books, and other artifacts of Christian life found at oasis towns bear witness to the scale and vitality of this, the northernmost expression of Chinese Christianity.

Christians from the Turkic and Mongolian tribes, such as the Ordos, whose cross is depicted on the following page, met here from at least the eighth century, when considerable communities of Uighurs and others were Christian. The White Huns who converted in the sixth century were also associated with this long corridor of Chinese power and influence. The Silk Road hosted the most diverse community in the world. Here Buddhists, Christians, Zoroastrians, Manichaeans, Taoists, shamans, practitioners of the Bon religion, and a host of variants on all these met and talked and traded. It was a truly cosmopolitan community. Here a transformation of a Buddhist Bodhisattva first took place. Avalokitesvara is the Bodhisattva of the beautiful *Lotus Sutra*. Originally a

This eleventh-century bronze cross for personal worship comes from the Ordos region of Mongolia close to the Silk Road. The Ordos people converted to Christianity from the tenth century onward. (© John Smith / CIRCA)

male deity of Indian Buddhism, he rose to become the most popular savior in Chinese Buddhism, in the process changing sex and significance. This transformation may well be due to the influence of the Christians of the Church of the East and their statues of Mary.

Avalokitesvara translates into Chinese as Guanyin. Guanyin is the most widely worshiped deity of any religion in China today. Beloved as a model of compassion and particularly associated with children, she is often depicted holding a child and is the favorite deity to whom people pray when they want to bear a child or ask protection for their children.

Until the ninth century, Guanyin was depicted as a man. Buddhism is as patriarchal as Christianity and women had no place within it. The Buddha even tried to stop them becoming nuns be-

A sixth-century stone carving of Guanyin in male form with attendants and Buddhist monks.

cause he held they were too low down the scale of reincarnation, well below being reincarnated as a man. In Indian Buddhism no woman appears in the pantheon of the Buddha, and in early Chinese Buddhism this male link was kept and strengthened. Indeed, to this day, Guanyin is the only female in the Buddhist cosmology of China. Her appeal reaches far beyond Buddhism and she is loved and honored by Taoists as much as Buddhists as the goddess of mercy and compassion.

No other model of a female goddess, especially a child-carrying female deity, except for the Christian statues of the Virgin Mary was present in China at the time of Avalokitesvara's transformation.[59] Suffice it to say that the creation of a compassionate, merciful, beautiful goddess version of the male Guanyin may owe as much to the statues of the Virgin Mary brought and created by the Church in China as to Buddhist theology.

✧ A LAST RESURGENCE ✧

On the Silk Road, sometime prior to 1005, a group of Christians joined Buddhists and Manichaeans who also dwelt in and around the town of Dunhuang in hiding their treasured scriptures and paintings in caves in the desert. Invasion by Tibetan tribes and widespread destruction forced the various communities to hide their texts. Thus we can be pretty certain that more than 150 years after the Great Persecution of 845, Chinese Christians were still meeting, still reading their Sutras, and still worshiping, for they preserved the Sutras right up to that fateful time when they all felt life as they knew it was coming to an end.

In the ruined oasis cities scattered along the Silk Road in China today, remains have been found of Christian monasteries, tombs, and artifacts. Christian life continued here because the Chinese Christians were joined by Christians from the various tribes, many of whom had been converted at the same time the Church in China was growing. It was from these tribes that the final surge and renewal of the Church of the East in China came.

The great Mongol leader Genghis Khan is perhaps the very last person one might associate with either Christianity or, in particular, the revival of Christianity in the East. Yet it is directly due to him and in particular one of his daughters-in-law that the Church of the East once again briefly revived in Persia and Central Asia.

This eighteenth-century statue of Guanyin as mother and protectress seated in her sacred cave illustrates the influence of the iconography of the Blessed Virgin Mary of the Nativity. (© John Smith/CIRCA)

Genghis Khan rose to power supported by the chief of the Keraits tribe, centered in the Karakorum region of present-day Mongolia. Indeed, Genghis Khan took as a wife a princess of the Keraits, who were Christian. They had been so since at least the early eleventh century. By the time Genghis Khan came to power in the late twelfth and early thirteenth century, they had all become Christians and traveled with their priests, who constructed felt chapels, religious versions of the Mongolian ger (felt huts).

Other Mongol tribes were also Christian or predominantly Christian. Thus, when Genghis Khan unified the Mongol tribes and burst out of Mongolia to conquer much of the world, a goodly proportion of his army was Christian. Many of his commanders were Christians, of which perhaps Chinkai, a Kerait born ca. 1171, is the most outstanding example. A faithful companion in arms of the Great Khan himself, he became secretary of state under Genghis Khan and ruled northern China for the Great Khan, Genghis's son.

As Mongol power pushed further and further west, it inevitably came into conflict with the ruling house and power bases of Islam. Mongol destructiveness and barbarity defy belief. When Samarkand fell to the Mongols in March 1220, the majority of the population, half a million people, were massacred and the skilled artisans shipped to Mongolia to work. When the Mongols captured the capital city of the Khwarizm kingdom, Gurganj, they not only massacred everyone in it but then drowned the city itself by diverting the Amu Darya River to create a lake over the city's remains.

Entering Persia proper, and thus coming into direct conflict with the caliphate of Islam based at Baghdad, the Mongols took Merv, one of the greatest and most ancient centers of Christianity in Persia. There they massacred seven hundred thousand people: men, women, and children. In 1221, Nishapur fell, another center of Christianity. There the records say that not only were all men, women, and children killed, but "even the dogs and cats were killed."[60]

Wherever the Mongol hordes went, the land was left desolate and the populations destroyed. Genghis Khan's grand plan in conquering much of northern China and sacking the city we now know as Beijing was to destroy every city, town, and even village to turn northern China into a vast pasture land for the rearing of Mongolian horses. He was eventually dissuaded from doing this by Chinese officials whom he recruited to plan this awful scheme.

This is not the place to cover the exploits of the Mongolian armies as they pushed across Central Asia, through into Russia and across to Poland and Hungary. Suffice it to say that their venture was an extraordinary one that very nearly destroyed Western Europe and that left Mongols in Russia right up until the seventeenth century. Indeed, their influence is visible to this day. The most famous church in Russia is the church of St. Basil in Red Square, with its dramatic cupolas and unique roofs. The design of this church, built to celebrate the final defeat of the Mongolians in Russia, is based on the colors and shapes of Mongolian felt huts!

The daughter-in-law of Genghis Khan, wife of his son Tolui, was Sorkaktani, a very devout Christian princess. Sorkaktani had three sons. One became the Great Khan and ruled Mongolia and its hordes. One became the conqueror and ruler of Persia. Her third son became emperor of China, Kublai Khan.

Under the sons of Sorkaktani, Christians were allowed to practice again. Sorkaktani's influence on her sons was enormous and they respected her faith and those who followed it. Only one, however, is thought to have come close to baptism: Hulegu, the son who conquered Persia. He favored the Christians above all others in his new kingdom. His wife was also a Christian princess, so he obviously felt great affinity with Christianity. He promoted the Christians and made contact with Rome, looking for a

Mongol-Christian alliance against their common foe, the Muslims of the Middle East. He had the tacit support of his brother the Great Khan, who had Church of the East priests in attendance upon him and many of whose greatest administrators were Christians.

Under Kublai Khan's rule, China settled down and experienced a period of peace and development. During his reign (1260–1294), Marco Polo came to China, where he reported finding in city after city "Nestorian Christians." We know from tombstones found across China that Christianity returned to many parts of China. The unanswerable question here is whether these Christians were Mongolian or Turkic people who followed in the wake of the armies, or whether they were Christians reemerging from centuries of persecution and hiding, feeling finally able to worship in public.

Marco Polo gives us a tantalizing hint that the latter may have been the case. He reports that he was told of a city, Fuzhou, where there were people who belonged to a strange sect or religion that had no idols, didn't worship fire (as the Zoroastrians do), and didn't follow Islam. Polo found this community and this is his report:

> For they had books, and Masters Mafeu and Marc reading in them began to interpret the writing and to translate from word to word and from tongue to tongue, so that they found it to be the words of the Psalter. Then they asked them whence they had that religion and order. And they answered and said, From our ancestors. They had also in a certain temple three figures painted who were three Apostles of the seventy who went preaching through the world. And they said that those had taught their ancestors in that religion long ago and that that faith had already been preserved among them for seven hundred years, but for a long time they had been without teaching, and so were ignorant of the chief things.[61]

Polo brought them to the Court and there they were permitted to be listed and worship freely as Christians. Polo goes on to say that once this edict was proclaimed, it was found there were seven hundred thousand in the region who followed the Christian faith in secret or quietly. The beautiful cross on the cover of this book comes from this renaissance period of the Church of the East in China. It was carved in 1382 and erected in a Christian monastery southwest of Beijing. Although the inscription on the stele on which this is carved has been published, no picture of this cross has ever been published before. The ruins of the monastery are still visible, deep in a beautiful, almost secret valley a few miles south of Yan Shan.

Christianity has managed to survive many centuries underground in other countries, including Japan. The dates given in Polo's report exactly accord with the arrival of Aluoben in 635 and the discovery "seven hundred years" later of these Christians. Polo cannot have known of the early Church in China from other sources, and the Stone had not yet been discovered.

For a brief period, under the patronage of Sorkaktani's sons, it looked as if Christianity in Central Asia and Persia would rise again and become the dominant religion, reuniting with Christian Europe to form a vast Christian world. But it was not to be. The Mongols were defeated by the Marmaluks of Egypt in 1260 at the battle of Ain Jalut, near Nazareth. The apparently invincible Mongol advance was halted and turned. From that day, the Mongolians in Central Asia and Persia began to turn toward Islam.

In China, when the Yuan Dynasty of the Mongols collapsed in 1368, so to a great extent did the Church. As the power of the Khans waned, so did the Church's, although the Church of the East kept a strong presence on the coast of China around Xiamen right into the fifteenth century.

One last story must be told.

In 1280, two Christians from China, priests from the monastery and cathedral in Beijing, traveled west to visit the Holy Land. One of them, 645 years after Aluoben arrived in China, became patriarch of the whole Church of the East, taking the title Mar Yaballaha III. His companion, Mark, was sent to the Pope to plead for an alliance against the Muslims and ended up celebrating Mass in 1287 for King Edward I of England at his Court in France. The Christians of China had traveled a long way since 635.

During the period of the Mongols' rule, other Christians arrived for the first time in China. Roman Catholic religious orders, foremost of which were the Franciscans, were sent by the Pope in response to concern about the Mongols and then in response to the suggestion of a Mongol–Christian West alliance against Islam.

When the next major wave of Christianity, the Jesuit missions of the late sixteenth and seventeenth centuries, reached China, they knew of the Franciscan missions but knew nothing of the Church of the East. Though they found no Christians, they did meet some who made the sign of the cross over their food but had long forgotten why.

Postscript

When I began work on this book and pulled together the team who made it possible, I thought I knew what I was going to write about and translate. It seemed as if all we had left from the extraordinary adventure of the Church of the East in China was a stone, a handful of manuscripts, and a few passing references in Persian and Chinese sources. To be sure, there was more than enough in those precious remains to show the challengingly different way Christianity developed in China in comparison to the Christianity we tend to know in the West. But I was unaware of how much more we were to discover.

To find, buried in the early Jesus Sutras, lost books from other Christian encounters with different cultures and religions was the first surprise. These discoveries elevate the Jesus Sutras from mere objects of historical fascination for those interested in China to significant finds for an understanding of Christianity's evolution.

To discover how seriously the Church in China took karma and reincarnation, by showing that Jesus could offer salvation from the wheel of karma, was a further surprise. We knew something of this was in the Sutras. We had no idea how strong it was, nor

Graffiti found on the fourth floor of the pagoda, carved into a Tang Dynasty brick. It is a crude form of Syriac script. (© Martin Palmer/ CIRCA)

how much it shaped the telling of the Jesus story in China. It raises profound questions about whether we in the Western Church have perhaps been too narrow in our understanding of the meaning of Jesus.

The discovery of the Da Qin monastery, however, really changed our lives, and that story has only just begun. At the time of writing, we are planning a joint venture among our team, the China Heritage Arts Foundation of New York and Hong Kong, and the Chinese government to fully excavate the site and create jointly a Museum of the West in Ancient China beside the ruins. This excavation should reveal many things about the Church that have lain buried for centuries. For instance, we already know that there are a series of sealed underground rooms beneath the pagoda itself. We have identified where the church stood and where the burial ground was. Artifacts are coming to light that indicate the cross-currents of West and East on the site. And carved on the inside wall of the pagoda, on the third floor, we have found graffiti that seems to be Greek written in Syriac letters.

In many ways, the discoveries in this book mark the opening of a new chapter in the story of Taoist and Christian thought, because we now know far more about the meaning of the Sutras than before. With help from Taoist, Buddhist, and Confucian scholars from China and the United States we have been able to go deeply into the spiritual significance of the Sutras. As a result, we can honestly claim to have found, in *The Sutra of Returning to Your Original Nature*, a spiritual classic of both Chinese and Christian origin that warrants serious worldwide study.

More important perhaps is the contemporary relevance of the Jesus Sutras. Today, Christianity and Buddhism, Christianity and Taoism, Christianity and Shamanism are engaged in dialogue where once there was only denunciation. As Christians slowly and tentatively feel their way toward a more mature relationship with other faiths and cultures, the Jesus Sutras stand as a beacon showing it has been done before. Over the centuries, the Church, whether Roman Catholic, Orthodox, or Protestant, has tended to limit our versions and understandings of Jesus. A set story and interpretation has emerged. Today, many are beginning to discover that this "orthodox" picture of Jesus is only one of many. To this search for the different images and stories of Jesus, and explorations of what his life, death, and resurrection could mean, the Jesus Sutras offer their own extraordinary contributions. Here is a worldview of the Church unlike any other, a worldview free of much of the theological and social baggage of Western Christianity. The Jesus Sutras have the potential to call Christians, and others, to a greater integration of the spiritual with the practical. Their teachings on charity, vegetarianism, antislavery, equality of men and women, and care for nature all offer models of personal behavior that draw on the best in Christianity and in other ancient spiritual traditions.

The concept of Original Nature in the Jesus Sutras is also

timely. It does not claim we are all good all the time, but it does say that the idea of the Incarnation makes sense because, as St. Athanasius (ca. 296–373), one of the greatest of what the Church of the West called the Church Fathers in the fourth century, said, "God became human in order that we could become God." The Jesus Sutras offer salvation from what we have made of ourselves— salvation from karma or from the burden of "Original Sin"—because beneath the layers of our inadequate actions lies an original nature that is good. These spiritual, theological, psychological, philosophical, and ethical insights are in the Jesus Sutras, often beautifully and simply portrayed in accessible images, stories, and concepts. They await our discovery and seek to prompt discussion and exploration by releasing us from the idea that we already know what we are and what God is.

As Christianity starts its third millennium, it urgently needs to broaden its understanding of who Jesus is and why the Church exists. The Jesus Sutras, voices from the Church's first millennium, unheard in the second millennium, could be a turning point for the Church or Churches of the third millennium.

At the end of St. John's Gospel are these words: "There were many other things that Jesus did; if all were written down, the world itself, I suppose, would not hold all the books that would have to be written" (John 21:25). From China have come hints of what it was St. John meant. After a thousand years, the Jesus Sutras have returned to us to shed light on the past, speak to our present, and, possibly, help shape our future.

Notes

Unless otherwise indicated, all translations are by Eva Wong, Zhao Xiao Min, and the author. We all relied, however, on the pioneering work of A. C. Moule and P. Y. Saeki and their early translations of the Nestorian Chinese scriptures. Their work was invaluable to us in sorting out the complex history of the Taoist Christians.

1. A. C. Moule, *Christians in China before the Year 1550* (London: 1930); P. Y. Saeki, *The Nestorian Documents and Relics in China* (Tokyo: The Academy of Oriental Culture, Tokyo Institute, 1937).
2. A detailed account of finds at Dunhuang is recorded in Paul Pelliot, *Les Grottes de Touen-Houng* (Paris: Librarie Paul Geuthner, 1921).
3. Samuel Hugh Moffett, *A History of Christianity in Asia* (San Francisco: Harper, 1992), 301.
4. *The Suppressed Gospels and Epistles of the Original New Testament of Jesus Christ,* trans. Archbishop Wake and other learned Divines (London: Hancock, 1863).
5. In A. C. Graham, trans., *Poems of the Late T'ang* (London: Penguin, 1965), 97.
6. In Mark Elvin, *The Pattern of the Chinese Past* (Stanford, CA: Stanford University Press, 1973), 55.
7. Peter Chunghang Chiu, "An Historical Study of Nestorian

Christianity in the Tang Dynasty between 635–845" (Ph.D. diss., University of Michigan at Ann Arbor, 1987), 126–27.

8. An imperial edict of 638 recorded in the *Tang History of A.D. 960* described the arrival and name of Aluoben and the facilities made available to him; quoted in Moule, 65.

9. In Moule, 71.

10. Chris Scarre, gen. ed., *Past Worlds: Atlas of Archaeology* (New York: HarperCollins, 1988), 262.

11. Max Muller, ed., *The Sacred Books of the East* (Oxford: Oxford University Press, 1890), vol. 35, bk. 2, ch. 2, p. 63.

12. From Robert van de Weyer, comp., *Celtic Fire* (London: Daron Longman & Todd, 1990).

13. The Book of Common Prayer, 240–41.

14. In a classic Antioch tradition attempt at compromise, Nestorius records the following: "When I came here, I found a dispute among the members of the church, some of whom were calling the Blessed Virgin Mary Mother of God, while others were calling her Mother of man. Gathering both parties together, I suggested that she should be called Mother of Christ, a term which represented both God and man, as it is used in the gospels." See F. Loofs, *Nestoriana* (Cambridge, England: Cambridge University Press, 1912; quoted in Moffett, 1: 173).

15. Cyril bribed his way back into power at a cost that Moffett estimates to have been "the amount of three million dollars in today's reckoning" (175).

16. In his enthusiasm as a Christian but also, no doubt, with a view to creating the beginnings of an excuse for an invasion, Constantine wrote to Shah Shapur in 315: "I rejoice to hear that the fairest provinces of Persia are adorned with Christians. . . . Since you are so powerful and pious, I commend them to your care, and leave them in your protection" (Theodoret, *Ecclesiastical History;* quoted in Moffett, 138).

17. Zoroastrians still see conversion as a fatal weakening of the faith that has been entrusted to them, as I know from my discussions with Zoroastrians in India. See Khojeste P. Mistree, *Zoroastrianism: An Ethnic Perspective* (Mumbai, India: Good Impressions, 1998).

18. A typical Victorian view was expressed in 1863: "It was the misfortune, perhaps a judicial one, of southern and eastern Asia to be vis-

ited in early ages by false apostles, deeply tainted with heresy: and to this fact has been attributed a large share of the multiplied disasters which have marked the course of religion in these ill-fated countries." See T. W. M. Marshall, *Christian Missions: Their Agents and Their Results* (London: Longman, Green, Longman, Roberts & Green, 1863), 61.

19. Stephen Neill, *A History of Christian Missions,* vol. 6 of *Pelican History of the Church* (London: Pelican, 1964).

20. Quoted in Moffett, 1: 202.

21. This story may be an invention of the early Church in Persia, but it is reported by Eusebius, writing in 324, probably drawing on an earlier account in the *Doctrine of Addai,* author unknown.

22. Another important book written by Tatian was his polemical *Oration against the Greeks.*

23. John Marshall, *The Buddhist Art of Gandhara* (Cambridge, England: Cambridge University Press, 1960), ch. 4, p. 6.

24. As Michael Wood illustrated in his epic TV series *In the Footsteps of Alexander the Great* in 1997 and further developed in his book of the same name (London: BBC Books, 1997).

25. Bardaisan of Edessa.

26. William Smith, *The History of the Holy Jesus and the Lives and Deaths of the Holy Evangelists and Apostles* (London: Trary, 1713).

27. J. N. Farquhar, *The Apostle Thomas in India According to the Acts of Thomas* (Kerala, India: Syrian Churches Series, 1972), 57.

28. See Moffett, 1: 29 and elsewhere.

29. "Buddhism exerted a strong influence, probably ousting the Church from the East of Tibet in the eighth century." See E. C. D. Hunter, "The Church of the East in Central Asia," *Bulletin of the John Rylands University Library of Manchester,* 78, no. 3 (1996): 141.

30. See ibid., 136.

31. Arthur Waley, *Translations from the Chinese* (New York: Knopf, 1941), 61.

32. John K. Fairbank and Edwin O. Reischauer, *China: Tradition and Transformation* (Sydney, Australia: George Allen Unwin, 1979), 82.

33. Ibid., 104.

34. Martin Palmer with Elizabeth Breuilly, trans., *The Book of Chuang Tzu* (London: Arkana, 1996), 20. The Pinyin form of Chuang Tzu is Zhuang Zi, but we have kept the more familiar romanization.

35. Ibid., 146–47.

36. Arthur Waley, *Translation from the Chinese* (New York; Knopf, 1941), p. 140.
37. W. E. Soothill, trans., *The Lotus Sutra of the Wonderful Law* (Oxford: Clarendon, 1930).
38. Author's translation from the *Platform Sutra of the Sixth Patriarch*.
39. I am grateful to Joseph Needham's *Science and Civilisation in China* (Cambridge, Eng.: Cambridge University Press, 1956), vol. 2, for these details.
40. Geshe Kelsang Gyatso, *Clear Light of Bliss: Mahamudra in Vajrayana Buddhism,* trans. by Tenzin Norbu (London: Wisdom Press, 1982), 18–19.
41. Ian Gillman and Hans-Joachim Klimkeit, *Christians in Asia before 1500* (Richmond, England: Curzon Press, 1999), 223–24.
42. According to Gillman and Klimkeit, the priest is probably an Iranian (see ibid., 225–26).
43. *Within the Four Seas* (London: George Allen Unwin, 1969), 90.
44. Palmer and Breuilly, 72–73.
45. From Alexander Carmichael, *Carmina Gadelica* (1099; repr. Edinburgh: Floris Books, 1992).
46. Kevin Crossley-Holland, ed., *The Anglo-Saxon World* (Oxford: Oxford University Press, 1984).
47. This means "tied up in Syriac" and so unavailable to the Chinese Christians.
48. Martin Palmer, *Living Christianity,* trans. by Jay Ramsay from Irish Gaelic (Shaftesbury, England: Element Books, 1993), 74.
49. Palmer and Breuilly, 269–70.
50. I am grateful to Xinru Liu, *Silk and Religion* (Delhi: Oxford India Paperbacks, 1998), for this insight.
51. Livia Kohn, ed., *The Taoist Experience* (Albany: State University of New York Press, 1993), 20.
52. Manuel Kornroff, ed., *The Travels of Marco Polo* (New York: Boric and Liveright, 1926).
53. Quoted in Moule, 75–76.
54. Translation by author.
55. Translation by author.
56. Moffett, 1: 313.
57. From "Ta sung seng shih luch," in Samuel N. C. Lieu and J. C. B. Mohr, *Manichaeism in the Later Roman Empire and Medieval China* (Tubingen, Germany: Paul Siebeck, 1992), 265.

58. Saeki, 320–21.

59. Martin Palmer and Jay Ramsay, with Man-Ho Kwok, *Kuan Yin* (London: Thorsons, 1995).

60. Rene Grousset, *The Empire of the Steppes* (New Brunswick, NJ: Rutgers University Press, 1970), 241.

61. Moule, 142.

Bibliography

Archbishop Wake and other learned Divines, trans., *The Suppressed Gospels and Epistles of the Original New Testament of Jesus Christ* (London: Hancock, 1863).

Bowerstock, G. W., Peter Brown, and Oleg Grabar, eds., *Late Antiquity: A Guide to the Postclassical World* (Cambridge, Mass.: Harvard University Press, 1999).

Chunghang Chiu, Peter, *An Historical Study of Nestorian Christianity in the Tang Dynasty between 635–845* (Ph.D. diss., University of Michigan, 1987).

Elvin, Mark, *The Pattern of the Chinese Past* (Stanford, CA: Stanford University Press, 1973).

Gillman, Ian, and Hans-Joachim Klimkeit, *Christians in Asia before 1500* (Richmond: Curzon Press, 1999).

Graham, A. C., trans., *Poems of the Late T'ang* (London: Penguin, 1965).

Hawkes, David, *The Songs of the South: An Anthology of Ancient Chinese Poems by Qu Yuan and Other Poets* (Harmondsworth: Penguin, 1985).

Lieu, Samuel, and J. C. B. Mohr, *Manichaeism in the Later Roman Empire and Medieval China* (Tubingen: Paul Siebeck, 1992).

Liu, Xinru, *Silk and Religion* (Delhi: Oxford University Press, 1998).

Marshall, John, *The Buddhist Art of Gandhara* (Cambridge: Cambridge University Press, 1960).

Moffett, Samuel Hugh, *A History of Christianity in Asia* (San Francisco: Harper-Collins, 1992).

Moule, A. C., *Christians in China before the Year 1550* (London: 1930).

Needham, Joseph, *Science and Civilisation in China,* vols. I–III (Cambridge: Cambridge University Press, 1952).

Neill, Stephen, *A History of Christian Missions,* vol. 6 of *Pelican History of the Church* (London: Pelican, 1964).

Palmer, Martin, *Living Christianity* (Shaftesbury: Element, 1993).

Palmer, Martin and Elizabeth Breuilly, trans., *The Book of Chuang Tzu* (Harmondsworth: Penguin, 1996).

Palmer, Martin, Jay Ramsay, and Man-Ho Kwok, trans., *Tao Te Ching.* (Shaftesbury: Element, 1994).

Pelliott, Paul, *Les Grottes de Touen-Houng* (Paris: Libarie Paul Geuthner, 1921).

Saeki, P. Y., *The Nestorian Documents and Relics in China* (Tokyo: The Academy of Oriental Culture, Tokyo Institute, 1937).

————. *The Nestorian Monument in China* (London: Society for Promoting Christian Knowledge, 1916).

Wallis Budge, Sir E. A., *The Monks of Kublai Khan, Emperor of China* (London: Religious Tract Society, 1928).

Index

Page numbers appear in italic for illustrations.

MARTIN PALMER is the director of the International Consultancy on Religion, Education, and Culture (ICOREC), which specializes in religious, environmental, educational, and developmental projects and works with a variety of international organizations, such as the World Wide Fund for Nature, UNESCO, and the World Bank. He is also secretary general of the Alliance of Religions and Conservation (ARC), which assists eleven world faiths in developing environmental and conservation projects worldwide. He is the author of many books on religious topics and one of the foremost translators of ancient Chinese texts, having published translations of the *Tao Te Ching, I Ching, Chuang Tzu,* and *Kuan Yin.* He has written new liturgies for churches and is regularly interviewed for British television and radio. He is one of BBC World Service's regular commentators and, in 1997, won the Sandford Prize for religious broadcasting for his Good Friday meditation, which combined pagan and Christian imagery.

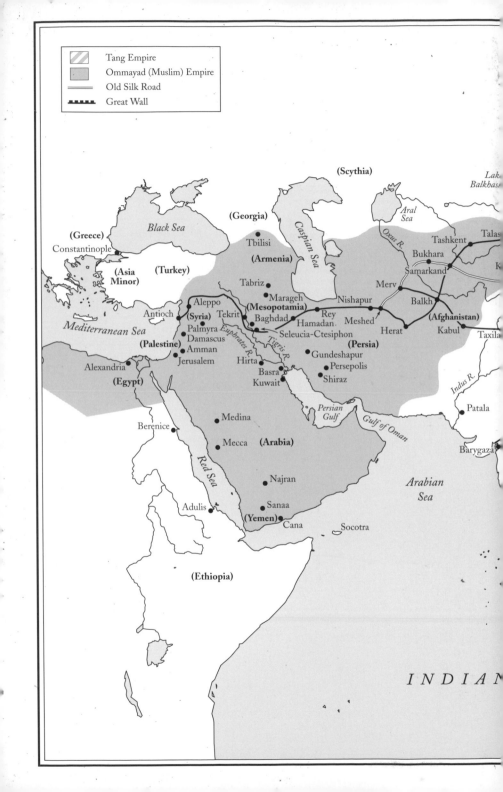

Legend:
- Tang Empire
- Ommayad (Muslim) Empire
- Old Silk Road
- Great Wall

(Scythia)

Lake Balkhash

Black Sea

(Georgia)

Aral Sea

Caspian Sea

(Greece)

Constantinople

Tbilisi

(Armenia)

Tashkent

Talas

Oxus R.

Bukhara

(Asia Minor)

(Turkey)

Tabriz

Merv

Samarkand

K

Mediterranean Sea

Antioch

Aleppo

Tekrit

Maragheh

(Mesopotamia)

Nishapur

Balkh

(Syria)

Baghdad

Rey

Meshed

(Afghanistan)

Palmyra

Hamadan

Seleucia-Ctesiphon

Herat

Kabul

Damascus

Euphrates R.

Tigris R.

(Persia)

Taxila

(Palestine)

Amman

Jerusalem

Hirta

Gundeshapur

Indus R.

Alexandria

Basra

Persepolis

(Egypt)

Kuwait

Shiraz

Patala

Persian Gulf

Gulf of Oman

Berenice

Medina

Mecca

(Arabia)

Barygaza

Red Sea

Arabian Sea

Najran

Adulis

Sanaa

(Yemen)

Cana

Socotra

(Ethiopia)

INDIAN